in company 3.0

UPPER INTERMEDIATE STUDENT'S BOOK

B2

in company 3.0 at a glance

Third edition Student's Book:

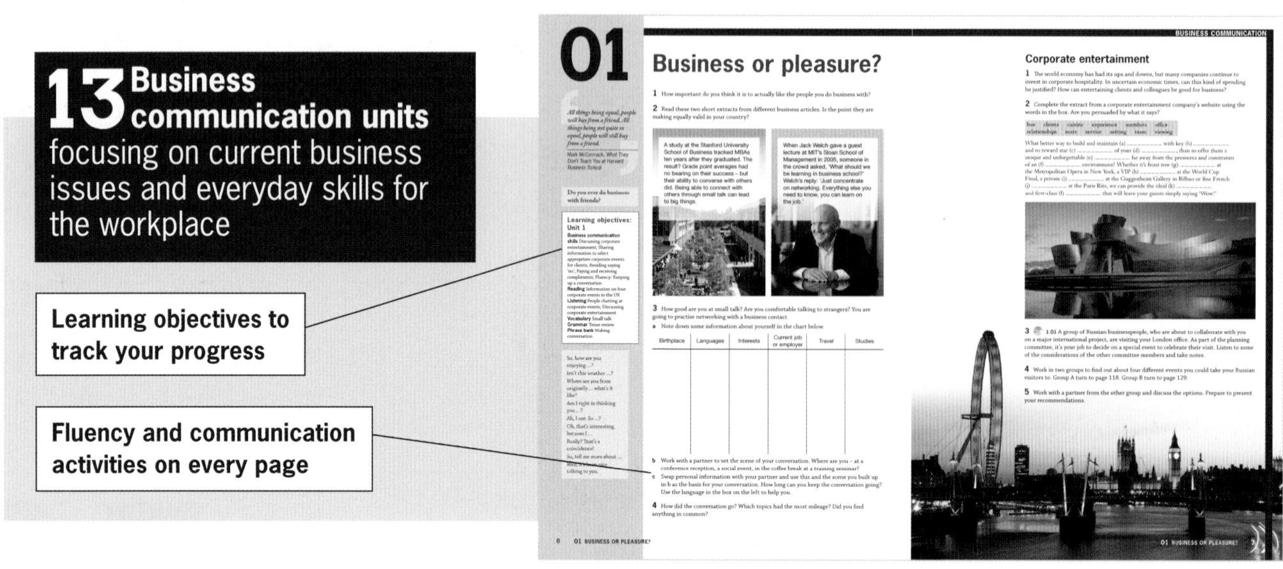

13 Business communication units focusing on current business issues and everyday skills for the workplace

Learning objectives to track your progress

Fluency and communication activities on every page

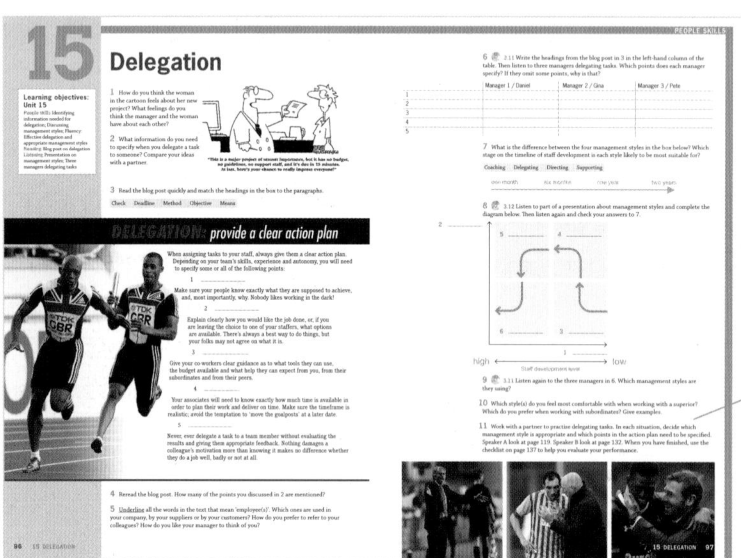

5 People skills units focusing on functional Business English language and interpersonal skills

Roleplay activities consolidate the skills learnt

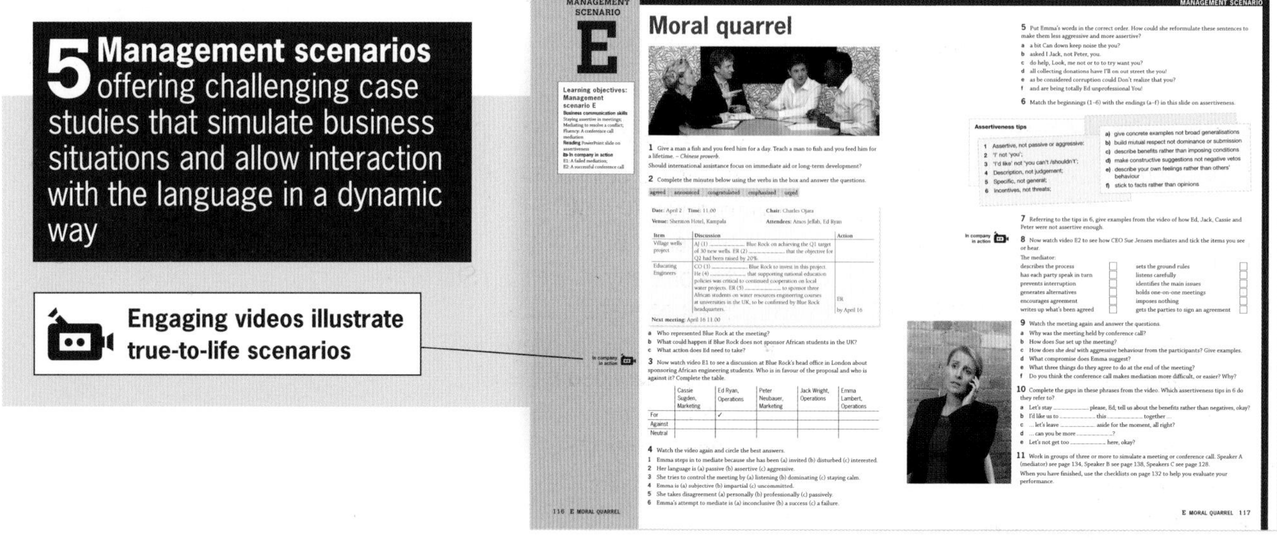

5 Management scenarios offering challenging case studies that simulate business situations and allow interaction with the language in a dynamic way

Engaging videos illustrate true-to-life scenarios

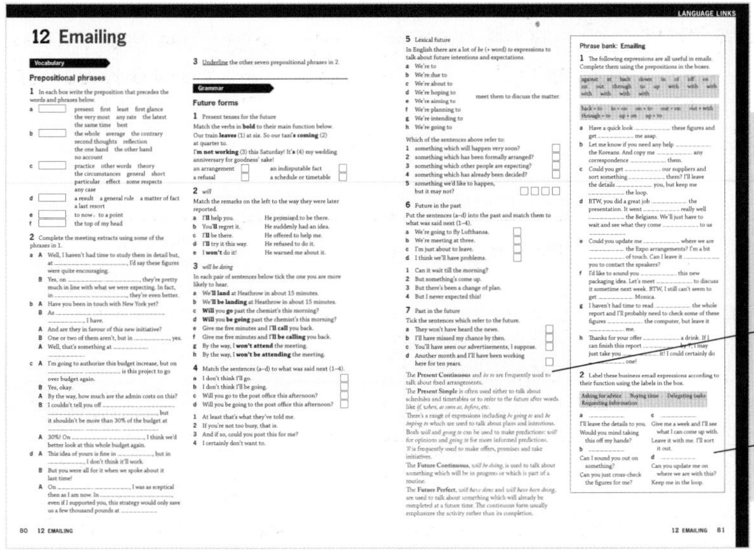

13 Language links consolidating grammar and extending vocabulary from the Business communication units

Grammar reference with detailed explanations of key points

Phrase bank of key take-away phrases for quick revision

Extra material

- Additional material for communicative activities
- Self-evaluation forms for Management scenario activities
- Listening scripts

New Online Workbook and Student's Resource Centre

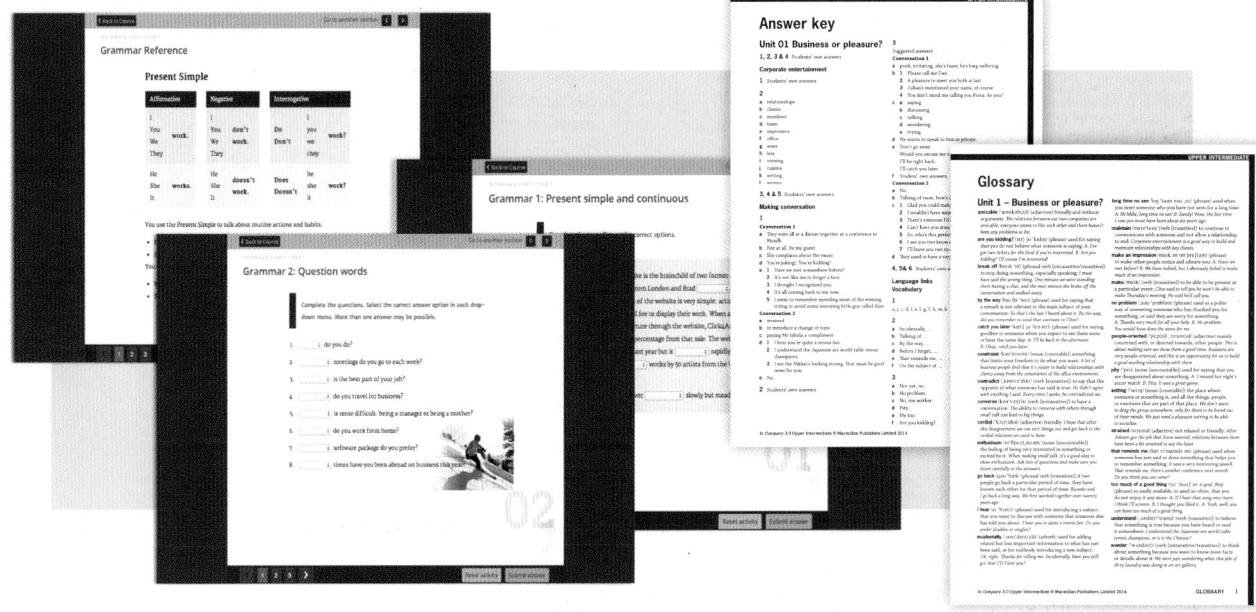

Online Workbook

Everything you need to build and expand on the Student's Book material outside the classroom, and all accessible online:

- Interactive activities to practise:
  - Vocabulary
  - Grammar
  - Reading
  - Writing
  - Listening
- Automatic gradebook
- Grammar reference

Student's Resource Centre

An extensive collection of resources, all available to download:

- Student's Book audio
- 'In company in action' – Student's Book scenario videos
- 'In company interviews' – additional video material
- Glossary
- Answer key
- Phrase banks

Contents

Unit	Business communication skills	Reading and listening	Language links
01 Business or pleasure? p6	Discussing corporate entertainment Sharing information to select appropriate corporate events for clients Avoiding saying 'no' Paying and receiving compliments **Fluency** Keeping up a conversation	**Reading** Information on four corporate events in the UK **Listening** People chatting at corporate events Discussing corporate entertainment	**Vocabulary** Small talk **Grammar** Tense review **Phrase bank** Making conversation
02 Information exchange p13	Describing attitudes to and content of meetings Paraphrasing information Pointing out discrepancies Dialogue-building using the language of meetings **Fluency** Breaking bad news and writing a report In company interviews Units 1–2	**Reading** Meeting: breaking bad news **Listening** A meeting: problems with a product Five meetings: discrepancies The language of meetings	**Vocabulary** Meetings **Grammar** Conditionals **Phrase bank** Debating issues
03 People skills: Rapport p20	Strategies and techniques to build rapport **Fluency** Building rapport with a colleague	**Reading** Top tips for building rapport Training manual checklists **Listening** Two meetings to discuss teleworking	
Management scenario A: Culture clash p22	Identifying potential cultural differences Avoiding a culture clash **Fluency** A meeting to discuss a merger	**Reading** Cultural sensitivity checklist **In company in action** A1: A culture clash A2: Positive cross-cultural understanding	
04 Voice and visuals p24	Doing a quiz on how to command attention Giving feedback on a presentation Using visuals in a presentation Analyzing the voice in presentations **Fluency** Giving a speech	**Reading** Articles on voice and visual impact **Listening** Voicemail Presenters giving information in different ways Radio programme: drama for business A Shakespeare speech	**Vocabulary** Presentations **Grammar** Modal verbs **Phrase bank** Describing and commenting on visuals
05 Problems on the phone p31	Discussing phone usage and its usefulness Dealing with 'chatterboxes' Complaining and dealing with complaints Toning down 'flames' Speculating about a problem **Fluency** Solving problems on the phone	**Reading** Article on 'chatterboxes' **Listening** Someone dealing with a 'chatterbox' Someone dealing with a customer complaint People discussing a problem People solving a problem	**Vocabulary** Phone, tablet and email **Grammar** Complex question formation **Phrase bank** On the phone
06 Leading meetings p37	Discussing dynamics of meetings Disagreeing diplomatically **Fluency** Chairing a meeting In company interviews Units 4–6	**Reading** Article on behaviour in meetings Disagreement strategies **Listening** Radio programme: alternative approaches to meetings Managing meetings	**Vocabulary** Companies and capital; The financial pages **Grammar** Linking and contrasting ideas **Phrase bank** Chairing meetings
07 People skills: Coaching p44	Discussing the role of a coach The GROW model of coaching **Fluency** Coaching your colleagues	**Reading** Article on professional coaching **Listening** Four extracts from a coaching session	
Management scenario B: Coach crash p46	Giving feedback on a presentation Coaching dos and don'ts **Fluency** Past-present-future presentations with coaching	**Reading** Coaching dos and don'ts **In company in action** B1: A failed presentation B2: Successful coaching	
08 Promoting your ideas p48	Discussing attitudes to public speaking Discussing national stereotypes Describing what makes a good talk Discussing innovation in your company **Fluency** Presenting an idea for a product or service	**Reading** Website extract: *Intrapreneurs* **Listening** Presenters talking about what makes them nervous People comparing audience expectations of presentations Presentation: a new business idea	**Vocabulary** Phrasal verbs **Grammar** The passive **Phrase bank** Pitching an idea
09 Relationship-building p55	Discussing first impressions Completing a questionnaire on networking Practising networking skills Getting out of the office **Roleplay** Visiting a colleague's home	**Reading** Questionnaire: Are you an effective networker? Article on sport and business **Listening** Three small talk conversations People chatting at golf Conversation: visiting someone's home	**Vocabulary** Social English **Grammar** Multi-verb sentences **Phrase bank** Networking

Unit	Business communication skills	Reading and listening	Language links
10 Making decisions p63	Discussing making decisions in difficult situations Doing a quiz on life-and-death decisions Giving advice on worst-case scenarios or workplace dilemmas Inserting missing articles into two texts **Fluency** Holding a crisis management meeting In company interviews Units 8–10	**Reading** Website extract: Worst-case scenarios Company crises **Listening** Advice on surviving worst-case scenarios Decision-making meetings Case study: Coca-Cola crisis	**Vocabulary** Marketing **Grammar** Articles **Phrase bank** Decision-making
11 People skills: Stress p70	Analyzing attitudes to stress in the workplace Identifying techniques for managing stress **Fluency** Helping a staff member in a stressful situation	**Reading** Article on helping colleagues manage stress **Listening** Talk on stress management Eight managers counselling their staff	
Management scenario C: Pitch and persuade p72	Identifying effective pitching techniques Using Cialdini's six principles of influence **Fluency** Pitching a new project	**Reading** Article on building donor circles **In company in action** C1: A failed pitch C2: An effective pitch	
12 Emailing p74	Discussing how to deal with emails Correcting errors in an email Shortening and simplifying an email Adding the personal touch to an email Choosing an appropriate email style **Fluency** Writing and answering emails	**Reading** Extracts on emailing **Listening** Podcast: what your emails say about your career prospects Radio programme: The biggest email blunders ever made	**Vocabulary** Prepositional phrases **Grammar** Future forms **Phrase bank** Emailing
13 Making an impact p82	Identifying effective presentation openings Identifying rhetorical techniques Rephrasing to add impact Identifying ways of closing a presentation **Fluency** Producing a promotional presentation for a new country	**Reading** Book extract on opening a presentation **Listening** Presentation openings Extracts from political speeches Closing remarks from four presentations	**Vocabulary** Metaphor **Grammar** Rhetorical techniques **Phrase bank** Opening and closing a presentation
14 Out and about p89	Discussing business travel and packing habits Identifying ellipsis in conversation Striking up a conversation Telling an anecdote **Fluency** Chatting over a business lunch In company interviews Units 12–14	**Reading** Extracts from *The Accidental Tourist* **Listening** People talking about their worst flying experiences Conversations over lunch	**Vocabulary** Storytelling **Grammar** Narrative tenses **Phrase bank** Sharing anecdotes
15 People skills: Delegation p96	Identifying information needed for delegation Discussing management styles **Fluency** Effective delegation and appropriate management styles	**Reading** Blog post on delegation **Listening** Presentation on management styles Three managers delegating tasks	
Management scenario D: Change champion p98	Discussing implementing change successfully Identifying the stages for managing change **Fluency** Meetings to implement change	**Reading** PowerPoint slide on managing change **In company in action** D1: Imposing changes D2: Managing change	
16 Teleconferencing p100	Discussing potential uses of tele- and videoconferencing facilities Discussing action in a crisis Completing the minutes of a teleconference **Roleplay** Holding a teleconference	**Reading** Website extract: Business benefits of *TelePresence* Emails about a film shoot **Listening** An unexpected phone call An emergency teleconference	**Vocabulary** Teleconferencing, Personnel and production **Grammar** Reporting **Phrase bank** Teleconferencing
17 Negotiating deals p107	Negotiating a tricky situation Identifying negotiating tactics **Fluency** Negotiating a contract In company interviews Units 16–17	**Reading** Analysis of a negotiation Article about the music business **Listening** Negotiations People talking about negotiating strategy Meeting: signing a new band	**Vocabulary** Negotiations **Grammar** Diplomacy and persuasion **Phrase bank** Negotiating
18 People skills: Mediation p114	Discussing the qualities of a good mediator Identifying the stages of mediation **Fluency** Mediating between colleagues	**Reading** Article about causes of conflict at work **Listening** Poor and positive mediation	
Management scenario E: Moral quarrel p116	Staying assertive in meetings Mediating to resolve a conflict **Fluency** A conference call mediation	**Reading** PowerPoint slide on assertiveness **In company in action** E1: A failed mediation E2: A successful conference call	
	Additional material p118	**Listening scripts** p139	

01

All things being equal, people will buy from a friend. All things being not quite so equal, people will still buy from a friend.

Mark McCormack, *What They Don't Teach You at Harvard Business School*

Do you ever do business with friends?

Learning objectives: Unit 1

Business communication skills Discussing corporate entertainment; Sharing information to select appropriate corporate events for clients; Avoiding saying 'no'; Paying and receiving compliments; Fluency: Keeping up a conversation
Reading Information on four corporate events in the UK
Listening People chatting at corporate events; Discussing corporate entertainment
Vocabulary Small talk
Grammar Tense review
Phrase bank Making conversation

So, how are you enjoying ...?
Isn't this weather ...?
Where are you from originally ... what's it like?
Am I right in thinking you ...?
Ah, I see. So ...?
Oh, that's interesting, because I ...
Really? That's a coincidence!
So, tell me more about ...
Well, it's been nice talking to you.

Business or pleasure?

1 How important do you think it is to actually like the people you do business with?

2 Read these two short extracts from different business articles. Is the point they are making equally valid in your country?

A study at the Stanford University School of Business tracked MBAs ten years after they graduated. The result? Grade point averages had no bearing on their success – but their ability to converse with others did. Being able to connect with others through small talk can lead to big things.

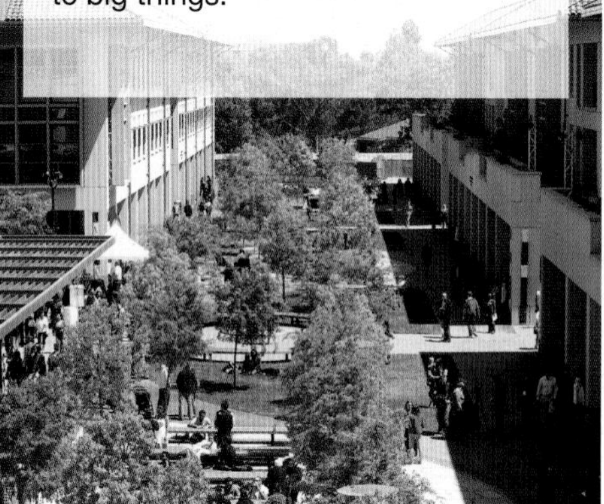

When Jack Welch gave a guest lecture at MIT's Sloan School of Management in 2005, someone in the crowd asked, 'What should we be learning in business school?' Welch's reply: 'Just concentrate on networking. Everything else you need to know, you can learn on the job.'

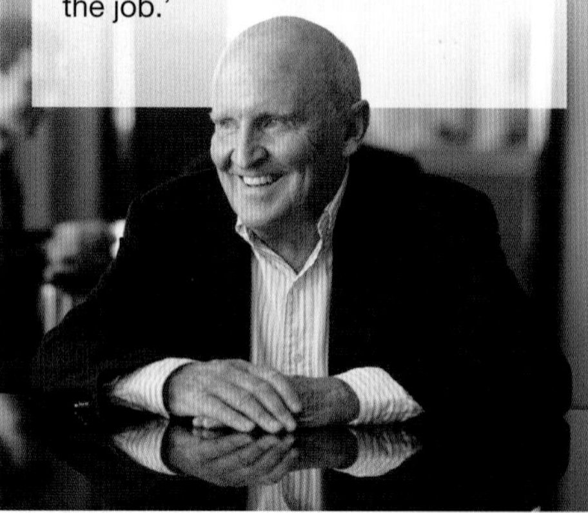

3 How good are you at small talk? Are you comfortable talking to strangers? You are going to practise networking with a business contact.

a Note down some information about yourself in the chart below.

Birthplace	Languages	Interests	Current job or employer	Travel	Studies

b Work with a partner to set the scene of your conversation. Where are you – at a conference reception, a social event, in the coffee break at a training seminar?

c Swap personal information with your partner and use this and the scene you built up in b as the basis for your conversation. How long can you keep the conversation going? Use the language in the box on the left to help you.

4 How did the conversation go? Which topics had the most mileage? Did you find anything in common?

Corporate entertainment

1 The world economy has had its ups and downs, but many companies continue to invest in corporate hospitality. In uncertain economic times, can this kind of spending be justified? How can entertaining clients and colleagues be good for business?

2 Complete the extract from a corporate entertainment company's website using the words in the box. Are you persuaded by what it says?

box	clients	cuisine	experience	members	office
relationships	seats	service	setting	team	viewing

What better way to build and maintain (a) ________ with key (b) ________ and to reward star (c) ________ of your (d) ________, than to offer them a unique and unforgettable (e) ________ far away from the pressures and constraints of an (f) ________ environment? Whether it's front row (g) ________ at the Metropolitan Opera in New York, a VIP (h) ________ at the World Cup Final, a private (i) ________ at the Guggenheim Gallery in Bilbao or fine French (j) ________ at the Paris Ritz, we can provide the ideal (k) ________ and first-class (l) ________ that will leave your guests simply saying 'Wow!'

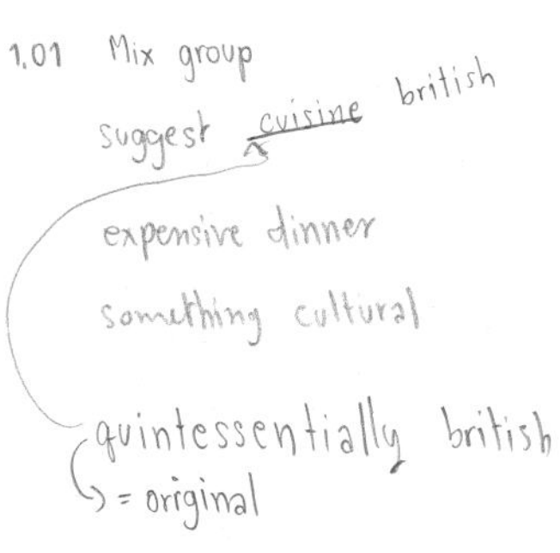

3 **1.01** A group of Russian businesspeople, who are about to collaborate with you on a major international project, are visiting your London office. As part of the planning committee, it's your job to decide on a special event to celebrate their visit. Listen to some of the considerations of the other committee members and take notes.

4 Work in two groups to find out about four different events you could take your Russian visitors to. Group A turn to page 118. Group B turn to page 129.

5 Work with a partner from the other group and discuss the options. Prepare to present your recommendations.

Making conversation

1 **1.02–1.03** Listen to some businesspeople chatting at two of the corporate events you discussed, and answer the questions.

Conversation 1

a What's the connection between Helen Keating, James McRae and Alan Sullivan?

b When Helen asks James 'Mind if I join you?', how does he reply?

N________ a________ a________. B________ m________ g________.

c What excuse does Helen make for leaving the rest of the party?

d Two of the following mean 'That can't be true'. Which two?

You're joking! [ ]
You're fooling! [ ]
You're kidding! [ ]

e Helen and James use several expressions to refer to memories. Can you remember the first three words of each expression? Contractions (*it's*, *you're* etc) count as one word.

1 ________ ________ ________ somewhere before?
2 ________ ________ ________ me to forget a face.
3 ________ ________ ________ recognized you.
4 ________ ________ ________ back to me now.
5 ________ ________ ________ remember spending most of the evening trying to avoid some annoying little guy called Alan.

Conversation 2

a How would you describe relations between Mr Ishida and Mr Thompson?

warm [ ] amicable [ ] cordial [ ] cool [ ] strained [ ] frosty [ ]

b Mr Thompson uses the word 'so' five times during the conversation:

So, Mr Ishida, let me freshen your glass.

So, how are you enjoying the match?

So, tell me, have you been to one of these big tournaments before?

So, shall we return to our seats?

So, do you still play?

Why does he need to use it so often? What's the equivalent word or expression in your own language?

c Mr Ishida says he's too old to play table tennis now. Mr Thompson replies 'Oh, I'm sure that's not true.' Is he:

paying Mr Ishida a compliment? [ ] calling Mr Ishida a liar? [ ]

d Mr Thompson tries to use his background knowledge to keep the conversation going. Complete his remarks below.

1 I h________ you're quite a tennis fan.
2 I u________ the Japanese are world table tennis champions.
3 I s________ the Nikkei's looking strong. That m________ be good news for you.

e What word is Mr Ishida avoiding by saying the following?

Not at the moment, thank you.

Not really.

Not especially.

Not any more.

As a matter of fact, …

2 Work with a partner. Practise avoiding saying 'no' by playing the no-no game.

THE no-no GAME

Prepare

Write down six false (but believable) statements about yourself, your job, your family, your interests, your company or your country. When you are ready, swap lists with a partner.

Your objective is to get the other person to say 'no'. Their objective is the same. Use the useful expressions below to help you to avoid saying 'no'.

Whoever says 'no' first loses.

Play

Imagine the two of you are chatting at a conference or corporate event. Take it in turns to make wrong assumptions about each other using the lists as a starting point but adding remarks of your own if you can.

***I hear** you're based in Rotterdam.*
***I understand** you're a keen golfer.*
***I believe** your company's about to be involved in a merger.*

Not very.
Not really.
Not especially.
Not exactly.
Not yet.
Not any more.
Not at the moment.
Not as far as I know.
Actually, ...
As a matter of fact, ...

3 **1.04–1.05** Listen to some businesspeople chatting at the other two corporate events you discussed and answer the questions.

Conversation 1

a How would you describe the Hamiltons? Compare your impressions with a partner.

b Put the words in the following greetings and introductions in the correct order, adding punctuation where necessary.

1 Dan call please me
2 meet last to both pleasure at a you
3 mentioned name Julian's course your of
4 Fiona calling me mind do don't you you you?

c It's common when someone joins a group at a party to tell them a bit about the conversation you've just been having. Complete the sentences with the words in the box.

discussing	saying	talking	trying	wondering

We were just
1 ____________ what a marvellous party this is.
2 ____________ these new tax laws they're bringing in.
3 ____________ about you – how are things?
4 ____________ what this pile of dirty laundry was doing in an art gallery.
5 ____________ to work out what this whole thing must have cost.

d Why does Dan say to Alistair 'I wonder if we could have a word?' when they're already talking?

e All the expressions below mean 'I'm going'. Which also mean 'but I'm coming back'? Some of them were in the conversation you just listened to.

It's been nice talking to you.	☐	Would you excuse me a moment?	☐
I'll have to be going.	☐	I'll be right back.	☐
If you'll excuse me.	☐	Is that the time?	☐
Don't go away.	☐	I'll catch you later.	☐

f Are you a fan of contemporary art?

Conversation 2

a Do Tom and Ricardo do a deal?

b What expression does Tom use to switch from discussing motor racing to discussing business?

T__________ o__________ races, how's the South African bid going?

c Complete the expressions below. They were all in the conversation you just listened to.

1 Glad ________ ________ make it.
2 I ________ ________ missed it for the world.
3 There's ________ ________ like you to meet.
4 Can't ________ ________ standing there with an empty glass.
5 So, ________ ________ person you wanted me to meet?
6 I ________ ________ two know each other already.
7 I'll ________ ________ two to chat. See you later.

d What do the following remarks tell you about Ricardo and Élise's relationship?

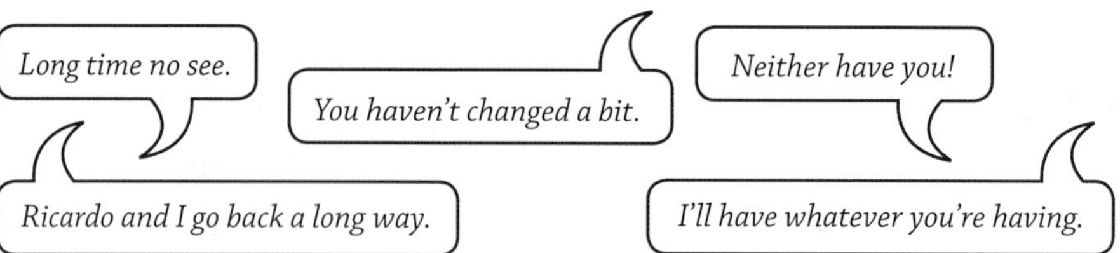

4 Work with a partner. Practise paying and receiving compliments.

You're looking well!
Great to see you again …
I (really) like your …! Where did you get it/them?
By the way, you did a great job in the meeting/presentation the other day.
Compliments on your brilliant project design!
You really know how to captivate an audience!
Great presentation style.

THE mutual appreciation GAME

Prepare

Spend a few minutes thinking of compliments you could pay your partner. Use the expressions on the left to help you.

Play

When you are ready,

- start exchanging compliments with your partner.
- respond to each compliment you receive in an appreciative but modest way.

See who can give the most compliments in under a minute!

5 They say 'Flattery will get you everywhere.' How important is it in your culture to give compliments? Can compliments be risky? How?

6 According to Dale Carnegie, author of the best-selling people skills book *How to Win Friends and Influence People*, 'You can make more friends in two months by becoming interested in other people than you can in two years by trying to get people interested in you.'

Work with a partner to practise keeping up a conversation.

- First choose just three 'hot buttons' from the list below – topics you are especially interested in talking about, but don't tell your partner what they are!
- Then take turns to ask each other questions from the list. Whenever your partner asks you about one of your hot buttons, you should speak enthusiastically about the topic for a minute or so. If the topic is not hot, then just reply very briefly and ask your next question.
- Whenever one of you hits a hot button, you score five points. When you miss, you lose one point.
- The game ends after ten minutes or when one of you has hit all the other's hot buttons. Whoever has the most points at the end of the game is the winner.

THE hot buttons GAME

Topics	Conversation starters	Hot or not?
WORK	How's business? I hear …	Hot / Not
RECENT NEWS	Have you heard about …? … news, isn't it?	Hot / Not
THE ECONOMY	I see the stock markets are … It's probably a good time to …	Hot / Not
SPORT	Are you into sport at all? Did you see the game/match on …?	Hot / Not
MUSIC	What kind of music are you into? Have you heard …'s latest album?	Hot / Not
MOVIES	Have you seen any good films lately? I quite liked …	Hot / Not
TRAVEL	Do you get to do much travelling? Have you ever been to …?	Hot / Not
FOOD/DRINK	Shall we get ourselves …? What would you like? How about …?	Hot / Not

01 Business or pleasure?

Vocabulary

Small talk

1 Put the conversation in the correct order.

a We were just talking about this new sports centre they're building. Do you play any sport at all, Kim? 1
b Oh, right. Thanks for telling me. Incidentally, have you still got my Coldplay CD? ☐
c Did you? Me too. I was never any good, though. ☐
d Me? Well, not really. I used to play a bit of football. ☐
e No, me neither. Talking of football, did you see the match last night? ☐
f Yeah, I sent it yesterday. Oh, that reminds me. Clive said to tell you he won't be able to make Thursday's meeting. He said he'd call you. ☐
g Against Real Madrid? No, I missed it. I had to go to a birthday party. ☐
h No problem. Oh, before I forget. I've got two tickets to see them in Manchester if you're interested. ☐
i Not yet, no. Why, are you doing something? ☐
j Pity. It was a great game. On the subject of parties, have you made any plans for New Year's Eve yet? ☐
k No, nothing special. By the way, sorry to talk business, but did you remember to send that estimate to Clive? ☐
l Are you kidding? Of course I'm interested! I've never seen them live. ☐
m Oops! Yeah, sorry. I meant to give it back to you. I'll bring it in tomorrow. Thanks for lending it to me. ☐

2 Find six expressions in 1 to guide the conversation or change the subject.

a I__________, …
b T__________ of …
c B__________ the w__________, …
d B__________ I f__________, …
e T__________ r__________ me, …
f O__________ t__________ s__________ of …

3 Which words and phrases in 1 could you replace with the following?

a Not so far.
b Not to worry.
c Nor me.
d Shame.
e So did I.
f Are you joking?

Grammar

Tense review

1 Try to complete the tense quiz in under five minutes.

1 *He* ***leaves*** *at five* means
a today **b** every day **c** either

2 *We'****re having*** *a meeting* means
a now **b** soon **c** either

3 *Profits* ***went up***. Are profits up now?
a yes **b** no **c** maybe

4 *Profits* ***have gone up***. Are profits up now?
a yes **b** no **c** maybe

5 *He'****s gone***. Is he here?
a yes **b** no **c** maybe

6 *I'****ve*** *just* ***been***. Am I back?
a yes **b** no **c** maybe

7 *When I arrived he* ***was*** *just* ***leaving***. Was he there when I arrived?
a yes **b** no **c** we don't know

8 *When I arrived he'****d*** *just* ***left***. Was he there when I arrived?
a yes **b** no **c** we don't know

9 *I'****ve tried*** *to phone her.* Am I still trying?
a probably **b** probably not **c** we don't know

10 *I'****ve been trying*** *to contact her all morning.* Am I still trying?
a probably **b** probably not **c** we don't know

2 Read the email and underline the best grammatical choice in each case.

From: Charles Wellcome
To: Deborah Newton, Stephen Clark, Willem Maes, Tatiana Korbutt
Subject: This year's client hospitality event

Dear all

As you (1) **know / are knowing**, the annual client hospitality event (2) **is fast approaching / will fast approach**. As of yet, we (3) **did not make / have not made** a final decision on where to hold it this year. One or two of you (4) **already came forward / have already come forward** with suggestions, which (5) **are currently considered / are currently being considered**. However, as we (6) **will have to / are having to** make the necessary arrangements quite soon, I'd like everybody's input on this asap.

CONTINUE ➤

◀ CONTINUE

What I particularly (7) **want / am wanting** to avoid is a repetition of the fiasco from last year's showjumping event. First, very few of our clients (8) **had / were having** even the remotest interest in the sport. And the atrocious weather (9) **meant / was meaning** that we (10) **walked / were walking** backwards and forwards through the mud between the show ring and the hospitality tent all day. The whole thing (11) **was / has been** a complete disaster. People (12) **still complained / were still complaining** about it six months later!

This year we (13) **have planned / had planned** to do something more cultural like going to the opera or even a musical, but (14) **I've wondered / I've been wondering** if this is a good idea. A musical event (15) **doesn't seem / isn't seeming** to be the best place to network or to have a quiet, friendly chat!

I (16) **do think / am thinking**, however, that an indoor event (17) **makes / is making** most sense, so can I ask you to (18) **think / be thinking** along those lines over the next few days? (19) **I've scheduled / I'd scheduled** a meeting for next Friday to discuss the matter further. So, (20) **I'm speaking / I'll speak** to you all then.

You use the **Present Simple** to talk about permanent facts (*I'm Spanish*), routines (*I get home at seven each evening*) and scheduled future (*The bus gets in at one*).

You use the **Present Continuous** to talk about current, perhaps temporary, activities and situations (*I'm staying at the Hilton*) or future arrangements (*I'm flying to Rome in the morning*).

Some 'state' verbs like *think, know, understand, need, want* and *seem* are not generally used in the continuous form unless the meaning is different: *I think* = I believe; *I'm thinking* = I'm considering something.

You use the **Present Perfect** to talk about things that started in the past and continue up to the present (*It's rained for a fortnight*), personal experiences no matter when they happened (*I've only ever snowboarded once*) and things which have an immediate consequence (*I've lost my car keys*). Words like *already*, *yet* and *since* are often in the same sentence as a present perfect verb.

You use the **Present Perfect Continuous** to talk about things that started in the past and may be recently completed or not yet completed (*She's been rearranging her office, I've been working here since January 2002*).

You use the **Past Simple** to talk about finished past actions or states (*I studied engineering at Oxford, I was a happy child*). Phrases like *last week, a year ago, in 2006,* etc make the time reference clear.

You use the **Past Continuous** to talk about an action in progress in the past (*The company was losing money*). The Past Continuous gives the background to more important events which are in the Past Simple at a specific time in the completed past.

You use the **Past Perfect** to emphasize that one event happened before another in the past (*By the time I left college, I'd already decided I didn't want to be a lawyer*).

will is a modal verb and, amongst its other uses, one of many ways of talking about the future (*I'll see you later*).

Phrase bank: Making conversation

Complete the tips on how to master the art of small talk with the words in the box.

break bring change compliment contradict start

1 Use what you already know about people to ________ up a conversation. ☐ ☐
2 Try to ________ people into conversation with others you know. ☐ ☐
3 Show enthusiasm; pay people you know well the occasional ________. ☐ ☐
4 Be careful not to ________ people too directly. ☐ ☐
5 ________ the subject smoothly by referring to what others have said. ☐ ☐
6 Don't ________ off the conversation too abruptly at the end. ☐ ☐

Now match two phrases to each of the tips above.

a I hear you speak Cantonese, is that right?
b Kenichi, there's someone I'd like you to meet.
c Well, it's been really nice talking to you.
d I'm afraid I'll have to be going. But let me give you my card.
e I understand you work for 3M.
f You're looking well. Been on holiday?
g Congratulations on the promotion, by the way!
h Funny you should say that, something very similar happened to me.
i Well, that's not entirely true, but I know what you mean.
j On the subject of the merger, have you heard the latest?
k Let's see what Max thinks. Max, we've got a question for you.
l Actually, it's not as bad as you might think.

02 Information exchange

If a problem causes many meetings, the meetings eventually become more important than the problem.

Arthur Bloch, *Murphy's Law*

How do you ensure that meetings are kept to a minimum?

Learning objectives: Unit 2

Business communication skills Describing attitudes to and content of meetings; Paraphrasing information; Pointing out discrepancies; Dialogue-building using the language of meetings; Fluency: Breaking bad news and writing a report
Reading Meeting: breaking bad news
Listening A meeting: problems with a product; Five meetings: discrepancies; The language of meetings
Vocabulary Meetings
Grammar Conditionals
Phrase bank Debating issues
In company interviews Units 1–2

1 Roughly how much of your working week do you spend in meetings?

2 Read the well-circulated web joke below. Is this anything like the meetings you take part in?

3 The language of business is constantly changing; phrases such as *face time*, *cloud computing* and *exit strategy* come and go. What are some of the current 'buzzwords' in your line of business?

4 With a partner, try to complete the buzzword dictionary definitions below by writing in the missing vowels.

1 A change of **m_nds_t** means completely rethinking your attitude and approach to something.
2 A company's **c_r_ c_mp_t_nc__s** are its strengths, the things it does particularly well.
3 **P_r_d_gm shift** is a fundamental change in the way something is done.
4 To be **pr__ct_v_** is to make things happen rather than waiting for them to happen. Always having Plan A, B or even C, if necessary!
5 To **syn_rg_z_** means to combine strengths and benefit from working together as a team.
6 To think **__ts_d_ th_ b_x** is to think in totally new and creative ways.
7 To **dr_ll d_wn** is to go into more detail.
8 Getting **b_y-_n** from people means getting their support for a proposal or project.
9 To take a business to **th_ n_xt l_v_l** means to expand it and make it more competitive.
10 You need to do a **r__l_ty ch_ck** when you've lost touch with the real world.
11 **Th_ b_tt_m li__** is the essential point in a discussion.
12 Looking at **th_ b_g p_ct_r_** is looking at the situation as a whole.
13 To **b_nchm_rk** is to use a successful company's standards to measure and improve your own.
14 To **r_mp _p** production or sales is to increase them.
15 **Emp_w_rm_nt** gives employees the confidence and authority to take control of their jobs.

5 1.06 You're going to play a game that's become popular with bored executives the world over – buzzword bingo! First, turn to page 119 and choose a bingo card. Then listen to a manager in a corporate sales meeting and cross off the buzzwords as he uses them. The first person to cross them all off and shout 'Bingo!' wins the game.

6 Some of the things you might really want to discuss in an information-sharing meeting are listed below, but the second word in each pair has been switched with another in the same column. Switch them back. The first two have been done for you.

a	b	c
1 production **margins**	1 quality **campaigns**	1 customer **budgets**
2 balance **appraisals**	2 sales **chains**	2 recruitment **setting**
3 market **channels**	3 advertising **control**	3 salary **support**
4 staff **sheets**	4 cost **development**	4 training **relations**
5 profit **methods**	5 supply **projections**	5 price **procedures**
6 distribution **trends**	6 product **cutting**	6 IT **reviews**

7 Work with a partner. Take turns to explain one of the terms in 6 and see if your partner can guess which one it is. How many can you get right in two minutes?

It's predicting how many products you think you'll sell.
'Market trends'?
No.
Oh, you mean 'sales projections'?
Right.

Making things clear

1 How direct are people from your country when it comes to doing business? Complete the diagram below with the nationalities in the box. Then check your answers on page 137.

American Brazilian British Chinese French
German Indian Italian Japanese Russian

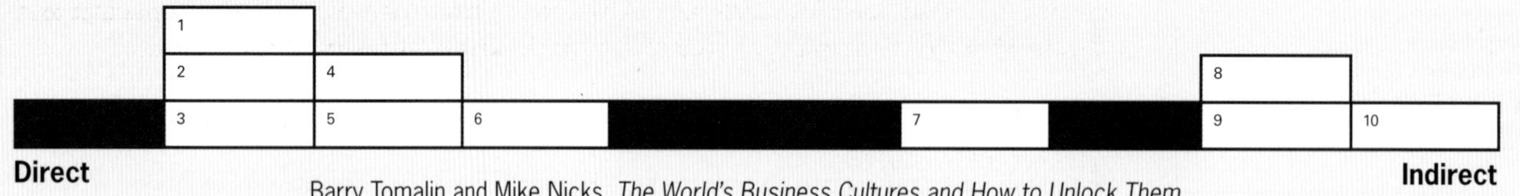

Barry Tomalin and Mike Nicks, *The World's Business Cultures and How to Unlock Them*

2 In meetings, especially in indirect cultures, people are sometimes reluctant to say exactly what they mean – especially if they have bad news! Match the vague statements to their blunt equivalents.

Vague

a I'm sorry to report that the project has not been a complete success.
b Technically speaking, we have run into negative profit.
c I think there's a general lack of consumer confidence.
d You know we've always been a market-driven organization.
e Now is not the time to expand, but to consolidate.
f There will have to be some restructuring of the department.
g We may also have to consider outsourcing production to cut costs.
h Of course, we won't be able to finalize anything today.

Blunt

1 Our assembly plant may be closed down too.
2 Sales are falling.
3 People are going to lose their jobs.
4 It's failed.
5 We'll have to hold another meeting!
6 We've made a loss.
7 Let's do nothing.
8 We've never had an original idea.

3 1.07 A computer games company has had problems with its latest product. Listen to an extract from their meeting and check your answers in 2.

4 Summarize the meeting you just listened to using the notes below. Listen again if you need to.

Quasar Online Gaming System

Considerable investment in design and marketing – project not a complete success – negative profit – disappointing sales – lack of consumer confidence – Sony and Nintendo innovate – we clone technology – do it cheaper – a market-driven organization – market massively oversupplied – bad time to expand – good time to consolidate – departmental restructuring necessary – possibly outsource – cut costs – assembly plant closure likely – schedule another meeting – final decision

5 Work with a partner. Take turns to read out the vague statements below. The other person should paraphrase them in a more direct way using the expressions in the box and the words in brackets.

In other words, ...	So what you're (really) saying is ...
What you (really) mean is ...	You mean ...

- **a** The results so far have been rather disappointing. (disastrous)
- **b** We may currently be overstaffed in the customer relations department. (lay-offs)
- **c** Head Office's reaction to the idea has not been as positive as we hoped. (hate)
- **d** Sales have not yet matched our original projections. (not selling)
- **e** The market doesn't seem to be as buoyant as it used to be. (dead)
- **f** The project is likely to cost rather more than we anticipated. (over budget)

Queries and comments

1 1.08 Listen to short extracts from five meetings. Each contains one piece of information that doesn't make sense. When each extract pauses, work with a partner and decide what the discrepancy is. Then listen to the rest of the extract and check.

2 Work with a partner to practise pointing out discrepancies. Speaker A see page 119. Speaker B see page 128.

3 1.09 Listen to an extract from a meeting. A CEO is breaking some bad news to the board. When the conversation pauses, write the board members' queries and comments using the notes in brackets to help you. Then continue listening and check. The first one has been done for you as an example.

- **a** (say/fall short/projections again?)
  Are you saying they've fallen short of projections again?
- **b** (suggest/introduce/price cuts?)
- **c** (surely/not say/time/phase them out!)
- **d** (this mean/should/invest more/new technology?)
- **e** (tell us/could be lay-offs?)
- **f** (mean some kind/job-share scheme?)
- **g** (so/say/should/spend more/R&D)
- **h** (this mean/think/centralize distribution?)
- **i** (hope/not suggest/situation/hopeless)

4 The following phrases and expressions were all in the meeting you just listened to. Reverse the meaning of each by changing the word or words in bold. The first one has been done for you as an example.

- **a** **disappointing** figures
  encouraging figures
- **b** **fall short of** projections
- **c** **miss** our targets
- **d** run at **a loss**
- **e** phase them **out**
- **f** the unions **oppose** it
- **g** **slide into** debt
- **h** **overseas** distributors
- **i** **inflated** prices
- **j** **volatile** markets

5 Turn to page 141. Look at the listening script of the meeting you listened to in 3 and answer the questions.

a How many examples of conditional sentences and expressions are there?
b Apart from *if*, which three words are used to link the conditional to the main clause?
c Only one of the conditional sentences refers to the past. Which one?
d Why is the past tense used in the following example from the meeting?
Even if we decided to do that, and it's a big if, it would take time to implement.
e *If only it was that simple* (line 29) means:
I wish it was that simple. ☐ I doubt it's that simple. ☐
f *We're not really in a position to invest in anything, even if we wanted to* (lines 30–32) means:
We don't want to invest in anything. ☐
Wanting to invest would make no difference. ☐

The language of meetings

1 Work with a partner. One word will complete each of the following extracts from meetings. Can you agree what it is? If you need help, turn to page 122.

a	A scheduling meeting			
	A	Right. Basically, the		is this: the contract is ours if we want it.
	B	But we're not in a		to take on another project right now, are we?
	A	I know. Jan, what's your		on this?
b	An IT meeting			
	A	Look, it's not just a		of software, Alessandro.
	B	Of course not. It's also a		of hardware. The entire system needs upgrading.
	A	But that's out of the		We can't afford that kind of capital outlay.
c	A marketing meeting			
	A	Sales are down. One		would obviously be to cut our prices.
	B	That's no longer an		for us. We're barely breaking even as it is.
	A	Well, then we've no		but to rethink our whole marketing strategy.
d	An HR* meeting			
	A	Well, there's no easy		to this, but how about voluntary redundancy?
	B	I don't think that's the		but maybe we could reduce people's hours.
	A	That might have been the		if we didn't already have a strike on our hands!
e	A strategy meeting			
	A	Now, let's not make a		out of this. What if we just pulled out of Sudan?
	B	Well, I've no		with that, but our partners won't be happy.
	A	No, but that's not our		is it? The political situation is just too unstable.
f	A CRM** meeting			
	A	I'll get straight to the		We're getting too many customer complaints.
	B	I agree with you. But the		is we don't have the staff to deal with them.
	A	That's beside the		We shouldn't be getting them in the first place!
g	A crisis meeting			
	A	I'm afraid the		is serious. And if the press get hold of the story, …
	B	Look, we'll deal with that		if and when it arises. Let's not panic just yet.
	A	You're right. What this		calls for is calm and careful planning.
h	A budget meeting			
	A	The		is, we're simply not spending enough on R&D.
	B	As a matter of		we've doubled our R&D budget this year.
	C	That may be so, but the		remains we're losing our technological lead.

* **Human Resources**
** **Customer Relationship Management**

2 1.10 Listen to the meeting extracts in 1 and check your answers.

3 Now decide which of the words in the box on page 122 will complete the following sentences and match them to what they mean.

a	That's a matter of ______________.	You're wrong!
b	I think that raises a different ______________.	I disagree!
c	Yes, but look at it from my point of ______________.	That's unimportant!
d	Actually, that might not be a bad ______________.	That's irrelevant!
e	That's not an ______________.	Good point!
f	What gave you that ______________?	What about me?

Breaking the bad news

I've been asked to inform you that ...
It seems/appears that ...
I'm afraid that ...
It's felt that ...
The following options are being explored ...
The suggestion is that ...
The basic idea is to ...
In addition, what's being proposed is ...
This would obviously mean ...

1 Your company was recently acquired by a former competitor in a hostile takeover. The new board of directors has decided it's time for a serious shake-up. Each of you has been chosen to announce at a special interdepartmental meeting some of the changes they would like to see implemented. Speaker A turn to page 118. Speaker B turn to page 128. Speaker C turn to page 133. The phrases on the left may help you to prepare.

2 When you're ready, take turns in your group to present the proposals. They could be controversial, so:

- put them forward one step at a time and get reactions from the group before moving on to the next step
- invite discussion of each proposal and take notes on any comments or alternative suggestions
- even though you yourself may not be in favour of the proposal you put forward, you should at least initially show loyalty to your new bosses by sounding positive.

In company interviews
Units 1–2

3 Write a memo to the board outlining the reactions to the proposals you presented at your meeting.

02 Information exchange

Vocabulary

Meetings

Metaphor: discussion is a journey

1 A lot of the language of discussion refers to journeys. Read the conversation and underline the references to movement and travel. There are 20.

Ian returns to the boardroom to find the meeting in chaos ...

Ian Sorry about that. Had to take a phone call from Bangkok. So, are we any nearer a decision?

Erik Not yet, but we're getting there. I think we're more or less on the right track, anyway.

Sonia Are we? I'd say we've got a long way to go yet. We just seem to be going round in circles.

Erik Well, we were making good progress before we got sidetracked, Sonia. Now, returning to the question of logistics ...

Ella Sorry, but could I just go back to what I was saying earlier about freight charges?

Sonia Hang on, hang on. Aren't we getting ahead of ourselves here? We haven't got as far as discussing transportation yet, Ella ...

Erik We don't seem to be getting very far at all!

Ian The conversation seems to have drifted a little while I was away ... I can't quite see where all this is heading.

Erik We've certainly wandered away from the main topic. Now, logistics ...

Sonia I was just coming to that. In my opinion, this whole plan is totally impractical.

Ian I don't think I like the direction this discussion is going in. Okay, look, we've covered a lot of ground this morning, but I think that's about as far as we can go at the moment.

Erik Now, just a minute! We haven't come this far to break off now, surely ...

Idiomatic expressions

2 In the fixed expressions below, delete the word you wouldn't expect to hear.

a So, what do you **reckon** / **guess**?
b I wouldn't go quite as **far** / **much** as that.
c Where do you **stand** / **sit** on this?
d Well, that goes without **saying** / **speaking**.
e I don't mind **either** / **each** way.
f I'm afraid it's not **so** / **as** simple as that.
g Any **responses** / **reactions**?
h The way I **view** / **see** it is this.
i I **wouldn't** / **couldn't** say that.
j **Yes and no** / **No and yes**.
k I **can't** / **couldn't** say, to be honest.
l I'd like us to **share** / **spare** our views on this.
m Oh, come **on** / **off** it!
n Well, I haven't **given** / **taken** it much thought.
o I'm **for** / **with** you there.
p To my **meaning** / **mind**, it's like this.
q To **a point** / **an extent** you're right.

3 Categorize the expressions in 2 according to their purpose.

1 asking for an opinion ☐ ☐ ☐ ☐
2 giving an opinion ☐ ☐ ☐
3 giving no opinion ☐ ☐ ☐
4 agreeing ☐
5 disagreeing ☐ ☐ ☐
6 half-agreeing ☐ ☐ ☐

Grammar

Conditionals

Put a cross next to the ending (1–3) which isn't grammatically possible and then correct it. The first one has been done for you.

a As long as we're well prepared, ...
1 we've got nothing to worry about. ✓
2 we couldn't go wrong. ✗
3 we'll be fine. ✓

we can't go wrong.

b I'll send them an email ...
1 if you'll tell me what I should say.
2 if you think it's worth it.
3 provided I hadn't lost their address.

______

c If you're going out, ...
1 you're going to miss the meeting.
2 you'd better take an umbrella.
3 I come with you.

______

d Do that ...
1 and you'll regret it.
2 if you'll get the opportunity.
3 – we'll lose business.

______

e I'd stay and help you ...
1 if I'm not going out this evening.
2 if I hadn't promised Jo I'd meet her.
3 if you asked me nicely.

______

f I'd be grateful ...
1 if you could sort this out for me.
2 if you'd keep this to yourself.
3 if you don't tell anyone about this.

______

g If he actually said that to her, ...
1 she'd kill him.
2 I'd have been very surprised.
3 he must have been mad.

____

h I wouldn't have asked you ...
1 unless I trusted you.
2 if I'd known this would happen.
3 if you didn't say you wanted to do it.

____

i If it hadn't been for him, ...
1 I'd still be working at Burger King.
2 I'd have got that job.
3 I hadn't had a chance.

____

You can use any tense in either half (clause) of a **conditional sentence.**

As well as *if, unless, as long as* and *providing/provided (that)*, you can also use *and* as a conjunction in a conditional (*Do that* ***and*** *we'll get complaints*) or no conjunction at all (*Do that – we'll get complaints*).

Conditional clauses can come either first or second in the sentence. However, with *and* or no conjunction, conditional clauses come first.

You can put *will* or *would* in the conditional clause *(If you'**ll** wait here, I'**ll** go and get her for you; I'**d** be grateful if you'**d** give this matter your serious attention)*, but this is unusual.

The **Past Simple** in a conditional can refer to the past (*Even if I **did meet** her, I'm afraid I don't remember her*), to a future possibility (*If I **resigned** tomorrow, I could get another job within the week*) or to an unreal situation *(If I **spoke** Italian, I'd phone her myself, but I don't)*.

Conditionals with the **Past Perfect** can refer to the effects of the past on the more recent past (*If you'**d made** a backup, we wouldn't have lost the whole document*) or on the present (*If I'**d got** that job, I could be earning a fortune now*).

Phrase bank: Debating issues

A small number of words account for quite a lot of the language of meetings and discussions. One noun will complete each of the sets of expressions below:

a ____________

I agree with you up to a ____________.
That's beside the ____________.
That's not the ____________.
That's just my ____________.
The ____________ is ...
Okay, ____________ taken.
I'll get straight to the ____________.
Good ____________.

b ____________

That's out of the ____________.
Good ____________!
It's not a ____________ of that.
It's not just a ____________ of ...
It's also a ____________ of ...
The (real) ____________ is ...

c ____________

We're not in a ____________ to ...
What's your ____________ on this?
This puts us in a very difficult ____________.
I'm in no ____________ to ...

d ____________

The ____________ is ...
The ____________ remains that ...
As a matter of ____________, ...
In actual ____________, ...
Despite the ____________ that ...
In view of the ____________ that ...

e ____________

We've no ____________.
That's not an ____________.
One ____________ would be ...
____________ two would be ...
Another ____________ would be ...

f ____________

There's no ____________.
What's the ____________?

03 Rapport

Learning objectives: Unit 3

People skills Strategies and techniques to build rapport; Fluency: Building rapport with a colleague
Reading Top tips for building rapport; Training manual checklists
Listening Two meetings to discuss teleworking

1 What is the man in the cartoon trying to do? What is he doing wrong?

2 What strategies or techniques can you use to build rapport with people who are different from you?

3 Read the web article below and decide on a one-word title for each tip. How many of the techniques you discussed in 2 are mentioned?

Five top tips for building rapport

1 ______________

Even if you're having a bad day, don't forget the basics: make eye contact, smile and be sincere. Be sensitive to cultural differences in areas like greeting people, respecting personal space and making small talk.

2 ______________

Set your personal fashion sense aside until the weekend and try to look like the other person. This could mean 'dressing to impress' in formal business meetings, but also dressing down in a technical or creative workplace. Your clothes, hair, make-up, nails, jewellery, beard or tattoos all send messages about you and your values.

3 ______________

Use your emotional intelligence to create empathy. Developing an awareness of how feelings and emotions influence attitudes and behaviour will allow you to accentuate similarities and minimize differences between yourself and other people.

4 ______________

Take time to find common ground. Finding a connection through your education, experience, family or interests brings you closer and helps build trust. But always be sincere; in the long run, inventing shared interests or experience will only lead to trouble!

5 ______________

Matching and mirroring the other person's speech, behaviour and thought processes is something that comes naturally to good communicators. Adapt your body language and the way you listen and speak to synchronize with the person you are dealing with.

4 Look at the photographs and describe the body language. Which of the five techniques in 3 are being used?

5 1.11 Listen to a director from Head Office in the US talking to the HR manager of a subsidiary in southern Europe about a new teleworking policy. Discuss the questions with a partner.

a How does each person speak? Describe their voices.
b Imagine a video of the meeting. What do you think Jacob and Helena look like? Describe their body language.

6 1.11 Listen again and answer the questions.

a How do Jacob and Helena feel about the new policy and about each other?
b Why do Jacob and Helena fail to build rapport?

7 Complete the checklist from a training manual using the words in the box.

compromise crossed deep husky mirroring outcome restricted small staccato subtle

Matching and mirroring

Observe, match and mirror the following:

- [ ] Gestures: with the hands or the head, large or (1) ________, expansive or (2) ________
- [ ] Posture: relaxed or tense, leaning forward or back, arms or legs together, apart or (3) ________
- [ ] Facial expressions: positive or negative, open or closed, overt or (4) ________
- [ ] Breathing: fast or slow, shallow or (5) ________, regular or irregular
- [ ] Voice: high or low, loud or soft, clear or (6) ________
- [ ] Speech: slow or fast, fluid or (7) ________, confident or hesitant
- [ ] Key words and phrases

Mirror, pace, lead

- [ ] Mirror: adapt your gestures, posture, expressions, voice, etc to the other person.
- [ ] Pace: make subtle changes, moving towards a (8) ________ that is comfortable for both of you. If the other person does not follow you, go back to (9) ________.
- [ ] Lead: when the other person has moved towards your pace, lead them towards the desired (10) ________.

8 How easy to use are the tips and techniques in 3 and 7? Do you find any of them insincere or even manipulative? Why? Which of the tips and techniques could you use the next time you need to build rapport with someone?

9 1.12 Listen to a second version of the meeting in 5. How have Jacob and Helena changed the way they communicate? How do you imagine their body language has changed?

10 Work with a partner to practise your rapport-building skills. Speaker A see page 138, Speaker B see page 129.

MANAGEMENT SCENARIO

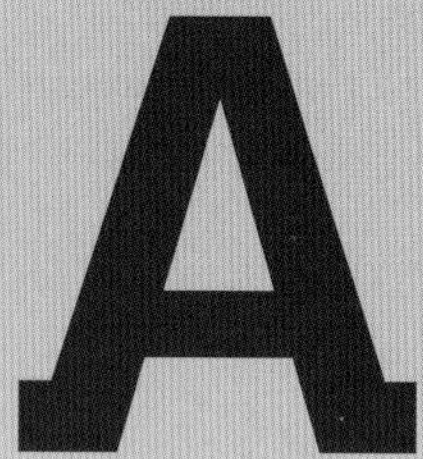

Culture clash

Learning objectives: Management scenario A

Business communication skills Identifying potential cultural differences; Avoiding a culture clash; Fluency: A meeting to discuss a merger

Reading Cultural sensitivity checklist

In company in action
A1: A culture clash;
A2: Positive cross-cultural understanding

1 How would you describe your organization's culture? Are your colleagues different from the people in other departments or companies you have worked in? Think about relationships, attitudes and communication styles.

2 Read the memo below and answer the questions.

a What kind of organizations are GWA and Blue Rock?
b Why have they merged?
c Why do you think Sue Jensen wrote the memo?
d What kind of culture clashes should managers anticipate when staff from two different organizations share office space?

Re: Merger

From: Sue Jensen, CEO
To: All staff
Re: Merger

As you are all aware, our merger with Global Water Aid was completed last month. The first of many synergies we hope to achieve will begin on Monday when staff from GWA's headquarters will be moving into our London office. This will mean a certain amount of reorganization to fit everyone in, but we expect everything to be up and running in 48 hours.

GWA and Blue Rock share the same goals: to build a world where every man, woman and child has access to safe drinking water and sanitation. GWA have over 40 years of experience of developing sustainable solutions to water, sanitation, and hygiene problems. Although Blue Rock is a much younger organization, I'm sure I don't need to remind you of our recent achievements in building partnerships, lobbying national and local government and setting up clean water programmes in the developing world. Together, we will be even stronger; with more resources, more expertise and more diverse talents at our disposal, our vision of a world with clean water for all has just come a step closer.

I know I can count on you to give our new colleagues a warm welcome.

In company in action

3 Now watch video A1 to see the first meeting between Ed Ryan of Blue Rock and Jack Wright of Global Water Aid. While you watch, tick the cultural differences that are referred to.

power distance	☐	age and gender roles	☐	dress code	☐
communication style	☐	attitudes to time	☐	attitudes to humour	☐
body language	☐	personal space	☐	attitudes to socializing	☐

4 Put Ed and Jack's words in the correct order. Which cultural difference in 3 does each phrase illustrate?

- **a** around ceremony don't here on stand We.
- **b** busy one That's very woman! assistant Your?
- **c** Minister the So, meeting today you?
- **d** joking only Relax, I'm!
- **e** at back be by desk forty-five I'm my one supposed to.
- **f** along bring don't her too Why you? / merrier more, The the!

5 Match the beginnings (1–6) with the endings (a–f) in this slide on cultural sensitivity.

CULTURAL SENSITIVITY CHECKLIST

1 understand your own culture and	a observing and analysing other cultures
2 suspend judgement while	b common values, beliefs, goals and attitudes
3 identify and share	c be aware of differences with others
4 respect differences and resist	d be inclusive – prefer 'we' to 'I' or 'you'
5 use language sensitively;	e keep trying however difficult it may be
6 be objective and positive;	f the temptation to make converts

6 Using the checklist above, give examples of how Ed and Jack could have avoided a culture clash.

Have you experienced similar situations, for example when working abroad or with different nationalities? Give examples of what went wrong, or how you avoided a clash.

In company in action

7 Now watch video A2 to see a second meeting between Ed and Jack and answer the questions.

- **a** How have Ed and Jack's attitudes to their own and to each other's cultures changed since their first meeting?
- **b** What do they decide to suggest?

8 Complete the phrases from the video and then match each phrase (1–6) to the positive attitude or cross-cultural understanding (a–f) it illustrates.

1 we got off on the wrong ______	a sharing common attitudes to management
2 when the cat's ______	b accepting limitations
3 I'd better try to blend in with the ______	c sharing common goals
4 to take a leaf out of your ______	d showing willingness to adapt
5 if it can't be ______	e recognizing mistakes
6 after all, we're all in this ______	f being prepared to learn from another culture

Committee meeting

9 Work in small groups. You have been invited to join a committee to help staff adapt to a merger between your two companies. Speaker A see page 118, Speaker B see page 120, then discuss the agenda below. When you have finished, use the checklists on page 123 to help you evaluate your performance.

AGENDA

1 **For discussion – cultural differences and potential problems:**
Power distance
Gender/age roles
Dress code
Time
Socializing

2 **For decision – policy and guidelines for the new organization:**
Work organization: office hours and layout
Equal opportunities
Dress code
Compensation
Socializing

04 Voice and visuals

I do not object to people looking at their watches when I am speaking. But I strongly object when they start shaking them to make certain they are still going.

Lord Birkett, British judge

How do you keep your audience's attention when you give a presentation?

Learning objectives: Unit 4

Business communication skills Doing a quiz on how to command attention; Giving feedback on a presentation; Using visuals in a presentation; Analyzing the voice in presentations; Fluency: Giving a speech
Reading Articles on voice and visual impact
Listening Voicemail; Presenters giving information in different ways; Radio programme: drama for business; A Shakespeare speech
Vocabulary Presentations
Grammar Modal verbs
Phrase bank Describing and commenting on visuals

1 When you stand up to speak in public, what keeps an audience interested in what you're saying? Expertise or enthusiasm? Visual impact or vocal range? PowerPoint or natural presence?

2 You are going to read about power and public speaking. First test your communicative awareness below by underlining the correct information.

Test your communicative awareness

1 The attention span of the average audience member is *15 / 50* minutes.
2 People in an audience are distracted roughly every 12 *seconds / minutes*.
3 The best listeners are the *Germans and Swiss / Chinese and Japanese*.
4 Using visual aids makes your message *twice as / four times more* memorable.
5 It's been proved that presentations with visuals are *23% / 43%* more persuasive.
6 The brain processes images *40,000 / 400,000* times faster than text.
7 It's a *fact / myth* that only 7% of a presentation is what you actually say.
8 People generally prefer *lower / louder* voices.
9 Mrs Thatcher was trained to speak in a *lower, more authoritative / softer, friendlier* voice.
10 *Dutch / Spanish* women have the lowest female voices.
11 *Men's / Women's* voices are gradually getting deeper.
12 What people *see / hear* overrides what they *see / hear* every time.
13 Images and speech are processed by the *same / opposite* sides of the brain.
14 For over 100 years the US presidential election has been won by the taller candidate *70% / 90%* of the time.

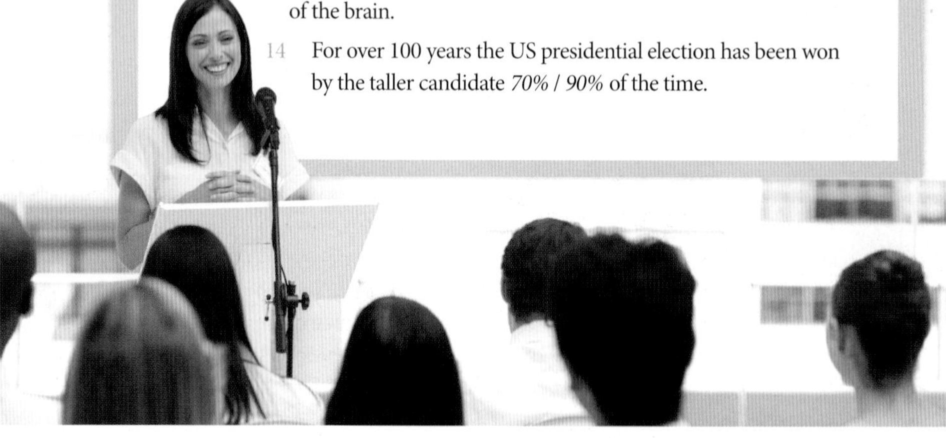

3 Work with a partner to check your answers in 2. Each read a different web article opposite. Then share your information.

4 Do any of the points mentioned in the articles surprise you? If true, what are the implications for a business presenter?

5 Highlight the following in the article you read and explain why you chose them to your partner:

- three new words you'd like to remember
- three new phrases you'd like to remember

VOICE LESSONS

IS ANYBODY LISTENING?

Long before it is born, a baby can recognize its mother's voice. And it is said that our sense of hearing is the last to fade before we die. As unique as our fingerprints, our voice is a key component of our personality. Indeed, the word 'personality' itself comes from the Latin 'persona', which literally means 'through sound'.

But, in our televisual age, we tend to shut out what we hear and be over-influenced by appearances. Maybe that's why in nearly 90% of US presidential elections since 1900, the taller, usually better-looking, candidate has been the winner! The attention span of the average audience member is just 15 minutes. In the more self-disciplined and data-hungry cultures of Germany and Switzerland it might be half an hour. But even the most attentive listener is distracted roughly every 12 seconds.

HOW LOW CAN YOU GO?

Is there anything we can do to hold their attention? There is some evidence to suggest that a low voice is preferred in both men and women. Former British Prime Minister Margaret Thatcher famously hired a voice coach to lower her voice. And, except in Japan, where higher female voices are preferred, it can be no coincidence that over the last 50 years, as women have risen to higher management positions in the workplace, their voices have measurably deepened – in the Netherlands, where women have achieved almost equal opportunity, especially so.

AN ORATOR AS PRESIDENT

The US presidential elections in both 2008 and 2012 were classic cases of the triumph of the charismatic voice, with Barack Obama putting the art of rhetoric into the spotlight. His catchphrase 'Yes, we can' has passed into American history and he has already been described as the greatest orator of his generation. But New York professor Ekaterina Haskins has a theory about that. 'I've been going through his speeches textually,' she says. 'The text alone cannot tell us why they are so powerful. It is about delivery.' Philip Collins, who used to be Tony Blair's speech writer, agrees. It's 'the way he slides down some words and hits others – the intonation, the emphasis, the pauses and the silences.' To become leader of the western world Obama's only visual aid was himself. The rest was voice.

VISUAL IMPACT

TRUTH, LIES AND VISUAL AIDS

It's the oldest cliché in communication training: 55% of the message is how you look, 38% is how you sound and a mere 7% is what you say. But it's wrong! The original research on which this myth is based was carried out at UCLA in the 1970s. Involving just a handful of volunteers, the experiments actually focused on how people judge others' feelings and had nothing to do with creating impact in a talk. So if your suit, slides and winning smile fail to impress, take it easy. All is not lost.

What is true is that, if your body language is saying one thing and your words another, people will believe what they see. When we're nervous or ill-prepared, our body language tends to give us away.

POWERPOINTLESS?

Of course, good visual aids do powerfully reinforce your message. In fact, according to a study by 3M, audiences shown visuals are four times more likely to remember what you said and 43% more likely to be persuaded by it.

But it depends what you show them. The typical list of bullet points, for example, can actually compete with you. At one stage, this became such a problem at Sun Microsystems that CEO Scott McNealy banned the use of PowerPoint. Images, on the other hand, are mentally processed 400,000 times faster than text and appeal to the opposite side of the brain, making them the perfect accompaniment to speech.

A WHOLE NEW IMAGE

No-one knows this better than ex-US vice-president Al Gore. Once the invisible man of American politics, after his presidential election defeat in 2000, Gore returned to his true passion and began an environmental lecture tour that literally took the world by storm. Ditching PowerPoint for Apple Keynote, he created a set of dramatic visuals, video clips and computer simulations that caused a sensation around the world. Speaking to a thousand different audiences, in what Fast Company magazine has called 'one of the most remarkable personal turnarounds of all time', Gore went on to become the champion of the green movement, the star of the Oscar-winning movie *An Inconvenient Truth* and winner of the Nobel Peace prize. He readily admits that he owes it all to a slide show.

Giving feedback

1 Work with a partner to practise giving and receiving feedback on a presentation. Speaker A see page 120. Speaker B see page 138.

2 **1.13** Listen to the voicemail from your Taiwanese client following the presentation in 1. Discuss his reaction with a partner.

Visuals

1 When you give presentations, what visuals do you use?

DVDs | flipchart | handouts | PowerPoint slides | samples | websites

2 Read the book extract. Do you share the author's doubts?

Death by PowerPoint

Are you risking 'Death by PowerPoint'? This is when you inflict on your defenceless audience endless bullet-pointed slides, keywords and clipart that look pretty, yet cumulatively create a numbing effect and loss of impact. Beware of spending more time on the technology than on preparing yourself. Remember, you are the presentation.

Adapted from *The Ultimate Business Presentation Book* by Andrew Leigh

3 All the expressions below can be used to comment on a visual in a presentation. Complete them using the verbs in the box.

draw | give | have | learn | mention | notice | point | put | see | show

Introduction	________ a look at this. As you can ________, ...
Highlights	One thing you'll immediately ________ is that ...
	I'd particularly like to ________ your attention to ...
	I'd also like to ________ out ...
	And perhaps I should ________ ...
Context	Just to ________ you some of the background to this ...
	To ________ this into some kind of perspective ...
Conclusions	Clearly then, what these figures ________ is ...
	The lesson we can ________ from this is ...

4 Draw a simple graph or chart relating to an interesting aspect of the business you're in, the company you work for, or your country's economy. Use some of the expressions in 3 to present it to the class.

Voice

1 How might pausing sometimes be the most effective thing a speaker can do? Read what communication expert Courtland Bovée has to say about the power of the pause.

> A pause is more than just a way to vary your speaking rate. It's also an important way to add emphasis and meaning to selected phrases and sentences. You can insert a pause to allow an audience a moment to think about an idea, to indicate a shift to a new idea or to a new section of your speech, or to heighten anticipation of your next idea.
>
> From *Contemporary Public Speaking* by Courtland L. Bovée

2 **1.14** Listen to three presenters speaking in different ways. Decide which presenter sounds:

1 fluent and confident.
2 fluent but boring.
3 hesitant.

a There's a whole market in Eastern Europe just there for the taking. ☐
b Quite frankly, the results we've been getting are absolutely incredible. ☐
c Now, I'm sure I don't need to tell you just how crucial this is. ☐
d Net profits are up 97% – yes, 97%. ☐
e Would you believe that so far we've not been able to sell a single unit? ☐
f Miss this deadline and we'll lose the biggest client this company's ever had. ☐

3 Why does the boring presenter sound so monotonous?

4 What exactly is the hesitant presenter doing wrong?

5 **1.15** Work with a partner. Listen again to the fluent and confident versions. One of you should mark the pauses like this: | The other should <u>underline</u> the stressed words. Compare your results. What's the connection between where we pause and what we stress?

6 **1.16** Deliver all the sentences in 2 in a fluent and confident way. Experiment with longer pauses and stronger stresses. Then compare your version with the recording.

7 **1.17** According to Swedish businessman Jan Carlzon, 'All business is show business.' Listen to an extract from a radio programme on how several training companies have taken his opinion literally, and discuss the questions.

a Would William Freeman's advice help you face a business audience?
b What does Michael Lame think classically trained actors can teach business people?
c According to Richard Olivier, what makes someone a brilliant speaker?
d Which of the trainees' opinions would be closest to your own?

8 Work with a partner to make your Shakespearian debut! Read through the Shakespeare speech on page 28 and take turns to be the actor and director. Don't worry – the speech has been slightly modernized!

- Decide where you are going to pause – mark short pauses like this: | longer pauses like this: || and very long pauses like this: |||
- <u>Underline</u> the words you are going to stress: usually nouns and verbs, but sometimes, for dramatic effect, you can stress pronouns and conjunctions.
- Highlight in different colours parts of the text you really want to project, even shout, and parts you want to say quietly or perhaps whisper.
- Try the speech a few times, the actor speaking, the director giving advice and feedback. When you are ready, have fun performing it!

9 1.18 Listen to the speech below. How does your performance compare with the recorded version?

10 Prepare a 90-second presentation on a work or business topic that is important to you. Try to keep some of the power and drama from your Shakespeare speech in your voice as you present.

Kenneth Branagh as King Henry in *Henry V*

The story so far:

The English army has fought a long hard campaign in France and now they face their final battle at Agincourt. They are heavily outnumbered and the soldiers are exhausted and almost ready to surrender. Henry's generals, Bedford, Exeter, Warwick, Talbot, Salisbury and Gloucester, do not really believe they can win. Henry knows he must somehow build confidence and self-belief in his troops if they are to stand even the remotest chance of victory. And so he tells his men not to wish for a bigger army, since all the glory can now be theirs …

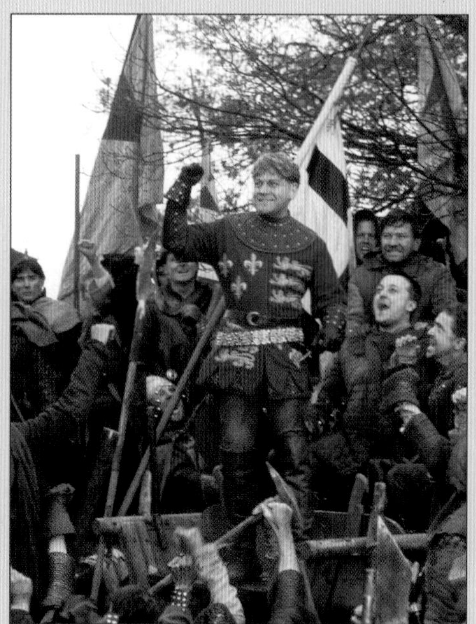

The motivation speech:

If we are going to die, we are enough
To cause our country loss; and if to live,
The fewer men, the greater share of honour.
This day is called the Feast of Crispian.
He who survives this day, comes safely home,
Will hold his head high when this day is named
And stand up at the name of Crispian.
He that shall live today and see old age
Will celebrate it yearly with his neighbours
And say: 'Tomorrow is Saint Crispian'.
Then he'll roll up his sleeve and show his scars
And say: 'These wounds I got on Crispian's Day'.
Old men forget; yes, all will be forgotten;
But he'll remember all too well
What he achieved that day. Then will our names:
Harry the king, Bedford and Exeter,
Warwick and Talbot, Salisbury and Gloucester,
Be between cups of wine newly remembered.
This story will the good man teach his son;
And Crispian will never go by,
From this day to the ending of the world,
But we shall be remembered for it –
We few, we fortunate few, we band of brothers;
For he today who sheds his blood with me
Will be my brother. However poor and humble,
This day will make of him a gentleman.
And gentlemen in England, now in bed,
Will curse the fact they were not here,
And question whether they are really men,
While anyone speaks who fought with us
Upon Saint Crispian's Day!

04 Voice and visuals

Vocabulary

Presentations

Commenting on statistics

1 Put the following verbs and verb phrases in order from the best news to the worst.

almost halved	increased tenfold	more than tripled
nearly doubled	plateau'd	quadrupled

Sales have
a ______
b ______
c ______
d ______
e ______
f ______

Which of the above means the same as a *fourfold increase*?

2 Match the adjectives with ones which have a similar meaning and put them in order from the biggest to the smallest.

considerable	huge	massive	moderate
modest	reasonable	significant	slight

a
a ______ / ______
b ______ / ______
c ______ / ______
d ______ / ______
increase

3 Describe the following success rates using suitable adjectives from the box.

disappointing	disastrous	encouraging	miserable
phenomenal	promising	spectacular	unimpressive

a(n)
a ______ / ______ 95%
b ______ / ______ 65%
c ______ / ______ 25%
d ______ / ______ 3%
success rate

Metaphor: trends and developments

4 Complete the joke by matching each noun or noun phrase on the left to a verb or verb phrase on the right. Use a dictionary to check the literal and metaphorical meaning of the verbs, if necessary.

And on the stock market today ...

mountaineering equipment	totally collapsed
military hardware	were up and down
lifts	went up sharply
kitchen knives	peaked
but the housing market	boomed

After a nervous start ...

rubber	quickly recovered
medical supplies	shot up
the automotive industry	bounced back
rifles	picked up after lunch
and vacuum cleaners also	rallied

In some of the fiercest trading seen in the City ...

swimwear	hit rock bottom
mining equipment	completely dried up
ice skates	plunged
and the market for raisins	slipped a little

By close of trade ...

fireworks	remained unchanged
but paper products	fell dramatically
men's socks	were stationary
and theatre curtains	skyrocketed

5 Mark the verbs and verb phrases in 4 according to the trend they describe: up (↗), down (↘), up and down (/\↘), down then up (\/↗) and no change (→).

Grammar

Modal verbs

1 In each of the sentences below, delete the modal verbs that are incorrect.

a We ... now, but we can if we want.
(mustn't pay/don't have to pay/haven't got to pay)

b I ... my laptop, so I left it at the office.
(needn't take/didn't need to take/needn't have taken)

c We ..., if we'd known he wasn't coming in today.
(didn't need to wait/mustn't wait/needn't have waited)

d When I was a student, I ... for hours on end.
('d study/would have studied/used to study)

e I ... quite left-wing, but I've become more conservative.
(used to be/would be/must have been)

f I took my driving test three times before I ... pass.
(could/was able to/managed to)

2 Complete the conversation using the modal verbs in the box.

can't can't could have could have 'll 'll might must must have needn't have shouldn't won't would have wouldn't

A Ivan, (1) ____________ Alexis be here by now? It's gone four!
B Yeah, she (2) ____________ got held up somewhere.
A But (3) ____________ she have phoned?
B Well, you (4) ____________ thought so.
A I mean, we're only having this meeting for her benefit. If she doesn't come soon, we (5) ____________ bothered.
B Quite, though I (6) ____________ think what (7) ____________ held her up. I (8) ____________ ring her and see what's going on. That's funny, I (9) ____________ find her number. I (10) ____________ sworn I put it in my diary. It (11) ____________ be in here somewhere!
A Well, if you ask me, she (12) ____________ be coming now, anyway.
B Hang on. That (13) ____________ just be her now. I (14) ____________ go and check.

Modal verbs *have to, have got to* and *must* mean there's an obligation to do something.
don't have to and *haven't got to* mean there's no obligation to do something.
mustn't means there's an obligation not to do something.
I needn't have done means I did something but it wasn't necessary; *I didn't need to do* means it wasn't necessary so I didn't do it.
would do means *used to do* for repeated past actions.
She should have left means *I expect she's left* or *She's supposed to have left* or *It would have been a good idea if she'd left.*
You use *was able to* (not *could*) to talk about a specific past achievement.
That must be him is the opposite of *That can't be him.*
will is the most versatile modal verb and can be used for offers, spontaneous decisions, assumptions, predictions and to express willingness or determination.

Phrase bank: **Describing and commenting on visuals**

All the following phrases and expressions can be used to describe and comment on visual aids. Add them to the chart according to their function.

INTRODUCTION	HIGHLIGHTS
CONTEXT	**CONCLUSIONS**

a Have a look at this ...
b What these figures clearly show is ...
c I'd particularly like to draw your attention to ...
d As you can see, ...
e I think this demonstrates ...
f Just to give you the background to this ...
g I'd like to point out ...
h I'll just talk you through it ...
i To put this into perspective, ...
j What this means is ...
k The take-home message here is ...
l Okay, let's take a look at ...
m One thing you'll notice is ...
n The lesson we can learn from this is ...
o Let's run the video ...
p I'll just show you how this works ...

05 Problems on the phone

Most people spend more time and energy going around problems than in trying to solve them.

Henry Ford, founder of Ford Motor Company

What's your top tip for problem-solving?

1 It's been said that 'When the phone rings, there's usually a problem on the other end of it.' What sort of problems do people phone you with at work? Have you ever had to deal with a chatterbox? Share examples with a partner.

2 Complete the article below by underlining the correct words.

HOW TO GET RID OF **CHATTERBOXES** ON THE PHONE

We are living in the age of telephony. Over half the planet now owns a mobile. China has the biggest mobile phone market worldwide. Over 70% of the population uses a mobile phone. Whenever we want, wherever we want, we can get in (a) **communication / touch**.

But when we do, it seems we can never get to the (b) **point / business**. Up to two hours in every working day are wasted in small talk on the phone. And great skill and determination are needed to escape the deadly game of social chit-chat – 'How are you? … Settling (c) **in / down** to the new job? … How's Ellen? … And the kids? … Hasn't your eldest just gone to college? … How (d) **life / time** flies! … Oh, I hear you're moving house as well. … Did you have a nice holiday, by the way? … I suppose you haven't heard the (e) **last / latest**, then? … Well, I'm not supposed to say, but there's a (f) **rumour / gossip** going about …'

Of course, what you really want to say in these circumstances is, 'Look, I haven't got all (g) **year / day**. Either state your business or kindly get off the phone,' but professional courtesy forbids it. Here, then, is the definitive executive guide to getting rid of chatterboxes on the phone.

GETTING DOWN TO BUSINESS

The most tactful way of bringing the conversation round to the subject of business is to ask in a slightly louder than normal voice, 'What (h) **can / could** I do for you?' If you know the caller, you could try, 'I (i) **expect / believe** you're calling about …' and then mention anything you can think of. They, hopefully, will reply, 'Er, no, actually, it's about something else' and you can finally (j) **pull / cut** the chat and get down to business. Should this strategy fail, you may have to resort to a firmer, 'Was there (k) **nothing / something** you wanted to talk to me about?'

ENDING THE CONVERSATION

This is more difficult. The trick is not to seem too abrupt. 'Anyway, …', though a clear signal to most people that you want to end the call, is much too subtle for chatterboxes. Try instead, 'Well, I mustn't (l) **hold / keep** you', 'I'll let you (m) **get / go** on' or the more insistent, 'I'll have to let you (n) **go / leave** now.' If you feel that sounds a little too harsh, friendlier alternatives include, 'Well, (o) **listen / see**, it's been great talking to you', 'We must (p) **come / get** together soon' or, 'Oh, one last (q) **thing / point** and then I really must go.' Of course, with an incurable chatterbox this last alternative may be asking for trouble!

DRASTIC MEASURES

In genuine emergencies the following may be used: 'Ah, someone's just this minute (r) **dropped / stepped** into the office. I'll have to ring (s) **off / out**.' Or, 'I've got an international call just come (t) **in / over** on the other line. Can I call you back?' And, if all else fails, you can always try, 'Hello? Hello? Are you still (u) **there / here**?' Of course the secret with this one is that when the caller says, 'Yes, I'm still here,' resist the temptation to reply 'Well, I can't hear you!'

3 Do you agree with the article that small talk on the phone wastes time at work?

4 **1.19** Listen to someone trying unsuccessfully to get a caller off the phone. Raise your hand when you hear them use one of the expressions mentioned in the article in 2.

Learning objectives: Unit 5

Business communication skills Discussing phone usage and its usefulness; Dealing with 'chatterboxes'; Complaining and dealing with complaints; Toning down 'flames'; Speculating about a problem; Fluency: Solving problems on the phone
Reading Article on 'chatterboxes'
Listening Someone dealing with a 'chatterbox'; Someone dealing with a customer complaint; People discussing a problem; People solving a problem
Vocabulary Phone, tablet and email
Grammar Complex question formation
Phrase bank On the phone

5 Work with a partner to practise dealing with a chatterbox. Speaker A see page 120. Speaker B see page 128.

Dealing with complaints

1 In 2009 American businessman Howard Schaffer got so fed up wasting time trying to get the phones in his office fixed, he worked out it had cost him $5,481.16, billed the phone company for it and was paid! Have you ever wanted to do that to a company that wasted your time?

2 When was the last time you made a formal complaint about something? Was it in person, in writing or on the phone?

3 Put the following stages of handling a customer complaint into the most likely order:

suggest possible solutions	4
get the details	2
end on a positive note	6
agree on a course of action	5
greet and reassure the caller	1
listen and empathize	3

4 Which of the following expressions would be most inappropriate at each of the stages in 3? Delete one from each set of three below. Then underline which of the remaining two you prefer.

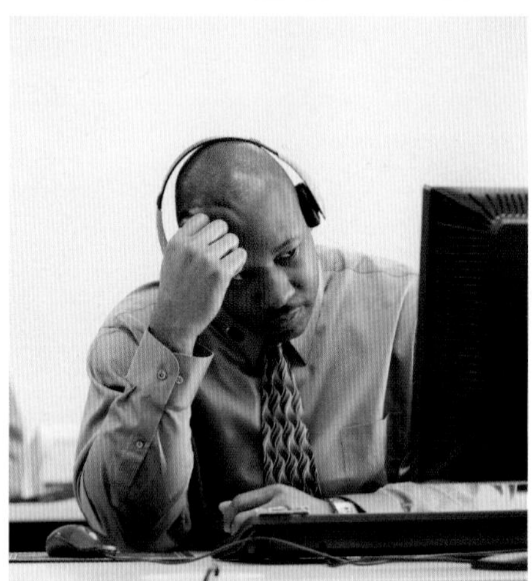

Stage 1

a How can I help you?
b What can I do for you?
c ~~What's the matter, then?~~

Stage 2

a Can you tell me exactly what the problem is?
b ~~What exactly is your problem?~~
c What seems to be the problem?

Stage 3

a ~~Tell me about it! I know just how you feel.~~
b I can understand exactly how you feel.
c I can understand how upset you must be.

Stage 4

a ~~Well, I suppose I could send you a new one, but I can't give you a refund. Sorry.~~
b I can't give you a refund, I'm afraid, but I can certainly send you a new one. How's that?
c Unfortunately, we're not authorized to give refunds, but what I can do is send you a brand new one. How would that be?

Stage 5

a Is that all okay for you?
b ~~Are you satisfied now?~~
c Are you happy with that?

Stage 6

a I'm so pleased we've managed to sort this out. Was there anything else?
b Glad to be of assistance. Is there anything else I can help you with?
c ~~Good. Anything else or is that it?~~

5 **1.20** Listen to a customer services adviser at iDeals, a computer supplies retail chain, dealing with a complaint. Compare what she says with your choices in 4.

6 A 'flame' is an angry or insulting email. Have you ever received or been tempted to write one?

7 Read the 'flames' with a partner. Imagine you wrote one to your partner, then phone him/her. Take turns to hold the conversations. Caller, be as direct as you like. Receiver, try to calm the caller down and deal with their complaint.

Why do you never answer your phone? May I suggest you turn your mp3 off occasionally?
What I want to know is, are you making any progress on the Samsung report or not? And if not, why not? No, don't even bother answering that. I already know you've been far too busy with more important matters to even get round to starting it. Correct?

Look, I asked you to type up this report ages ago and you know full well I've got to have it for Thursday's meeting with the people from head office.

This is the second time you've fouled things up and I'll be reminding you of that when your probationary period finally ends.

So, I'll ask you once again. WHEN WILL THE SAMSUNG REPORT BE READY?

For the third time this week, WHERE IS OUR ORDER?

We ordered $15,000 of shirts from you three – yes, three – months ago and so far what have you sent us? That's right, nothing! Not so much as an email to explain why it's taking so long. This is an utter disgrace.

You call yourselves the world's leading promotional products company and you can't even manage to organize 6,000 polo shirts with a simple company logo on. Frankly, it's pathetic. I notice you had no problem debiting our account for the $15,000, though.

I'm sure it's too much to expect an apology, but if I don't see those shirts within the next 48 hours, I'll see you in court. GOT IT?

8 Rewrite your email from 7 to make it more polite but equally assertive. Use the prompts below.

a Unfortunately / unable / reach / phone

Can / tell / managing / make / progress / Samsung report? // having / problems / please let / know / soon / possible // understand / been preoccupied / other matters / may not / even / made a start yet / although / hope / not / case

did ask / some time ago / this report / as you know / do need / urgently / Thursday's meeting / people / head office

not / first time / let me down / consequently / shall have / discuss / matter / when / probationary period ends

really must know today how / longer / going / take

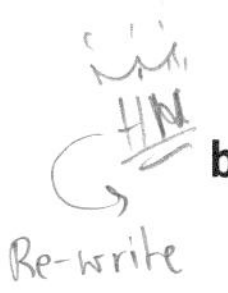

b again writing / regard / order / ref no 099X

records show / order / $15,000 / shirts / placed three months / but so far / received anything // Nor / sent / email explaining / reason / delay // afraid / quite unacceptable

You advertise / world's leading promotional products company // therefore / find / inability / take care / simple order like this both surprising / disappointing // notice / however / were more efficient / debiting / account / sum / $15,000

should like / delivery / 48 hours / together / apology // Otherwise / no alternative / hand / matter over / legal department // hope / made myself clear

9 Exchange the rewritten emails with your partner and hold the two telephone conversations again. How do these calls compare with the ones you had in 7?

Tackling problems

1 **1.21** Listen to an overheard telephone conversation. Take notes and, with a partner, try to work out what the problem is.

> It sounds like ...
> It seems as though ...
> There's been some kind of ..., by the sound of it.
> I'm not (exactly) sure whether ..., or whether ...
> It's definitely something to do with ...

2 **1.22** Now listen to both sides of the conversation in 1 and check your ideas.

3 You heard the following idiomatic expressions in 2. Can you remember the missing words? The first two letters are given. Use the definitions in brackets to help you.

a I'm working fl__________ out. (I'm working as quickly and as hard as possible.)
b It completely sl__________ my mind. (I completely forgot to do it.)
c We're sn__________ under at the moment. (We've got too much work to deal with.)

4 What would you do in Graham and Piotr's situation?

5 **1.23** Listen to Graham and Piotr's second conversation and compare your solutions with theirs.

6 Match the sentence beginnings (a–n) to the endings (1–14). You heard them all in 5.

a	Can you get hold	**1**	of sending someone else out here?
b	I don't suppose	**2**	to have a phone number for the promotions people?
c	Do you happen	**3**	getting some brochures to me in Polish?
d	Is there any chance	**4**	of the organizers?
e	I'll check	**5**	what I can do, but I can't promise anything.
f	I'll see	**6**	with Liz and see if she can spare Kim for a few days.
g	Would you mind	**7**	you remembered to put another laptop in?
h	Is there any point	**8**	the minute I get off the phone.
i	Are you absolutely	**9**	if we got a local Polish interpreter in?
j	I'll look into it	**10**	to me.
k	Could I ask you	**11**	in sending the ones we've got in Russian?
l	Would it help	**12**	to that right away.
m	I'll get on	**13**	to hurry that up a bit, please?
n	Leave it	**14**	sure we didn't order a reprint of the Polish ones?

7 Work with a partner to practise solving problems on the phone. Speaker A see page 120. Speaker B see page 130.

8 Would you follow up the phone calls you had in 7 with emails or meetings? Why? Do problems and complaints need all three methods of communication to get resolved?

05 Problems on the phone

Vocabulary

Phone, tablet and email

Complete the telephone conversation using the words in the box.

around as back by down down for in off
off off on on on on on on out out
out up up up up under

A design agency office is in chaos. The phone is ringing. Tina finally answers it.

A Hello? Tina Mallon.

B Tina. Thank goodness you're there!

A Hi, Geoff. What's (1) ______?

B Listen. I'm (2) ______ a bit of a mess here.

A Where are you?

B I'm just (3) ______ my way to see the people at FlexiPak and you'll never guess … I've left the file with the visuals in it back at the office!

A Oh dear … Well, can I fax them through to you at their office?

B No, I don't think they'd come (4) ______ properly.

A Geoff, I'm (5) ______ to my neck in it here. I can't access my email because the server is (6) ______ this morning. And I'm having some problems with my tablet, so that's not much help either! I'm rushed (7) ______ my feet, running (8) ______ trying to sort things (9) ______ with IT and get those posters (10) ______ to Milan by midday.

B Look, Tina, this is urgent. Could you go over the road to the print shop, scan the visuals and ask them to email them to me (11) ______ attachments? I'll give you FlexiPak's email address.

A Geoff, I'm sorry, but I'm really snowed (12) ______ here.

B Tina, I wouldn't ask you if I wasn't desperate. I haven't got time to come (13) ______ and pick them (14) ______.

A Well, maybe it would be easier just to send them (15) ______ courier. Hang (16) ______. Let me take (17) ______ the details. Which visuals do you need exactly? Hello? Geoff?

B Tina?

A Geoff? You're breaking (18) ______. Are you (19) ______ your mobile? I can't hear you!

B Hello? Oh, what's going (20) ______ with this phone? I can't be (21) ______ of range. I must be running low (22) ______ batteries. No, it's charged. Tina, can you hear me? I'll have to ring (23) ______ and look (24) ______ a payphone or something. Tina?

Tina hangs up, smiling.

A Now, maybe I can finally get (25) ______ with some work!

Grammar

Complex question formation

Polite question forms

Rewrite the requests and offers to make them sound friendlier and more polite using the words in brackets to help you. Make any necessary changes to grammar.

a Can you turn the air conditioning up a bit? (think/could)
Do you think you could turn the air conditioning up a bit?

b Can you help me? (wonder/could)
______

c Don't mention this to anyone else. (could/ask you)
______

d Can you do some overtime next week? (think/could/ask)
______

e Do you want me to put in a good word for you? (would/like me)
______

f Can you stop whistling while I'm trying to concentrate? (would/mind not)
______

g Is it okay to leave early today? (do/mind/if)
______

h Do you want me to give you a few days to think about it? (would/help/give)
______

i Can I ask you a personal question? (Would/mind/I)
______

j When is Mr Álvarez coming back? (happen/know)
______

k Can you lend me €50 until Friday? (don't suppose/could you?)
______

Being polite takes longer!

Modal verbs (*could, would*) soften a request that may be unwelcome.

'Type 1' conditionals (*Do you mind if I leave early?*) make requests more diplomatic.

'Type 2' conditionals (*Would you mind if I left early?*) make requests even more diplomatic.

Do you happen to know …? is useful when you're not sure the other person knows the answer to your question.

I don't suppose you could …, could you? is a good way of asking people to do you a favour.

Phrase bank: On the phone

Small talk on the phone

1 Put one word in each box below to make 30 things you could say to encourage a bit of small talk during a business call. Contractions (*You're, How's,* etc) count as one word.

a [ ] life / business / the family / it going / the new job / your golf doing / your course going?

b [ ] [ ] [ ] doing / keeping / enjoying Paris / getting on in Manila / settling down in Seville / settling in at Goldman Sachs?

c [ ] [ ] the promotion / the new baby / winning the Dubai contract / finally getting your MBA!

d [ ] [ ] [ ] moving house / getting married / about to visit Russia / about to sign a deal with Samsung, is that right?

e [ ] [ ] [ ] been on holiday / come back from Buenos Aires / opened a new office in Cologne?

f [ ] [ ] [ ] the news / the latest / from Ron lately / about the Asian situation?

g [ ] job on the Siemens report / luck with presentation tomorrow, by the way!

Getting down to business on the phone

2 Complete the ways of switching from small talk to business. The initial letters are given.

Subtle ↕ Direct

a A________,

b S________, w________ c________ I do for y________?

c I e________ y________ calling a________ …

d W________ there s________ y________ wanted t________ t________ to m________ a________?

Requesting assistance on the phone

3 Put the words in bold in the correct order.

a **mind you would** letting me know when they arrive?

b **hold you can of get** someone in accounts?

c **ask I could to you** arrange that for me?

d **chance there is any of** extending the deadline?

e **you suppose could don't I** speed things up a bit, could you?

f **have you happen do to** Alicia's mobile number?

g **sure can't absolutely you you are** do anything today?

Offering assistance on the phone

4 Complete the sentences using the pairs of verbs in the box.

check + see	help + give	leave + get	look + give
see + promise	worry + get		

a I'll ________ what I can do, but I can't ________ anything.

b I'll ________ with IT and ________ if they can help.

c Don't ________, I'll ________ on to it right away.

d I'll ________ into it. ________ me an hour.

e Would it ________ if I got someone to ________ you a hand?

f Why don't you ________ it with me and I'll ________ back to you?

Ending a call

5 Each sentence ending in bold has been switched with another. Switch them back to make eight ways of ending a call.

a I mustn't **let you go now**.

b I'll let you **get together soon**.

c Someone's just **come in on the other line**.

d We must **get on**.

e It's been great **running a bit late**.

f I'll have to **keep you**.

g I've got a call just **stepped into the office**.

h Listen, I'm **talking to you**.

06 Leading meetings

Either lead, follow or get out of the way.

Sign on the desk of Ted Turner, founder of CNN

What are the pros and cons of being a 'leader' or a 'follower'?

Learning objectives: Unit 6

Business communication skills Discussing dynamics of meetings; Disagreeing diplomatically; Fluency: Chairing a meeting
Reading Article on behaviour in meetings; Disagreement strategies
Listening Radio programme: alternative approaches to meetings; Managing meetings
Vocabulary Companies and capital; The financial pages
Grammar Linking and contrasting ideas
Phrase bank Chairing meetings
In company interviews Units 4–6

1 How much influence do you have at the meetings you participate in? When it comes to meetings, would you rather lead, follow or simply get out of the way?

2 Think about a regular meeting you attend and consider the following:

- Who is the most powerful person in the room? Does he/she actually lead the meeting?
- What are the seating arrangements – fixed or flexible?
- Does anyone tend to dominate the discussion? Is that ever a problem?
- Are there people who hardly speak at all? If so, why are they there?
- Who, if anyone, is the most 'dangerous' person in the room?

Explain to a partner how the meeting works. A simple diagram may help you.

3 Combine one word from each box to make ten common problems encountered in meetings. Do you have similar problems in your meetings?

communication communication group- hidden inadequate late over point- pulling time	+	agendas barriers breakdowns preparation rank runs scoring starts think wasting

1 communication barriers
2 communication breakdowns
3 ~~grou~~ group think
4 hidden agendas
5 inadequate preparation
6 late starts
7 over runs
8 point scoring
9 pulling rank
10 time wasting

Which of them mean:

a misunderstandings? ______
b failing to finish on time? ______
c competition between colleagues? ______
d the need to agree at all costs? ______
e secret intentions or objectives? ______
f using your status to get what you want? ______
g things which make people reluctant to talk? ______

4 Read the suggestion below. Does it strike you as a good idea? Which of the problems in 3 might it help to solve? Which would it probably make worse?

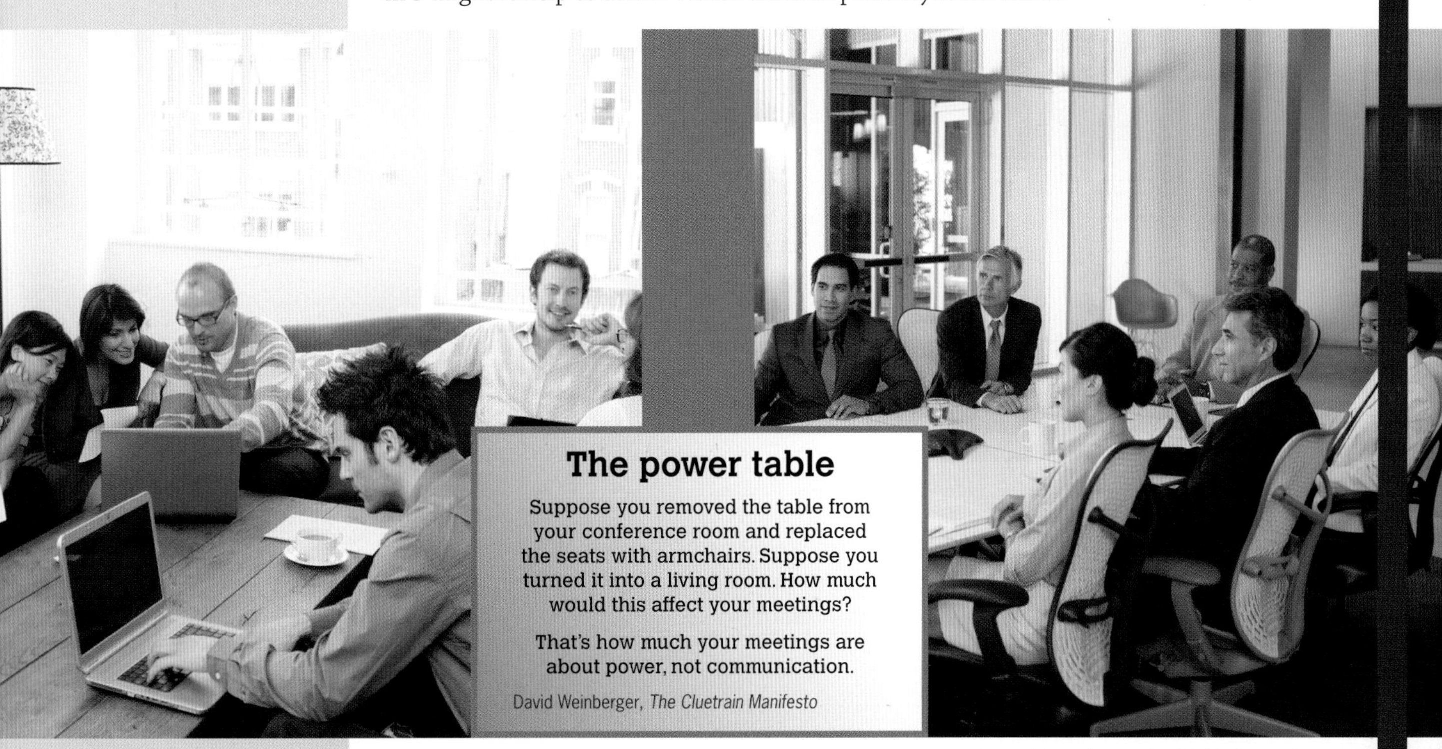

The power table

Suppose you removed the table from your conference room and replaced the seats with armchairs. Suppose you turned it into a living room. How much would this affect your meetings?

That's how much your meetings are about power, not communication.

David Weinberger, *The Cluetrain Manifesto*

5 Five alternative approaches successful companies have taken to the problem of meetings are listed below. What do you think they might involve?

a the non-stop meeting
b the virtual meeting
c the recreational meeting
d short stand-up meeting
e informal drinks and snacks meeting

6 **1.24** Listen to an extract from a business news programme and match the companies to the approaches in 5 that they adopted.

Ritz-Carlton	d
Yahoo	e
Michaelides & Bednash Media	a

7 Could any of the approaches in 5 and 6 work in your company? Would any be thought ridiculous? What could be the pros and cons of each meeting style? Discuss with a partner.

Chairing skills

1 Complete the following and compare with the other members of your group.

A meeting without a chairperson is like a Country *without a* leader.

2 Complete the collocations by writing the nouns and noun phrases in the right-hand boxes. They are all things the leader of a meeting might do.

the agenda · the final decision · the main goals · the meeting · the participants · points of view

an action plan · areas of conflict · follow-up tasks · the key issues · other speakers · troublemakers

	Verbs	Nouns		Verbs	Nouns
a	open close	the meeting	**g**	bring in shut out	other speakers
b	welcome introduce	the participants	**h**	anticipate avoid	areas of conflict
c	set stick to	the agenda	**i**	identify discipline	troublemakers
d	ask for summarize	Points of View	**j**	work out draw up	an action plan
e	establish define	the main goal	**k**	prioritize assign	follow-up tasks
f	deliberate over take	the final decision	**l**	explain focus on	the key issues

Which of the skills above are mostly about managing:

- the content of the meeting?
- the people present?

Write *C* or *P*.

3 What, in your opinion, is the single most important task of a chairperson? Read the article below. Does the author agree with you?

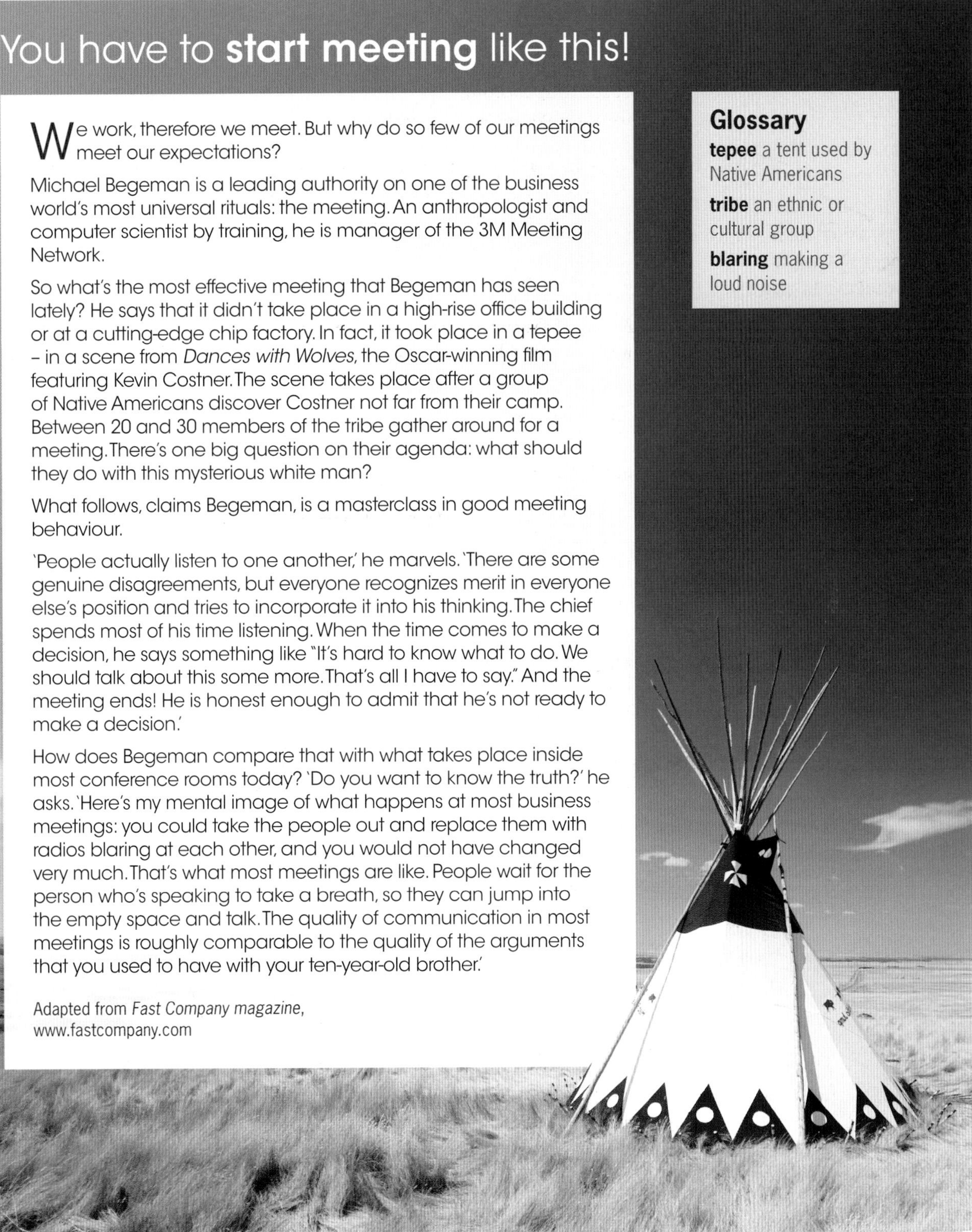

You have to **start meeting** like this!

We work, therefore we meet. But why do so few of our meetings meet our expectations?

Michael Begeman is a leading authority on one of the business world's most universal rituals: the meeting. An anthropologist and computer scientist by training, he is manager of the 3M Meeting Network.

So what's the most effective meeting that Begeman has seen lately? He says that it didn't take place in a high-rise office building or at a cutting-edge chip factory. In fact, it took place in a tepee – in a scene from *Dances with Wolves*, the Oscar-winning film featuring Kevin Costner. The scene takes place after a group of Native Americans discover Costner not far from their camp. Between 20 and 30 members of the tribe gather around for a meeting. There's one big question on their agenda: what should they do with this mysterious white man?

What follows, claims Begeman, is a masterclass in good meeting behaviour.

'People actually listen to one another,' he marvels. 'There are some genuine disagreements, but everyone recognizes merit in everyone else's position and tries to incorporate it into his thinking. The chief spends most of his time listening. When the time comes to make a decision, he says something like "It's hard to know what to do. We should talk about this some more. That's all I have to say." And the meeting ends! He is honest enough to admit that he's not ready to make a decision.'

How does Begeman compare that with what takes place inside most conference rooms today? 'Do you want to know the truth?' he asks. 'Here's my mental image of what happens at most business meetings: you could take the people out and replace them with radios blaring at each other, and you would not have changed very much. That's what most meetings are like. People wait for the person who's speaking to take a breath, so they can jump into the empty space and talk. The quality of communication in most meetings is roughly comparable to the quality of the arguments that you used to have with your ten-year-old brother.'

Adapted from *Fast Company magazine*, www.fastcompany.com

Glossary

tepee a tent used by Native Americans

tribe an ethnic or cultural group

blaring making a loud noise

4 How do you think Michael Begeman would describe the ideal meeting? You may want to refer to some of the terms in the box.

authority	consensus	decisions	diplomacy	disagreement
listening	patience	respect	teamwork	

5 In the article, Begeman points out that while 'there are some genuine disagreements' in the meeting, 'everyone recognizes merit in everyone else's position and tries to incorporate it into his thinking'. How can you avoid upsetting people you disagree with? How important is it in your culture for people to 'save face'?

6 Match the examples (a–j) on the right to the disagreement strategies (1–5) they exemplify.

1 ___ and ___ **2** ___ and ___ **3** ___ and ___ **4** ___ and ___ **5** ___ and ___

Disagreement strategies

1 Show support before you disagree
2 Disagree but ask for more detail
3 Check you've understood correctly
4 Be specific about your disagreement
5 Disagree but offer an alternative

Examples

a I think I'm going to go with Janine's idea, but tell me more about your idea first.
b That's not quite how I see it, but how about looking at this a different way?
c I'm not sure, but maybe I'm missing something. Run me through it again.
d I'm not against your whole idea, just the part about pricing.
e While I agree with a lot of what you say, I think you may be exaggerating the problem.
f I don't quite agree with you there. However, you've given me another idea.
g I'm not so sure I'm going to agree with this. I'd like to hear more about it, though.
h Before I answer that, let me just check I understand what you're saying.
i I can understand exactly how you feel, but at the moment it's just not an option.
j It's not so much your plan I have a problem with as how you intend to implement it.

Managing meetings

1 **1.25–1.27** A venture capital firm is discussing the start-up company it had talks with last week. Listen to three extracts from their meeting and answer the questions.

Extract 1

a Who's absent from the meeting and why?
b What are the two main goals of the meeting?

Extract 2

c What's the main area of conflict in the meeting?
d Who do you think the main troublemaker is?
e Whose side is Tania on – Pieter's or Jack's?

Extract 3

f Does timeofyourlife.com's business plan sound good to you?
g What follow-up tasks are assigned?
h In your opinion, how effective was the chairman of the meeting?

2 You heard the following idiomatic expressions in 1. Complete them by filling in the missing letters. Use the words in brackets to help you.

a I wanted his in________ on this one. (I wanted to hear his views.)
b We're interested in taking things fu________. (We'd like to progress with this deal.)
c I don't want us ru________ into anything. (We need to think about this carefully.)
d We've been th________ this. (We've discussed this in depth many times before.)
e The fi________ don't quite add up. (The financial part of a proposal is suspect.)

3 The following expressions are all useful in chairing meetings. Complete them by filling in the missing vowels.

Opening the meeting

a _kay, l_t's g_t st_rt_d, th_n, sh_ll w_?
b Th_nks f_r c_m_ng, _v_ryb_dy.

Setting the agenda

c _s _ s__d _n my _m__l, th_ p_rp_s_ _f t_d_y's m_ _t_ng _s t_ ...

d By th_ _nd _f th_s m_ _t_ng _'d l_k_ s_m_ k_nd _f d_c_s__n _n th_s.

Managing the discussion

e W_ s_ _m t_ b_ g_tt_ng s_d_-tr_ck_d h_r_.

f C_n w_ g_ b_ck t_ wh_t w_ wer_ d_sc_ssing e_rli_r?

g _kay, s_ j_st t_ s_mm_r_z_ wh_t w_'v_ s__d s_ f_r.

Managing other speakers

h Jack, c_ _ld Pieter j_st f_n_sh wh_t h_ w_s s_y_ng?

i _kay, _kay! L_t's _ll c_lm d_wn, sh_ll w_?

j Tania, wh_t's y_ _r p_s_t_ _n _n th_s?

Assigning follow-up tasks

k Pieter, c_n _ l_ _v_ th_t _n_ w_th y_ _?

l Tania, c_n y_ _ g_t b_ck t_ m_ _n th_t?

Closing the meeting

m I th_nk th_t's _bo_t as f_r _s we c_n g_ _t th_s st_ge.

n _'m _fr_ _d w_'ll h_v_ t_ st_p _t th_r_.

4 **1.25–1.27** Listen to the meeting extracts in 1 again and tick the expressions as you hear them. Which one is not used?

5 Play the Chairperson's game in groups. Flip a coin – heads move forward three spaces, tails move forward one space. Follow the instructions on the square you land on using appropriate chairing expressions. The first person to close the meeting is the winner!

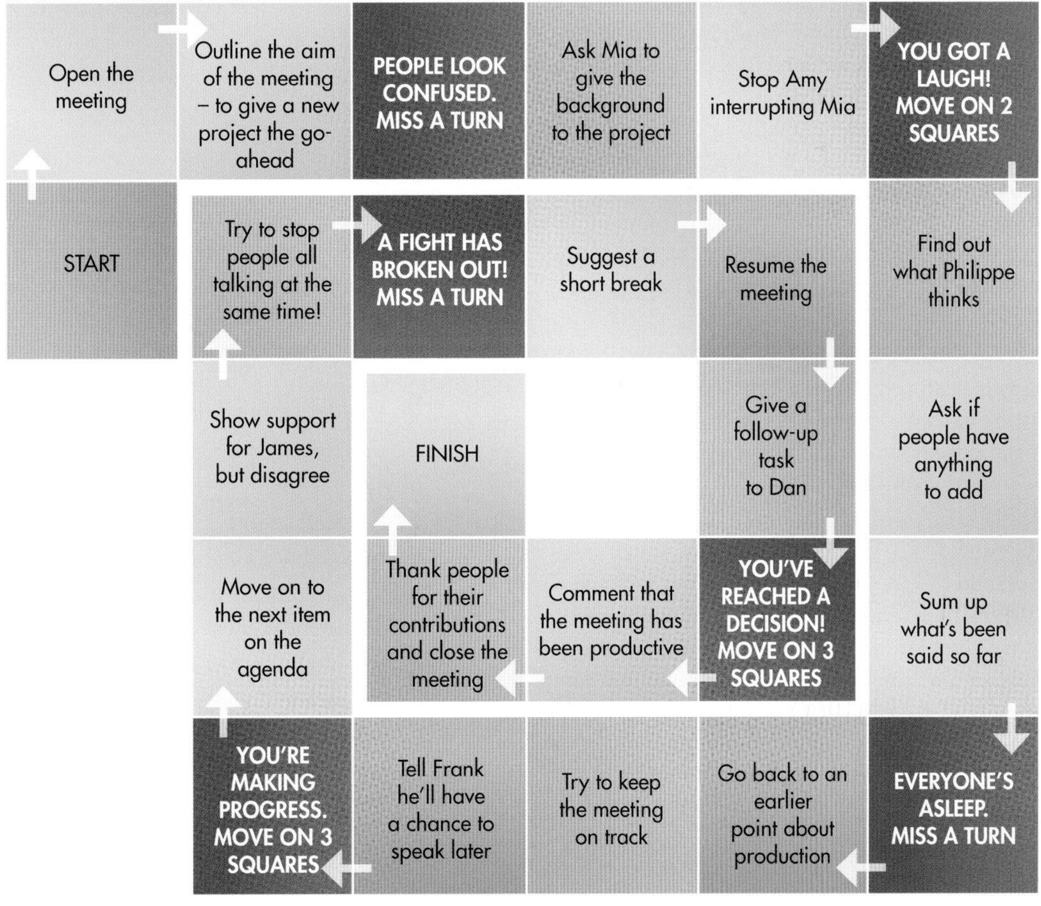

6 Work in groups of three. Take it in turns to lead three short meetings. Speaker A see pages 121 and 130. Speaker B see pages 121 and 136. Speaker C see pages 121 and 134.

06 Leading meetings

Vocabulary

Companies and capital

1 Group the verbs according to their meaning.

acquire build up buy into buy up de-layer establish expand found grow liquidate rationalize sell off start-up streamline wind up

set up	______	______	______
take over	______	______	______
restructure	______	______	______
develop	______	______	______
close down	______	______	______

2 A manager is comparing business in the past with business now. Complete what he says using the words in the box.

1–8 customer economy flatter global outsourced stakeholders vision value

9–16 effectiveness empowered flexibility functional layers learning total networked

'Well, the most important difference, obviously, is that nowadays we're all operating in a (1) ______ market, rather than simply a national one – the so-called borderless (2) ______. And the increased amount of competition means that this company, at any rate, has gone from being product-driven to much more (3) ______ oriented. And whereas we used to focus on price, now we focus on customer (4) ______. And where we used to set goals, we now have something called a corporate (5) ______. A lot of it is just a change in terminology but it certainly looks like we're doing something new!

A company's chief responsibility used to be to its shareholders, but these days we prefer to talk about (6) ______, not just the people with a financial stake in the company, but everyone who has an interest in the way it's run. A big change in the organization of this company is that we now have a much (7) ______ structure, instead of the old hierarchy. Everything used to be kept in-house. Now a lot of work is (8) ______. So, we're a (9) ______ company now, with fewer (10) ______ of management. For the most part, we work in cross-(11) ______ teams, which gives us much greater (12) ______. And we aim to have an (13) ______ rather than simply loyal workforce. That means we give training and development top priority. In fact, we like to think we're a (14) ______ company. For us, now, (15) ______ is a much more important concept than efficiency and we see product quality as just one part of a (16) ______ quality mindset.'

The financial pages

3 Match the heads (a–h) with the tails (1–8) of the following headlines.

a Disappointing pre- ☐
b Venture ☐
c $500m rights ☐
d Kagumi plan ¥200bn stock ☐
e Fears of another rise in base ☐
f Contex reject hostile takeover ☐
g Government crackdown on offshore ☐
h Record fourth- ☐

1 rates hit housing market
2 investments
3 tax profits for Kovak
4 bid from Avalon
5 quarter earnings tipped to top €90m
6 capital dries up
7 market flotation
8 issue to finance acquisition

4 Find words and phrases in 3 which mean:

a attempted acquisition by predator company ______
b exceed ______
c rate of interest charged by banks ______
d predicted ______
e strict new laws or measures ______
f profits for the period October to December ______
g affect badly ______
h money invested in a foreign country with lower tax ______
i when a company goes public and issues shares ______
j runs out ______

5 Divide the following into good (✓) and bad (✗) news.

a downturn in demand ☐
b sales boom ☐
c windfall profits ☐
d housing slump ☐
e upswing in the economy ☐
f economic recovery ☐
g rise in the cost of living ☐
h rise in the standard of living ☐
i stock market crash ☐
j credit crunch ☐

Grammar

Linking and contrasting ideas

Read the meeting extracts below. For each of the words or phrases in **bold**, underline the word or phrase in brackets that is similar in meaning. Don't change any grammar or punctuation.

a **A** Well, **in spite of** all these problems, I'd say we're still on target for a January launch. (despite / even though)

B What, **even though** we've hardly completed phase one trials? (in spite of the fact that / despite)

A Yes. **Although** obviously I'd have liked us to be further ahead by now, I'm confident we'll be ready in time. (However / Whilst)

B Well, I admire your optimism, Sergio, but **nevertheless**, I think we should make some kind of contingency plan. (all the same / however)

b **A** I'm afraid that, **because of** the strong euro, exports are down again this quarter. (consequently / owing to)

B And **as a result** our share price is falling. (consequently / owing to)

A Quite. Now, **whereas** we've been able to sustain these losses so far, we clearly can't do so indefinitely. (despite / although)

c **A** Right, well, **as** nobody seems to be in favour of this proposal, I suggest we just scrap it! (due to / seeing as)

B It's not that we're against it, Jakob, **although** it is an unusual idea. (though / whereas)

C Yes, I'd like to support you on this one, Jakob, **but** I can't help feeling you're rushing things. (whilst / and yet)

A Well, how much more time do you need? **In order to** put this before the board, I have to have your approval. (To / So that)

d **A** Now, I don't want to spend a lot of time on these new European guidelines. I do think we should go through them briefly, **however**. (though / although)

B The guidelines do affect all of us, Renata.

A **Even so**, we have more important things to discuss. (Whereas / Nevertheless)

e **A** Well, everybody, **thanks to** all your hard work, the campaign has got off to a great start. (as a result / as a result of)

B And **while** it's too early to say exactly how successful it will be, it's looking very good indeed. (whilst / as)

A Yes. **So as to** give you a clearer idea, I've prepared copies of our sales projections for year one. (so / in order to)

B The figures are broken down by country **so that** you can get the full picture. (since / in order that)

A And, **since** we're celebrating, the drinks are on me! (seeing as / because of)

You can use the following words and phrases:

- to make contrasts and contradictions

all the same	even though
although	however
and yet	nevertheless
but	though
despite	whereas
in spite of (the fact that)	while/whilst
even so	

- to express purpose or intention

in order to/that	so as to
to	so (that)

- to link cause and effect

as	owing to
as a result (of)	seeing as
because of	since
consequently	thanks to

Phrase bank: Chairing meetings

Complete the following chairing expressions.

a Bjorn, could you just fill us ______ ______ the background ______ the project?

b Janet, would you like to come ______ here or are you okay ______ that?

c Going ______ ______ what we were saying earlier, I'd just like to point ______ one thing.

d ______ ______ a minute, Jack – you'll get your chance in a moment.

e Let's break ______ here ______ a few minutes, shall we?

f Does anybody have ______ ______ ______ to add?

g Now, the Tokyo situation — Rashid, can you get ______ ______ me ______ that?

h And then there's the training report – Suzanna, can I leave that one ______ you?

i Okay, I think that about wraps things ______ for today. But we'll need to set ______ another meeting.

07

Coaching

Learning objectives: Unit 7

People skills Discussing the role of a coach; The GROW model of coaching; Fluency: Coaching your colleagues

Reading Article on professional coaching

Listening Four extracts from a coaching session

1 What kind of things can coaching help a businessperson with? What can't it help with? Work in a group to make two lists and briefly present your ideas to another group.

2 Look at the cartoon. In what ways is the man on the left like a personal coach? In what ways is he not like a coach?

3 What does a coach actually do? With a partner, underline the things involved in being a coach.

asking questions   building rapport   clarifying goals   establishing priorities
facilitating commitment to goals   fixing problems   focusing on action
giving advice   giving feedback   imparting knowledge   influencing behaviour
listening   setting goals   sharing experience   showing empathy   supporting
using intuition

4 Now read the article below and compare what it says with your answers in 1–3.

The Coach Approach

According to emotional intelligence guru Daniel Goleman, expertise in a professional field is no longer sufficient to guarantee success in your career. After all, many of the people you are competing with have pretty much the same level of expertise as you. They may also be as experienced and well qualified as you. What makes the difference career-wise is the possession of those all-important soft skills. And this is where a coach comes in.

Perhaps you are transitioning to a new role within your company. Suddenly, you require leadership or team-motivation skills. Or you are posted abroad and now need better intercultural awareness. Either way, there will be day-to-day issues, decisions, conflicts and personality clashes where you could also do with some support. Problems such as stress and burn-out may also be something a coach can help with, but remember – a coach is not a therapist. Personal hang-ups, difficulties at home and negative past experiences are not the business of coaching, which tends to focus instead on professional self-development, meeting future goals and overcoming present obstacles at work.

Nor is a coach the same thing as a mentor. A mentor, usually a more experienced executive in the same company, is there to offer advice and pass on some of their own hard-earned wisdom. Coaches do not give advice and needn't even have direct experience in their coachee's line of work – although, increasingly, managers themselves are required to coach members of their team.

So what exactly does a coach do? Perhaps the key skill is the ability to ask good questions in order to get you – the coachee – to work out what your own goals are and dedicate yourself to achieving them. This will mean prioritizing those goals and clarifying what action needs to be taken. It goes without saying that empathizing with your concerns, building a good relationship with you and really listening to what you have to say will be paramount.

A coach, then, is not a fixer, but a facilitator. The coach is there not to influence you but to smooth the path you have set yourself on, to help get you from where you are to where you want to be – quickly, comfortably and with the minimum of hold-ups. The coach is a vehicle for your success.

5 Work with a partner. Check you know what the highlighted words and phrases in the article mean. Try to work out the meaning of any you don't know from the context.

6 Look at the grid below, which shows a popular approach to coaching called the GROW model. Work with a partner and complete the chart with the phrases in the box.

- commit to specific actions
- decide on the conversation topic
- describe the current situation
- discuss alternatives
- give examples of present challenges
- identify possible obstacles to those alternatives
- put a timeframe on those actions
- set objectives for the session

GOAL	REALITY	OPTIONS	WAY FORWARD
1 ______	3 ______	5 ______	7 ______
2 ______	4 ______	6 ______	8 ______

7 Look at some of the things said during a coaching session. At what stage of the GROW process do you think the coach said them? Write *G*, *R*, *O* or *W*.

a So what alternatives do you think you have here? ☐
b So what are the steps you need to take now? ☐
c Okay, so what would you like us to work on today? ☐
d What's the most challenging thing about this right now for you? ☐
e Is there anything else you could be doing? ☐
f What precisely would you like to get from this session? ☐
g What's stopping you from pursuing these options? ☐
h In comparison with the ideal situation, where are you at the moment with this? ☐
i What do you think is the first thing you need to do? ☐
j On a scale from one to ten, how important would you say this issue is to you? ☐
k And when are you planning to take that first step? ☐
l Can you give me a few examples of what you're finding most challenging? ☐

8 2.01 Now listen to four extracts from a coaching session using the GROW model and check your answers in 7.

9 2.01 Listen again and make notes on how the coachee answers the coach's questions in 7.

10 Work in groups of three to practise your coaching skills. Turn to page 124.

MANAGEMENT SCENARIO

B

Coach crash

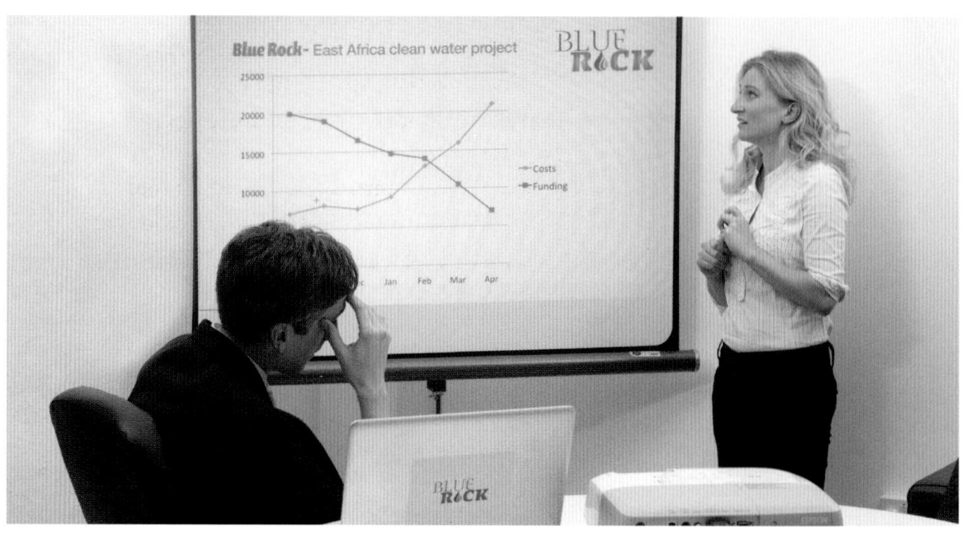

Learning objectives: Management scenario B

Business communication skills Giving feedback on a presentation; Coaching dos and don'ts; Fluency: Past-present-future presentations with coaching

Reading Coaching dos and don'ts

In company in action
B1: A failed presentation;
B2: Successful coaching

1 How does a sports coach give players feedback on their performance? Is it different in business?

2 Read the email below and mark the sentences *T* (true) or *F* (false). Then compare with a partner.

a The goal of the meeting is to secure more funding. ☐
b Cassie has plenty of time to prepare her presentation. ☐
c Cassie can see Peter for more information if necessary. ☐
d Peter seems to be a good coach. ☐

Hi Cassie,

We have a meeting on the 22nd with the lottery people: we're hoping to persuade them to increase their contribution to our East Africa clean water project. I know you're new to the team and I'm sorry it's short notice, but I'd like you to make a short presentation comparing our budgets and expenditure in the past, present and future. Obviously a successful presentation could be really influential in securing funding for the future of the project, so this is top priority; let's do a dry-run together on Friday just to iron out any problems. Let me know if you need any help, but remember I'm in Stuttgart today and tomorrow; I won't be back in London until Friday morning.

Thanks,

Peter

Peter Neubauer
Marketing Manager
Blue Rock
Tel: +44 (0)20 5689 5423
Mobile: +44 (0)7157 554 237

In company in action

3 Now watch video B1 to see Peter giving feedback on Cassie's presentation and then talking to CEO Sue Jensen. Which statements best describe each person? Tick the boxes.

	Cassie	Peter	Sue
Feels nervous	☐	☐	☐
Criticizes personal behaviour	☐	☐	☐
Makes excuses	☐	☐	☐
Is diplomatic	☐	☐	☐
Makes judgements	☐	☐	☐
Refuses to share responsibility	☐	☐	☐
Makes constructive suggestions	☐	☐	☐

4 Watch the video again and answer the questions.

a What does Peter say he likes about the presentation? Why?
b What does he dislike?
c What reasons does Cassie give for the presentation's weaknesses?
d How does Sue tell Peter he shouldn't shout at Cassie?
e What coaching skills (or lack of them) from the list in 3 do the following phrases illustrate?
  1 If I'd known there was a problem, I could've done something about it.
  2 Why did you speak in that funny little voice?
  3 Don't you think you're being a little hard on her?
  4 You might want to look through it.

5 Have you ever found yourself in Cassie, Peter or Sue's situation?

6 Work with a partner. Discuss how Peter could have improved his feedback to Cassie. Brainstorm a list of coaching dos and don'ts.

7 Speaker A see page 122, Speaker B see page 129. When you have finished, summarize what you have read for your partner. Compare what you read with your own list of dos and don'ts.

In company in action

8 Now watch video B2 to see Peter and Cassie working on the presentation again. Tick the points in the list of dos on page 122 that Peter implements.

9 Which coaching dos are illustrated by the following phrases?

a Have you got a few minutes to talk about it now?
b You go first.
c There were lots of really good points.
d I just wonder whether we still have too many slides?
e Shall we have a look through them together?

10 Prepare a three-minute 'past-present-future' mini-presentation asking for investment in your company, your association, your town or city, your sport or hobby, or your own idea, using the structure below.

The 'past-present-future' presentation

Introduction

The Past

The Present

The Future

Conclusion

With a partner, take turns making and giving feedback on your presentations. Use the checklists on page 133 to help you.

Speaker A: Make your presentation and listen to Speaker B's feedback.
Then give Speaker B your feedback on how well they coached you.
Speaker B: Listen to Speaker A's presentation then give your feedback.

08 Promoting your ideas

Surveys consistently put giving presentations near the top of the list of people's fears. Snakes, spiders, loneliness or even death have no comparison to the dreaded speaking in front of a group!

Forbes.com

What is your biggest fear?

Learning objectives: Unit 8

Business communication skills Discussing attitudes to public speaking; Discussing national stereotypes; Describing what makes a good talk; Discussing innovation in your company; Fluency: Presenting an idea for a product or service
Reading Website extract: *Intrapreneurs*
Listening Presenters talking about what makes them nervous; People comparing audience expectations of presentations; Presentation: a new business idea
Vocabulary Phrasal verbs
Grammar The passive
Phrase bank Pitching an idea

1 How important is it in your line of business to be able to present your ideas professionally? Do you enjoy giving presentations or generally try to avoid them?

2 **2.02** Listen to five experienced presenters talking about what still makes them nervous every time they give a presentation. Underline the speakers whose worries you share. Then compare concerns with a partner.

Speaker 1 Speaker 2 Speaker 3 Speaker 4 Speaker 5

3 Complete the following expressions from the extracts in 2 using a single verb.

a Your mind ____ blank.
b Your mouth ____ dry.
c Your mike ____ funny.
d The audience ____ quiet.
e Everything ____ wrong.

4 Which of the expressions in 3 means:

you can't think of anything? ☐ your microphone doesn't work properly? ☐

5 Complete the expressions from the extracts in 2.

about down down of out over to up up up

a You dry ____ completely.
b Your equipment breaks ____.
c You run ____ ____ time.
d You run ____ schedule.
e You pace ____ and ____.
f Your wave your arms ____.
g Your heart speeds ____.
h Your legs turn ____ jelly.

6 Someone once observed: 'There is nothing wrong with having nothing to say – unless you insist on saying it.' Read the text. Can you think of any less extreme ways of achieving the same objective?

KEEP IT SHORT AND SIMPLE!

According to ancient custom, the elders of a remote African village have to stand on one leg while addressing their audience at council gatherings. As soon as their second foot touches the ground, they must stop speaking immediately.

Audience analysis

1 **2.03–2.08** Listen to a group of businesspeople talking about audience expectations in different countries. Which countries do you think they're talking about? Match the countries to the extracts.

Country	**Extract**
USA	3
Germany	1
Japan	4
UK	5
France	6
Kuwait	2

Compare your ideas with a partner. Then check the answers on page 122. How do they compare with your discussion in 1?

2 In an increasingly global economy are certain national stereotypes still valid?

3 Match the phrasal verbs in these sentences. They were all in the extracts in 1.

a Wisecracks – that's what they tend to **go** 4
b The one thing you can't **do** 5
c The audience may **switch** 1
d They'll want you to **go** 8
e Anecdotes and amusing stories seem to **go** 7
f What matters is how you **come** 2
g Be too techie and they'll think you're **showing** 6
h You have to **keep** 3

1 **off** altogether.
2 **across** as a person.
3 **up** a certain level of formality.
4 **for**.
5 **without** is a sense of humour.
6 **off**.
7 **down** well.
8 **through** all the main points again.

4 Match the phrasal verbs in 3 to the meanings below.

a present yourself come across
b lose interest switch off
c be appreciated go down well
d try to impress show off
e like go for
f repeat go through
g maintain keep up
h manage without do with out

5 In your experience, what sort of thing do audiences in your country tend to go for? What doesn't go down so well?

6 You heard the following idiomatic expressions in 1. Complete them by filling in the missing letters. Use the words in brackets to help you.

a You should have all the technical information at your fingertips. (easily available)
b Give your presentation the personal touch. (aim it directly at your audience's needs)
c You'll get loads of interruptions, but just go with the flow. (let things happen)
d Don't get too carried awarded. (be overenthusiastic)
e Have a few gimmicks up your sleeve. (plan some clever surprises to attract attention)
f It really is essential that you do your homework. (prepare very carefully)

7 Which piece of advice in 6 do you think is the most important?

Innovation

1 How much of your company's business depends on innovation? Give a few examples.

2 Look at the extract from a website below. What do you think the title means? Now read the text. Does your company encourage this kind of initiative?

INTRAPRENEURS

Ideas are like insects – many are born, but few live to maturity. Because they closely resemble entrepreneurs, we call the people who turn ideas into realities inside an organization 'intrapreneurs'. Intrapreneurs are the hands-on managers who make a new idea happen.

Texas Instruments, well known for intrapreneurial successes, studied fifty of their successful and unsuccessful new product efforts. In each of their successes there were one or more dedicated intrapreneurs who persisted despite great obstacles. Similarly, the common denominator of their failures was that every one of them lacked a champion, an intrapreneur. Innovations just don't happen unless someone takes on the intrapreneurial role.

Gifford and Elizabeth Pinchot, www.pinchot.com

3 Find the words and phrases in the text which mean:

a describing people who don't just talk about it, but do it

b giving a lot of time and energy to something

c kept on trying to do something

d things that make progress difficult

e the only thing in common

f someone who supports and fights for an idea

4 What new ideas within your company or department have you been closely involved with recently?

5 It is important when presenting new ideas to be well organized and to give the information clearly. With a partner, complete the stages of a presentation with the words and phrases in the box.

a gap in the market · interest · the key message · the main product features · the new product · the objectives · the presentation · project approval · the Q&A session · some relevant statistics

1 Open	
2 Outline	
3 Arouse	
4 Quote	
5 Identify	
6 Introduce	
7 Describe	
8 Sum up	
9 Ask for	
10 Lead into	

6 **2.09–2.12** Two managers for MaxOut, an American chain of fitness centres, are presenting a new business idea to their board of directors. Listen to four extracts from their presentation and answer the questions.

Extract 1

a Are the presenters successful at arousing the curiosity of their audience? Why / why not?

b Is it more effective having two speakers instead of one?

c What advice would you give the speakers if they had to present in your country? Should there be more or less technical detail, humour, formality, audience involvement, 'hard sell'?

Extract 2

a What do these figures refer to? Do you find them surprising?

 1 a mere 13%

 2 a staggering 92%

b What do you think 'mere' and 'staggering' mean when they talk about figures?

c Complete the chart, which shows the results of the survey.

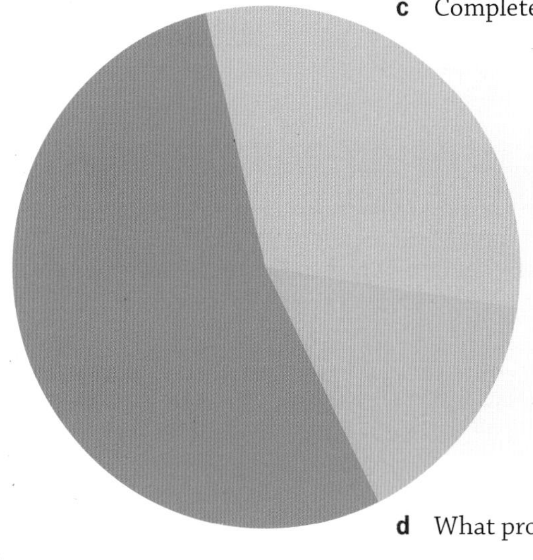

Nationwide survey

Reasons given for not becoming a member of MaxOut Health Clubs

d What product do you think the speakers are about to present?

Extract 3

a What is the product?

b How long has it taken to develop?

c Complete the product features chart.

Main product features

- weighs just over ____________
- fits easily into ____________
- assembles in ____________
- offers 35 different ____________

d What's the main selling point?

e In what ways do you think the product would benefit MaxOut's main business? Note down two to three possibilities. Share your ideas with a partner.

Extract 4

a Complete the extract below using the verb phrases in the box. The first one has been done for you.

> are currently being considered could be recorded ~~has been fully costed~~
> has been suggested is included is still being carried out
> would probably be reasonably priced

Okay, to wrap things up. The Micro-GYM (1) *has been fully costed* – a complete breakdown (2) ______ in the report. Product testing (3) ______, but we would obviously need the go-ahead from you before we proceed further with that. The Micro-GYM (4) ______ at around $35. It (5) ______ that exercise demonstrations (6) ______ on DVD and sold online. Both these suggestions would incur extra costs, but (7) ______.

b If you were on the board of MaxOut, would you give the new product idea the go-ahead? If not, what other information would you need before you were persuaded?

Pitching your idea

Work with a partner to present a new product idea.

Step One: Prepare

You'll find information on real concept products in the additional material section. Team 1 turn to page 131, Team 2 turn to page 135. Choose which product idea you want to pitch and decide what kind of company would be able to manufacture it. Find out or invent any supporting figures you'd like to refer to and create any simple visuals you'll need.

Step Two: Practise

Run through your pitch a couple of times. Use a similar presentation structure to the pitch you listened to in exercise 6. Some of the phrases and expressions in the phrase bank on page 54 may be helpful. Practise handing over to your partner after each phase of the talk.

Step Three: Perform

When you're ready, give your presentation. Make sure you invite questions at the end. Whose pitch was the most persuasive? Who gets the go-ahead?

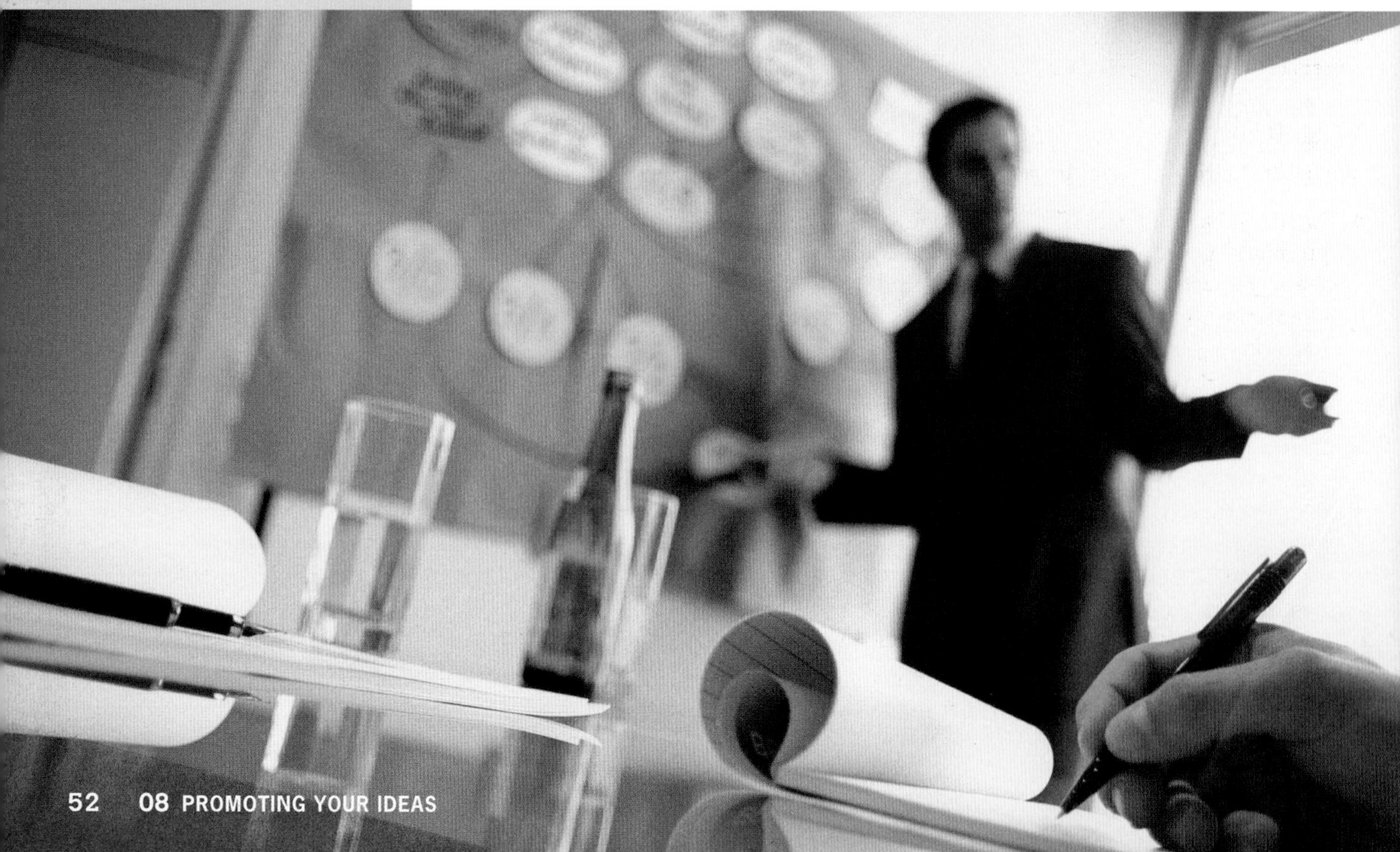

08 Promoting your ideas

Vocabulary

Phrasal verbs

1 The five most common verbs used in phrasal verbs are: *get, come, go, take* and *put*. Complete each set of sentences using one of these verbs in the Past Simple and a particle from the box. Use the definitions in brackets to help you.

across	around	down	for	in	into	into
off	off	on	on	on	out	out	over
over	through	through	under	up		

a We … ______ too much work. (accepted)
______ a few details. (wrote)
______ a bank loan. (obtained)
______ the project. (got control of)

b They … ______ the recession. (survived)
______ an accounting error. (discovered)
______ a lot of money. (inherited)
______ pressure to resign. (received)

c She … ______ to talk about training. (proceeded)
______ the figures with us. (checked)
______ the idea. (started to dislike)
______ option B. (chose)

d We … ______ the problem in the end. (avoided)
______ an argument. (became involved in)
______ a ton of paperwork. (completed)
______ well. (had a good relationship)

e They … ______ hours of work on it. (did)
______ the meeting. (postponed)
______ a press release. (issued)
______ most of the cash. (provided)

2 Some phrasal verbs have three parts. Complete the sentences using the pairs of particles in the box.

in for + back to	in for + down as	on about + on with
out of + ahead with	round to + on to	
up against + round to	up with + up for	

a I'm afraid I haven't got ______ doing that report yet, but I'll get ______ it as soon as I've finished these spreadsheets.

b I know there's no point going ______ it, but I really don't get ______ this new boss of ours.

c I'm not putting ______ this situation a moment longer – it's time I stood ______ myself!

d I know it's too late to back ______ it now, but I'm really sorry we went ______ this agreement.

e We seem to be coming ______ a lot of opposition from marketing at the moment, but hopefully they'll soon come ______ our way of thinking.

f I put ______ that promotion I was telling you about but they haven't got ______ me about it.

g I hear Jon's come ______ a lot of criticism from the board and may have to stand ______ chairman.

Grammar

The passive

1 Make the following extracts from reports more formal:

- use the passive
- replace the words in **bold** with an adverb from the box
- delete the subject

currently	formally	generally	provisionally
~~roughly~~	tentatively	thoroughly	unanimously
unofficially			

a Our site engineers estimate that construction will take **about** 18 months to complete.
It is roughly estimated that construction will take 18 months to complete.

b They've given us the go-ahead, but it's **not official yet**.
We've ______

c We're considering several options **at the moment**.
Several ______

d **Almost everyone** felt the project was taking too long.
It ______

e **Everyone** agreed that the proposal required further discussion.
It ______

f We have tested **every part** of the new software.
The ______

g The company will announce the plant closure at the **official** press conference next week.
The ______

h They've okay'd the training budget at this stage, but they **may change their minds**.
The ______

i They suggested that we could import the raw materials, **but stressed that this was only a suggestion**.
It ______

2 Make the accusations below less personal by removing all references to 'we' and 'you' and making any necessary grammatical changes.

a But we understood that you'd agreed to this.
But it was understood that this had been agreed.

b We assumed that you'd accept this.
It ______

c We stated quite clearly in the contract that you must make your payments on the first of the month.
It ______

d We presumed that you would comply with current health and safety regulations.
It ______

3 Rewrite the impersonal email below using only active verbs and replacing some of the more formal words and phrases with friendlier-sounding alternatives from the box.

each other	exchange views	from now on	get the chance
in this way	look forward	meet	pencilled in
seeing you there	up to speed	various	

From: Robert Masters
To: All departmental managers
Subject: Interdepartmental meeting

It has been decided that an interdepartmental meeting will henceforth be held every month. Heads of department will thus be able to network and generally be brought up to date on recent developments in other departments. Furthermore, they will be given the opportunity to have their voice heard on a number of matters relating to overall corporate strategy.

The first meeting is scheduled for next Thursday. Your attendance would be appreciated.

Robert Masters

You use the **passive** when you are more interested in actions, views and decisions than in the people who actually took them. The **passive** sounds more formal and objective than the **active**. For this reason it is frequently used in reports.

If the subject of the **active** sentence is *they, you, one, people, everyone* or *no one*, it is usually unnecessary to refer to it in the **passive**. *No one can do it* becomes *It can't be done ~~by anybody~~*.

When using reporting verbs in the **passive**, you need to insert the word *it*. *'They said there was absolutely no corruption'* becomes *'**It** was strongly denied that there had been any corruption'*.

The **active** generally sounds more personal than the **passive**. The danger is that in criticisms it can also sound more aggressive, and so in delicate negotiations the **passive** is often preferred to depersonalize potential conflict.

Phrase bank: Pitching an idea

Complete the crossword using the clues below.

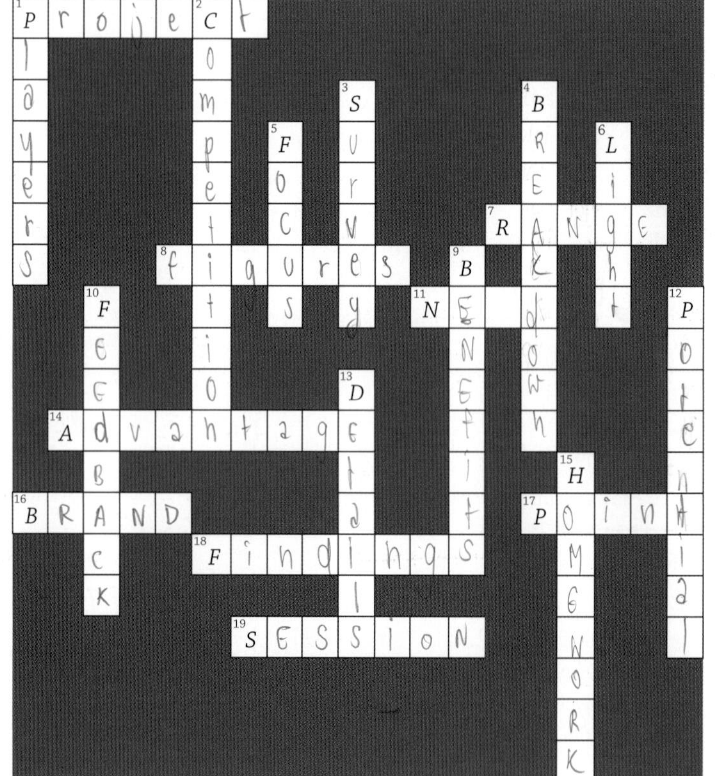

Down

1. We are one of the major __________ in our industry. (7)
2. We are constantly looking for ways to stay ahead of the __________. (11)
3. We did a nationwide __________ of our target customers. (6)
4. A complete __________ of costs is included in the report. (9)
5. We set up special __________ groups. (5)
6. What we need now is the green __________ from you. (5)
9. The main __________ of the product are clear. (8)
10. The __________ so far has been overwhelmingly positive. (8)
12. We think this product has enormous __________. (9)
13. Full __________ are in the report in front of you. (7)
15. Believe me, we've really done our __________ on this one. (8)

Across

1. As you know, we've been working on a __________ of our own for some time now. (7)
7. We think this would be an excellent addition to our current __________ of products. (5)
8. Let me quote you some interesting __________. (7)
11. The product meets a real __________. (4)
14. We need to maintain our competitive __________. (9)
16. This is a great opportunity for us to stretch our __________. (5)
17. I'm sure you'll agree this feature is a real selling __________. (5)
18. This chart highlights our main __________. (8)
19. Okay, we'd like to throw this __________ open now for questions and suggestions. (7)

Relationship-building

Never do business with anybody you don't like. If you don't like somebody, there's a reason.

Henry Quadracci, CEO of Quad/Graphics

Have you ever worked with someone you don't like?

1 In business, have you ever:

a felt an instant rapport with someone you've only just met?

b taken an immediate dislike to someone you've just been introduced to?

c misjudged someone by taking too much notice of the way they looked or sounded?

Tell the story to a partner.

2 How good are your networking skills? Complete the questionnaire using the pairs of verbs in the boxes. Then circle your answers. Compare your answers with a partner and then read the analysis on page 122.

QUESTIONNAIRE

ARE YOU AN EFFECTIVE NETWORKER?

crack + break
hover + wait
look + say
moan + complain
relax + let
talk + catch

1 You meet a group of business people for the first time. Do you:

a ______ them in the eye, smile and ______ hello?

b ______ in the background and ______ to be introduced?

c ______ a joke to ______ the ice?

2 You meet up with some colleagues after work. Do you:

a ______ shop and ______ up on all the latest gossip?

b ______ about work and ______ about the boss?

c ______ and ______ your hair down?

feel + mingle
introduce + slip
make + escape
persevere + find
stick + ignore
try + draw

3 You meet a fascinating person at a cocktail party. Do you:

a ______ to them like glue and ______ everyone else?

b ______ and ______ other people into the conversation?

c ______ obliged to go and ______ with other people?

4 You're stuck with a bore at a conference. Do you:

a ______ in the hope you'll ______ something in common?

b ______ some kind of excuse and ______?

c ______ them to someone else and ______ away?

cut + get
exchange + get
get + mention
give + keep
go + make
look + pretend

5 You see someone you don't get on with at a function. Do you:

a ______ the other way and ______ you haven't seen them?

b ______ over and ______ the effort to speak to them?

c ______ them a polite nod, but ______ your distance?

6 You're introduced to a potential client. Time is short. Do you:

a ______ the preliminaries and ______ straight to the point?

b ______ to know them a bit before you ______ business?

c ______ business cards and say you'll ______ back to them?

Learning objectives: Unit 9

Business communication skills Discussing first impressions; Completing a questionnaire on networking; Practising networking skills; Getting out of the office; Roleplay: Visiting a colleague's home

Reading Questionnaire: Are you an effective networker?; Article on sport and business

Listening Three small talk conversations; People chatting at golf; Conversation: visiting someone's home

Vocabulary Social English

Grammar Multi-verb sentences

Phrase bank Networking

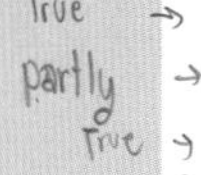

3 Discuss the following points of view with a partner:

a It's a cliché, but it's true: 'You never get a second chance to make a first impression.'

b It's not how you start; it's how you finish. Last impressions are what really count.

c They say 'humour is the shortest distance between two people'. But it can also be the furthest!

d As you travel round the world, you find that business and pleasure mix in very different ways.

4 **2.13** Now listen to four extracts of business people talking about the same points you discussed in 3. Make a note of anything you either find interesting or disagree with. Compare with a partner.

5 **2.13** You heard the following phrases in 4. Complete them then listen again to check.

a li___ ha___sh___

b soc___ bu___fl___

c lou___ aro___

d soc___ chit-___

e schm___

f wor___ the r___

6 Work with a partner. For each of the situations below, make a short list of things you could say.

a The person standing next to you in the hotel lobby is a good customer of your company. You've heard a lot about them from your new boss, who was about to introduce you, but suddenly had to take a phone call.

b You're at a trade fair. The person on the stand hasn't met you before. A friend gave you their name, told you they might be able to help you make some business contacts and said they'd mention you'd be dropping by to say hello.

c You unexpectedly bump into a very good friend at a conference who you haven't seen for ages. You've loads to talk about but unfortunately you were just on your way to a business appointment when you met them.

7 Compare lists with another pair.

8 **2.14–2.16** Listen to three short conversations. How quickly can you match them to the situations in 6?

Conversation 1 ☐ Conversation 2 ☐ Conversation 3 ☐

9 **2.14–2.16** Listen again to the conversations. How similar is the language the speakers use to the lists you made in 6? Look at the listening scripts on page 148 and underline any expressions you'd like to remember to use yourself.

10 You're going to act out one of the situations in 6 with a partner. First, work with him or her to build up your scenario.

- decide who's who
- establish exactly where you are
- agree on a few background details (names, shared acquaintances, past experiences, current business)
- you may find some of the language in the phrase bank on page 62 useful.

If you prefer, base your scenario on people and places you know.

11 When you're ready, take a couple of minutes to have each conversation. Try switching roles if you like. Which situations were the most challenging to deal with?

Getting out of the office

1 Can the golf course, tennis court or a sailing boat be a good place to do business?

Read the following three short business articles (on pages 57 and 58) and think about the questions in the boxes. Then discuss them with a partner.

How to beat your boss at tennis and survive

Competing with the boss outside the workplace is an ancient ritual designed to test your thinking, competitiveness and ability to fit in. Once it involved weapons, but today it involves tennis rackets. Your goal is to leave a good impression and that doesn't necessarily mean losing.

Before stepping onto the court, check two things: the boss's level of expertise and how much he cares about the game. It could be he's an A-tournament player so you'll have to sweat to survive. But if you judge your abilities superior, you'll have more decisions to make.

Even the game, if possible. Play to win but not to kill. It's one thing to beat the boss. It's another to take the match in straight sets six-love. This doesn't mean deliberately missing shots. But you might consider scaling back your 160 kph serve, if only because you want everyone to have a good time.

a Is it easy to fit in where you work? Is there a competitive atmosphere?

b Are you a good loser or do you always play to win?

c Would you lose a match just to please the boss?

Golf and business

Not everyone can play tennis, but everyone thinks they can play golf. In an age of health and enlightenment, golf has replaced the business lunch as the preferred vehicle for sealing deals. Sun Microsystems co-founder Scott McNealy is a scratch golfer and Bill Gates is devoted to the game.

So why is golf the preferred sport of business? In a word, relationships. 'Four to five hours on the golf course, and you get to know the character of your golfing partners – honesty, humility, ability to handle success and failure, approach to risk, desire to have fun,' says Miller Bonner, a public relations veteran. 'That translates into a successful business relationship.'

Marketing director Derek Van Bronkhorst has his own test of character on the links. 'Do they cheat?' he asks. 'If they cheat in golf, would you want to do business with them?'

d What's so wrong with a business lunch for sealing deals?

e Are you a golf fan or do you agree with Mark Twain that 'golf is a good walk spoiled'?

f What else might your opponent do to reveal their character on the golf course?

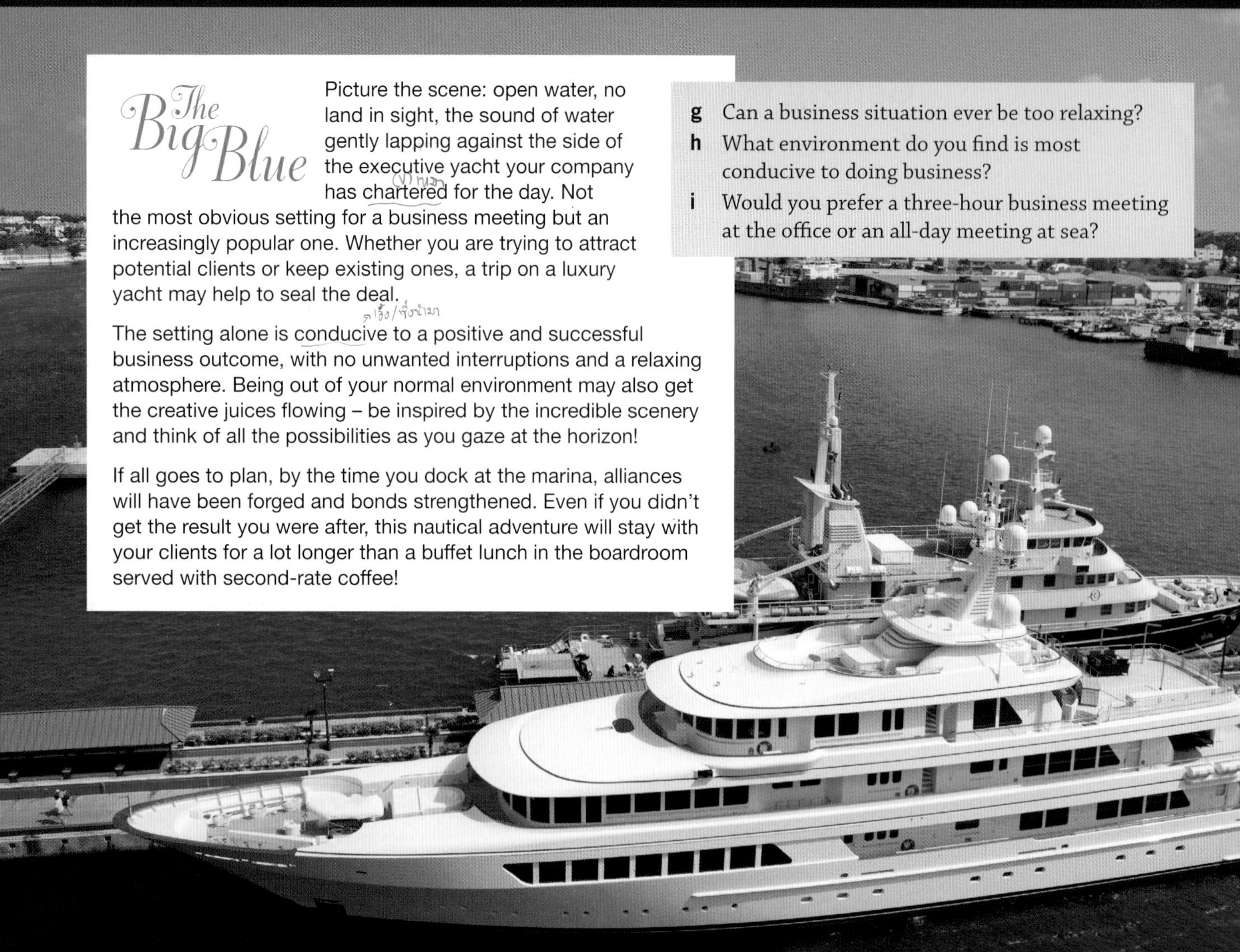

The Big Blue

Picture the scene: open water, no land in sight, the sound of water gently lapping against the side of the executive yacht your company has chartered for the day. Not the most obvious setting for a business meeting but an increasingly popular one. Whether you are trying to attract potential clients or keep existing ones, a trip on a luxury yacht may help to seal the deal.

The setting alone is conducive to a positive and successful business outcome, with no unwanted interruptions and a relaxing atmosphere. Being out of your normal environment may also get the creative juices flowing – be inspired by the incredible scenery and think of all the possibilities as you gaze at the horizon!

If all goes to plan, by the time you dock at the marina, alliances will have been forged and bonds strengthened. Even if you didn't get the result you were after, this nautical adventure will stay with your clients for a lot longer than a buffet lunch in the boardroom served with second-rate coffee!

g Can a business situation ever be too relaxing?

h What environment do you find is most conducive to doing business?

i Would you prefer a three-hour business meeting at the office or an all-day meeting at sea?

2 **2.17–2.18** Listen to a group of oil company executives chatting during a game of golf and answer the questions.

Extract 1

a According to the group, what are the benefits of a cup of coffee?

b Why are they only playing nine holes?

c How would you describe the men's attitude to the game?

Extract 2

a How's Craig playing today?

b What do Craig and Stella disagree on?

c What do you think Craig has to do if he wants the job?

3 Reorganize the words in **bold** to make correct sentences. They were all in the conversations in 2.

a We **be should thinking making probably of** a move quite soon.

b We **count staying can't weather fine the on** at this time of year.

c I **have have arranged lunch us to for** at the clubhouse.

d We **be get should able to around** the course in a couple of hours or so.

e You **be teamed been had must wishing you with up** Max.

f I **have have meaning been word you a with to about** this disposal operation.

g I **get would was mentioning wondering you when round to** that.

4 Work with a partner to practise mixing business and sport. Speaker A turn to page 123, Speaker B turn to page 131.

Visiting someone's home

1 What are the advantages and disadvantages of inviting a client or colleague to your home? Is it as common in your country as it is in Britain, Australia and the States?

2 **2.19–2.21** Listen to some people entertaining at home and answer the questions.

Extract 1

a Did Magda have a problem finding Anne's house?

b What do you think 'Martin's still slaving away in the kitchen' means?

c What do you think Magda brought as a present?

Extract 2

a What do you think 'The whole place was an absolute wreck when we moved in' means?

b What do you think Martin means by 'I had to rescue the starter'?

c What word does Anne use which means 'more to drink'?

Extract 3

a How does Magna describe the duck?

crispy ☐ juicy ☐ soggy ☐ tasty ☐ delicious ☐ tender ☐

b Who raises the subject of business? Complete the expression: I've been m________g to talk to you about this business in Poland.

c What excuse does Martin make to leave the two women to talk business?

d How many times does Magda indicate she's going to leave soon?

3 All the remarks below were in the conversation in 2. Work with a partner. See who can remember the most in just three minutes!

Arrival

L________t me take your coat.
Oh, I b________t you this.
You shouldn't h________e.
Come on t________h.
Oh, w________t a fabulous apartment!
Now, how about s________g to drink?
Make y________f at home.

The meal

Dinner's r________y when you are.
Sit w________r you like.
Now, there's more duck if you w________t it.
And help y________f to vegetables.
Mm, this is a________y delicious!
I'm g________d you like it.
You m________t let me have the recipe.

Farewells

Well, I o________t to be making a move soon.
You don't have to r________h off just yet, do you? How a________t some more coffee?
Okay, j________t half a cup. And then I really must be g________g.
Thank you b________h for a lovely evening. Next time you must come to my p________e.
T________e care now.

A dinner invitation

Work with a partner. Act out the situation of a business person (the guest) visiting the home of a colleague (the host) from arrival to departure. The host is the guest's immediate boss. Before you start, establish:

- what company you work for (name, location and main business activity)
- exactly what your roles are at work
- how business is doing and what problems or opportunities your company currently has.

You both have an ulterior motive for the dinner. Guest see page 131. Host see page 123.

Step 1 This is the host's living room. Host, welcome your guest, ask about their journey, make them feel at home and try to keep the conversation going. Guest, make up any information you like about the journey, make some positive comments about the apartment, ask questions and show interest in the answers.

Step 2 This is the dinner. Host, explain what the food is. Guest, compliment your host on the meal.

Step 3 Guest, take your leave, thank your host. Host, say goodbye to your guest and thank them for coming. Conclude any business you discussed during the evening or arrange to meet to discuss it again.

09 Relationship-building

Vocabulary

Social English

1 Complete the conversation extracts from a dinner party using the pairs of verbs in the boxes.

got + joking   is + accept   looking + ask   makes + think
mean + talking   reckon + is   's + be   see + doing
tells + going   think + happen

A So, what do you (1) ______ is going to ______ with this Ukrainian contract then?

B Good question. You know, something (2) ______ me we're not ______ to get it.

A Oh, really? What (3) ______ you ______ that? It (4) ______ not like you to ______ so pessimistic.

B Well, for one thing, we've gone in way too high. My guess (5) ______ they'll ______ a lower tender.

A Mm. By the way, have some more meat – there's plenty of it. You know, I don't (6) ______ price ______ really the issue.

B No?

A No. I (7) ______, we're ______ long-term here. This is a seven-year project, maybe longer.

B So?

A So, reliability is what they'll be (8) ______ for, if you ______ me. They'll pay more for that.

B You've (9) ______ to be ______. This is one of the most price-sensitive markets in Eastern Europe. The way I (10) ______ it, we'll be ______ well just to get part of the contract. They'll probably get a local firm in to do the main work.

A Hm, well, that's bad news ...

can't + say   had + would   hear + going   is + getting
knew + coming   might + known   's + help
shouldn't + saying   stop + get   suppose + heard

A I (11) ______ you've ______ the news about Alex?

B About her leaving to join HP? Well, we (12) ______ that was ______, didn't we?

A I suppose so. The word (13) ______ that Eduardo's ______ her job now. You know, I (14) ______ a feeling he ______.

B Mm. I (15) ______ really ______ I'm surprised. He's had his eye on it for a while. And, anyway, if you get engaged to the executive vice-president's daughter, it (16) ______ bound to ______ your career prospects, isn't it?

A He's what? I (17) ______ have ______! He'll (18) ______ at nothing to ______ a promotion.

B Well, you didn't (19) ______ this from me, but there's a rumour ______ around that ... well, maybe I (20) ______ be ______ this, but ...

A No, no, go on!

2 Underline eight new expressions in 1 that you could use yourself.

Grammar

Multi-verb sentences

1 Decide which of the verbs below precede the infinitive with *to*, the *-ing* form or both and tick (✓) the appropriate boxes. The first one has been done for you.

	to do	doing		to do	doing
agree	✓		manage		
admit			enjoy		
suggest			hope		
try			miss		
put off			avoid		
aim			expect		
stop			promise		
refuse			go on		
carry on			fail		
remember			dislike		

2 Complete the conversation using the correct form of the verbs in brackets.

A Hi, James. Client meeting overran a bit, did it?

B Mm. And Lucy and I stopped (1) ______ (have) a coffee on the way back.

A Oh, right.

B By the way, did you remember (2) ______ (send) those invoices off?

A What invoices?

B Stuart! I distinctly remember (3) ______ (ask) you to deal with the invoices. They should have gone last week.

A Well, I've been a bit busy trying (4) ______ (fix) this wretched computer!

B Okay, look, stop (5) ______ (do) whatever you're doing and deal with them now, would you? And what's wrong with the computer?

A No idea. It keeps crashing.

B Well, have you tried (6) ______ (ask) Callum about it?

A Of course I have. I've been trying (7) ______ (get) through to him all morning. But he's like you, isn't he? He's never in!

3 Complete the conversation using an appropriate preposition and *-ing* form from the boxes below.

about about of in on

being having making putting telling

A Of course, Tim succeeded _____ _____ a complete fool of himself at the party.

B Did he?

A Oh, yes. Well, he will insist _____ _____ those tasteless jokes, won't he? The president's wife was not amused.

B Well, he can forget _____ _____ in for that promotion, then, can't he?

A Hm, not much chance of that here, anyway. You know I complained _____ us _____ to work another weekend?

B Mm, I hear Angela went mad about it.

A Yeah, she practically accused me _____ _____ disloyal to the company! Can you believe it?

B Sounds like her.

Some **verbs** can precede both the **infinitive** and the *-ing* **form**, but the meaning usually changes (*I **like to** work out twice a week* = I think it's a good idea; *I **like** work**ing** out* = I enjoy it).

Some verbs normally followed by the *-ing* form change to infinitive without *to* when there's an indirect object (*I suggest **stopping** now – I suggest we **stop** now*).

When a verb is followed by a preposition other than *to*, the *-ing* form is usually used (*They apologized **for** not **getting** back to us sooner*).

Modal verbs always precede the other verbs in a sentence and are followed by the infinitive without *to* (*You **must** be wishing you'd never come to work here!*).

Certain expressions always precede the *-ing* form: ***It's no good** complain**ing**; **There's no point (in)** complain**ing**; **What's the use of** complain**ing**?*

A number of expressions take the past form: ***I'd rather** you **didn't**; **It's time** we **went**.*

A number of expressions of intention take the infinitive with *to*: ***I'm planning to** do it later; **I've been meaning to** have a word with you.*

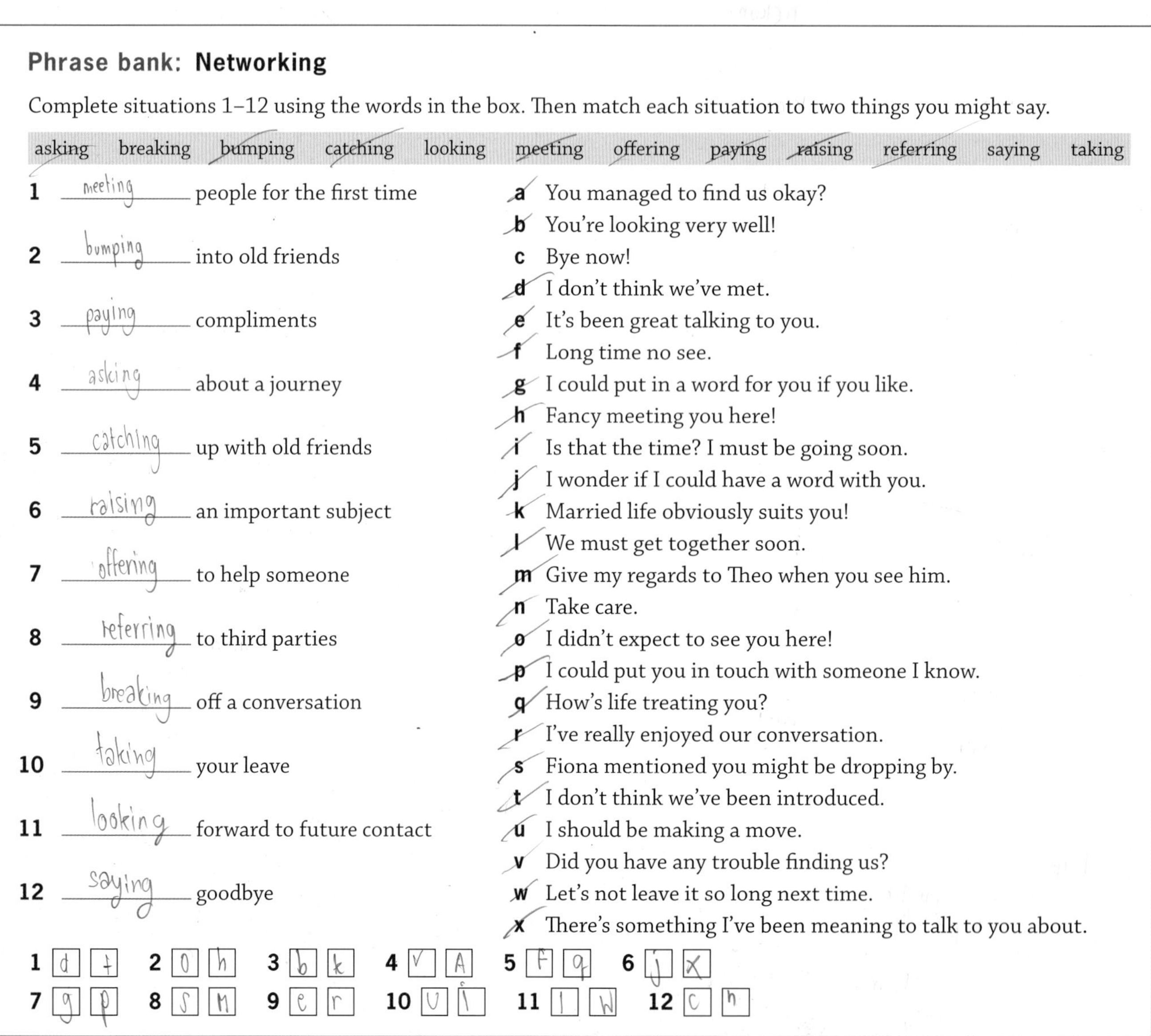

Phrase bank: Networking

Complete situations 1–12 using the words in the box. Then match each situation to two things you might say.

asking breaking bumping catching looking meeting offering paying raising referring saying taking

1 _____ people for the first time
2 _____ into old friends
3 _____ compliments
4 _____ about a journey
5 _____ up with old friends
6 _____ an important subject
7 _____ to help someone
8 _____ to third parties
9 _____ off a conversation
10 _____ your leave
11 _____ forward to future contact
12 _____ goodbye

a You managed to find us okay?
b You're looking very well!
c Bye now!
d I don't think we've met.
e It's been great talking to you.
f Long time no see.
g I could put in a word for you if you like.
h Fancy meeting you here!
i Is that the time? I must be going soon.
j I wonder if I could have a word with you.
k Married life obviously suits you!
l We must get together soon.
m Give my regards to Theo when you see him.
n Take care.
o I didn't expect to see you here!
p I could put you in touch with someone I know.
q How's life treating you?
r I've really enjoyed our conversation.
s Fiona mentioned you might be dropping by.
t I don't think we've been introduced.
u I should be making a move.
v Did you have any trouble finding us?
w Let's not leave it so long next time.
x There's something I've been meaning to talk to you about.

1 ☐ ☐ 2 ☐ ☐ 3 ☐ ☐ 4 ☐ ☐ 5 ☐ ☐ 6 ☐ ☐
7 ☐ ☐ 8 ☐ ☐ 9 ☐ ☐ 10 ☐ ☐ 11 ☐ ☐ 12 ☐ ☐

10 Making decisions

Standing in the middle of the road is very dangerous – you get knocked down by the traffic from both sides.

Margaret Thatcher

Do you find decision-making easy or difficult?

Learning objectives: Unit 10

Business communication skills Discussing making decisions in difficult situations; Doing a quiz on life-and-death decisions; Giving advice on worst-case scenarios or workplace dilemmas; Inserting missing articles into two texts; Fluency: Holding a crisis management meeting
Reading Website extract: Worst-case scenarios; Company crises
Listening Advice on surviving worst-case scenarios; Decision-making meetings; Case study: Coca-Cola crisis
Vocabulary Marketing
Grammar Articles
Phrase bank Decision-making
In company interviews Units 8–10

1 When was the last time you were faced with a difficult decision and were unable to make up your mind? How did you decide in the end, or was the decision made for you?

2 You may be a cool-headed decision maker in the office, but would you know what to do in a real life-or-death situation? Read the following extract from an unusual website and discuss the questions.

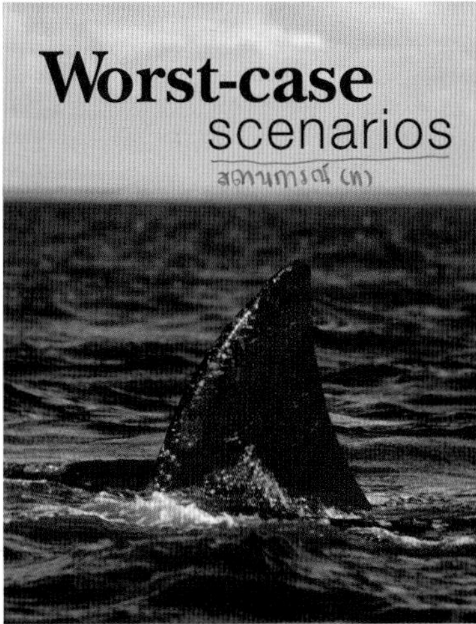

The principle behind this site is a simple one: you just never know.

You never really know what nasty surprises life has in store for you – what is lurking around the corner, what is hovering over your head, what is swimming beneath the surface. You never know when you might be called on to perform an act of extreme bravery and to choose life or death by your own actions.

But when you are called, we want to be sure that you know how to react. We want you to know what to do when the pilot passes out and you have to land the plane. We want you to know what to do when you see that shark fin heading toward you …

www.worstcasescenarios.com

a What kind of things 'lurking around the corner', 'hovering over your head' or 'swimming beneath the surface' do you think the website is referring to?

b Have you ever found yourself in a really dangerous situation where you needed to act quickly? Tell the story.

c What worst-case scenario would you least like to face:
1 at work? **2** in life?

3 Work in two groups. Hold an emergency meeting to decide what decisions you'd make in real life-and-death situations. There are four items on your 'agenda' and you have just five minutes to decide what action to take. Group A your worst-case scenarios are below and on page 64. Group B turn to page 124.

1 On a driving holiday in India you lose control of your hire-car travelling downhill at 70 mph on a mountain road. You've no brakes and there's a 300m drop to the valley below. Do you:
- a try to jump out of the car and roll to safety?
- b steer away from the cliff edge and into the mountainside to stop the car?
- c steer into the crash barriers on the cliff edge to slow the car down?

2 On a trek in the Chilean Andes you get cut off from the rest of your group and become hopelessly lost. As you try to work out which direction to take, you are confronted by a hungry mountain lion. Do you:
- a lie down and play dead?
- b shout and flap your coat at the animal?
- c run and hide (maybe find a tree to climb)?

3 During a flight over the Grand Canyon in a private plane, your pilot passes out and you have to land the plane yourself. You manage to reach the airfield. Do you:

a keep the nose of the plane pointing above the horizon as you descend to the runway?
b slow down to about 60 mph as you touch down and then hit the brakes hard?
c keep the plane at a steady altitude of 150 feet as you approach the beginning of the runway?

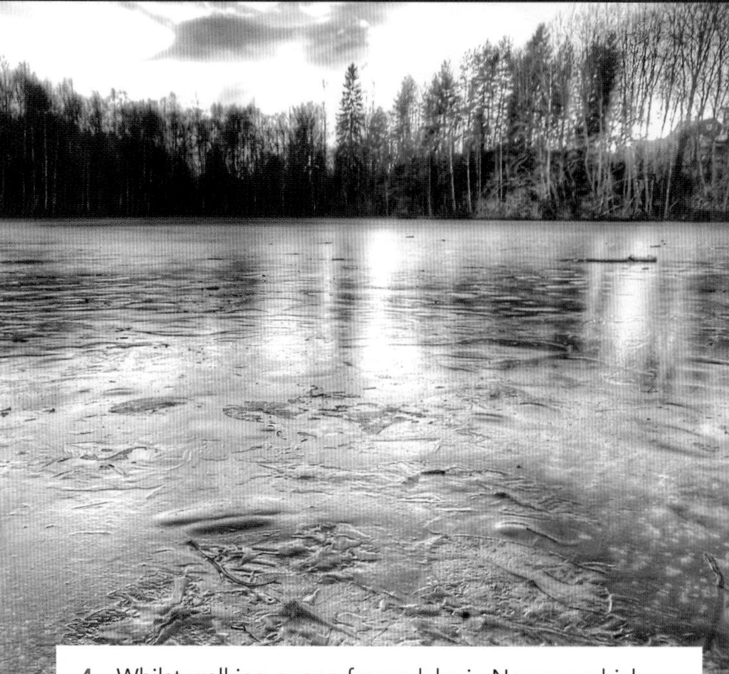

4 Whilst walking over a frozen lake in Norway, which you were assured was perfectly safe, you fall through the ice and are in danger of drowning. Do you:

a attempt to pull yourself out?
b move about in the water to generate body heat?
c stay calm, conserve energy and cry for help?

4 Work with a partner from the other group. Briefly summarize the scenarios you faced and the decisions you took.

5 **2.22–2.29** Now listen to some advice on how to survive the eight worst-case scenarios in 3. How many lives did you lose? Which group did better?

6 Put the following expressions on the scale below according to how likely they are. Most of them were in the advice you just listened to. The first one has been done for you.

a You've a good chance.
b You don't stand a chance.
c There's a 50-50 chance.
d Your chances are slim.
e You're in with a chance.
f The chances are remote.
g You've blown your chances.
h There's a fair chance.
i There's an outside chance.
j It's a million-to-one chance.
k No chance!

(a)

more likely ← **possible** → **less likely**

7 Complete expressions a–n using the nouns and verbs in the boxes. They were all in the advice in 5.

bet circumstances idea mistake move point thing

a Your best ____________ is to shout and flap your coat at the animal.
b Do not in any ____________ try to stand up on the ice.
c It's a good ____________ to brake as soon as you've gained control of the steering.
d There's not much ____________ trying to force the door open.
e By far the most sensible ____________ to do is to open the car window.
f Just grabbing on to the nearest person with a parachute is not a smart ____________.
g It's a common ____________ to think the shark's nose is the best area to target.

do forget make put resist take think

h Don't even ____________ about jumping from a moving vehicle.
i ____________ the temptation to run from a mountain lion.
j ____________ any ideas of playing dead out of your mind.
k ____________ sure that the nose of the plane is six inches below the horizon.
l ____________ care to land on your back to avoid breaking it.
m ____________ about trapping air inside a sinking car.
n You'd ____________ much better to strike at the eyes or gills.

8 Work with a partner. Practise using some of the expressions in 6 and 7 by advising them on how to handle one of the following situations. Don't worry if you can't give expert advice!

Worst-case scenarios

- on a round-the-world cruise the ocean liner you're on hits an iceberg and starts to sink
- during a trip across the Australian Outback, your car breaks down in the middle of nowhere
- a poisonous snake has crawled into your sleeping bag

Workplace dilemmas

- your boss is working you to death
- a colleague is taking the credit for all your ideas
- you've been passed over for promotion – again!
- there's a rumour your company is about to announce redundancies

The decision-making process

'Gentlemen, I take it we are all in complete agreement on the decision here.' Alfred P. Sloan, the head of General Motors, looked around the committee room table. His senior managers nodded in assent. 'Then,' continued Sloan, 'I propose we postpone further discussion of the matter until our next meeting to give ourselves time to develop disagreement and perhaps gain some understanding of what the decision is about.'

John Adair
Effective Decision-Making

1 Read the anecdote about Alfred P. Sloan, the man who built General Motors into the biggest company in the world. What point is being made about group decisions?

2 **2.30–2.32** Listen to extracts from three different decision-making meetings and answer the questions.

1 An industrial dispute
a Why is Dan so concerned about a strike?
b Who's the calmest person at the meeting?

2 Political instabilities
a What's Hans's objection to the proposal?
b What's Andrea worried about?

3 A product recall
a Whose side is Laura on?
b Do you think Simon has already made up his mind?

3 You heard the following idiomatic expressions in 2. Can you remember the missing words? The first two letters are given. The meaning of the idioms in brackets may help you.

a the ball is in their co____________ (we're waiting for someone else to make a decision)
b jump to co____________ (decide too quickly without considering all the facts)
c when it comes to the cr____________ (when a decision finally has to be made)
d sit on the fe____________ (refuse to support either side in an argument)

4 The following remarks were also all in the meetings in 2. Replace the words and phrases in **bold** with similar ones from the box.

advantages and disadvantages | alternative | come to | complete support | I don't think we should make a decision | information | intuition | the main thing | opinions | plan | pool our ideas | serious thought | stand by | suggest | undecided | we need to take our time on this | we're running out of time | we unanimously agree

a Look, **time is short** ______. So let's **put our heads together** ______ and see what we can **come up with** ______.

b Okay, we've weighed up the various **pros and cons** ______. Now it's time to **reach** ______ a decision and **stick to** ______ it.

c **I don't want us rushing into things** ______. This whole issue requires **careful consideration** ______.

d I take it **we're all in agreement** ______ that **our first priority** ______ is to safeguard the well-being of our personnel.

e Well, then, I don't see we have any **option** ______ but to give this proposal our **full backing** ______.

f I'd like your **input** ______ on this before committing us to any definite **course** ______ of action.

g I'm **in two minds** ______ about it. At this stage **I think we should keep our options open** ______.

h Well, in the absence of more reliable **data** ______, I think I'm going to have to go with my **gut instinct** ______ on this one.

Crisis management

1 What sort of crises can companies be faced with these days? Can you think of recent examples of any of the following?

accusations of fraud | a consumer boycott | an environmental disaster | a hostile takeover bid | insider trading | a lawsuit | mass redundancies | a product recall

2 Work in two groups. Group A read about a crisis at McDonald's, Group B at Mercedes. Twenty-five articles (*a, an* and *the*) are missing from each text. Write them in. If you do the exercise correctly, both groups should use *a, an* and *the* the same number of times.

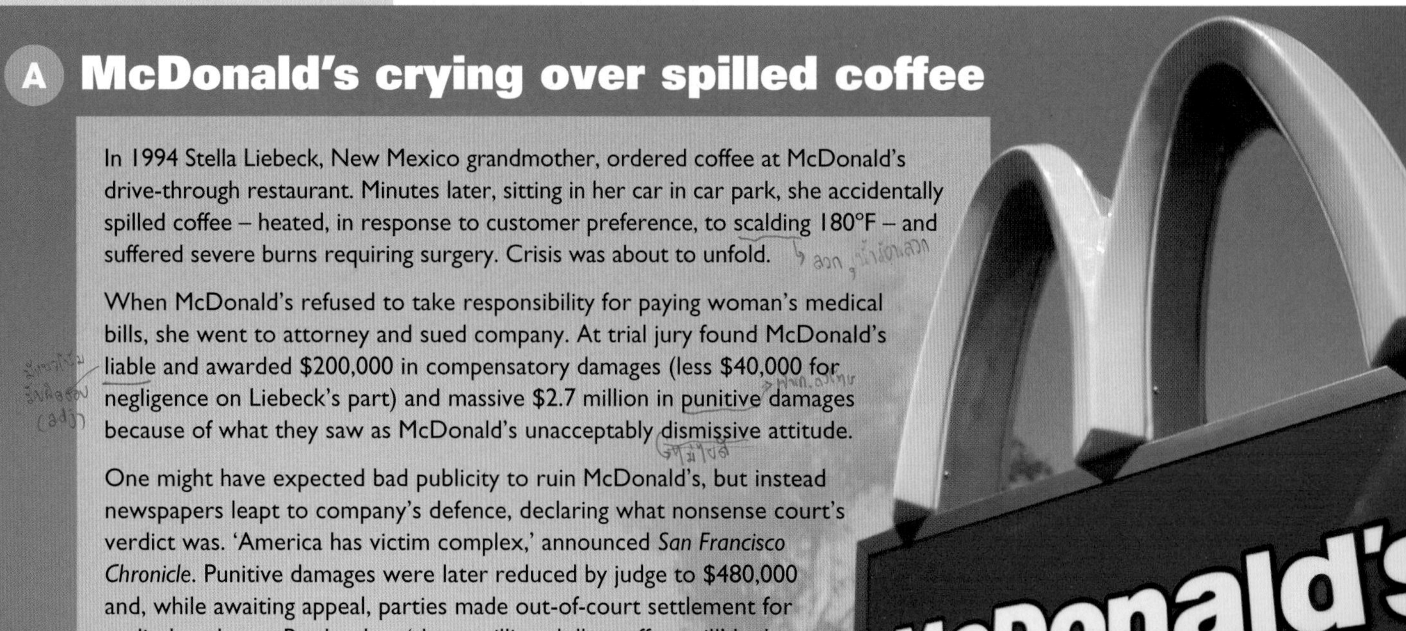

A McDonald's crying over spilled coffee

In 1994 Stella Liebeck, New Mexico grandmother, ordered coffee at McDonald's drive-through restaurant. Minutes later, sitting in her car in car park, she accidentally spilled coffee – heated, in response to customer preference, to scalding 180°F – and suffered severe burns requiring surgery. Crisis was about to unfold.

When McDonald's refused to take responsibility for paying woman's medical bills, she went to attorney and sued company. At trial jury found McDonald's liable and awarded $200,000 in compensatory damages (less $40,000 for negligence on Liebeck's part) and massive $2.7 million in punitive damages because of what they saw as McDonald's unacceptably dismissive attitude.

One might have expected bad publicity to ruin McDonald's, but instead newspapers leapt to company's defence, declaring what nonsense court's verdict was. 'America has victim complex,' announced *San Francisco Chronicle*. Punitive damages were later reduced by judge to $480,000 and, while awaiting appeal, parties made out-of-court settlement for undisclosed sum. But by then 'three million dollar coffee-spill' had already passed into corporate legend.

B Mercedes *on a roll*

In automotive industry trend for many years has been towards smaller, more economical vehicle. So in autumn of 1997, Daimler-Benz introduced new economy model, Mercedes 'A Class'. It was car designed to compete with ever-popular Volkswagen Golf. But just before November launch, disaster struck.

Swedish auto magazine had conducted what they called 'elk test' on new car. Test is standard in Sweden to make sure cars can steer to avoid large deer crossing road. But at just 60 kph 'A Class' overturned, injuring both test drivers. Storm immediately blew up in press and on TV, as buyers waiting to take delivery cancelled their orders. For Mercedes it was not only financial but image crisis too.

Daimler responded quickly, adding wider tyres, electronic stability mechanism and stronger anti-rollbars – all at no extra cost to customer. Highly successful advertising campaign and public support from Niki Lauda, ex-formula one racing champion, helped to restore consumer confidence in 'A Class' but at cost of hundreds of millions of dollars.

3 Summarize the story you read in 2 to a member of the other group. What lessons can be learned from how the companies behaved?

4 Which are the best things a manager can do in a crisis? Which do you think are good advice? Match the following collocations.

a	deny	someone	**g**	admit	honest
b	stay	time	**h**	take	data
c	delegate	calm	**i**	make	charge
d	buy	decisive	**j**	act	quickly
e	blame	everything	**k**	collect	nothing
f	be	responsibility	**l**	be	promises

5 Work in groups to act as crisis management consultants to the Coca-Cola Company. It is May 1999 and the world's most famous brand is in trouble ...

Step 1

 **2.33** Listen to the first part of the case and answer the questions.

a How many Cokes are sold each day?
b How would you describe Coca-Cola's advertising strategy?
c What has just happened?
d Which markets are directly involved in the crisis?
e Calculate how much those markets are worth in annual sales.

Step 2

 **2.34** Listen to the second part of the case and answer the questions.

a What do the following figures refer to?
+25% -13%
b What is the significance of these figures?
c What have the inspectors at the Belgian bottling plant found?
d What is the toxicologist's verdict?
e Who is benefiting from Coca-Cola's current problems?

Step 3

Hold a meeting to decide what recommendations to make to your client. As well as the information you have just heard, read the article and agenda on page 121.

10 Making decisions

Vocabulary

Marketing

The marketplace

1 Complete the adjectives by writing in the missing vowels. The adjectives range from positive to negative.

	b__m_ng	thr_v_ng	+
	h__lthy	b__y_nt	
The market is	v_l_t_l_	_npr_d_ct_bl_	
	w__k	sl_gg_sh	
	fl_t	d_pr_ss_d	–

2 Complete the sentence using some of the adjectives in 1 and information that is true for you.

The market for __________ *in* __________ *is* __________, *whereas the* __________ *market is* __________.

3 Complete the collocations by writing a noun from the box before each set of three nouns below.

advertising	brand	distribution	market	marketing

a __________ mix / drive / strategy
b __________ forces / research / share
c __________ network / channels / costs
d __________ campaign / expenditure / agencies
e __________ awareness / loyalty / stretching

4 Which collocations in 3 are the following examples of?

a Omnicom, Publicis, Doyle Dane Bernbach, Dentsu
b competition, the state of the economy, political stability
c 'the four Ps': product, place, price, promotion
d wholesalers, retailers, sales reps
e Virgin Cola, Camel watches, Ferrari sunglasses

5 Listed below are some of the terms commonly used in marketing departments, but the second word in each collocation has been switched with another in the same column. Can you switch them back? The first two have been done for you.

a market **outlet**	**g** subliminal **relations**
b competitive **brand**	**h** price **marketing**
c retail **challenger**	**i** niche **analysis**
d mass **sensitivity**	**j** public **advertising**
e price **market**	**k** consumer **market**
f leading **advantage**	**l** permission **war**

6 Which of the terms in 5 refer to:

a the number two player in a market after the market leader?
b the importance the customer gives to prices?
c a small number of customers requiring a particular type of product or service?
d the shop or store through which products are sold to the consumer?
e a method of persuading consumers to buy by invisible, psychological means?
f getting customers' permission before sending information to them?

7 The verbs and verb phrases in the box all form strong collocations with 'the market'. Put them into the most likely chronological order. One of them has been done for you.

be squeezed out of	break back into	compete in
~~dominate~~	enter	target

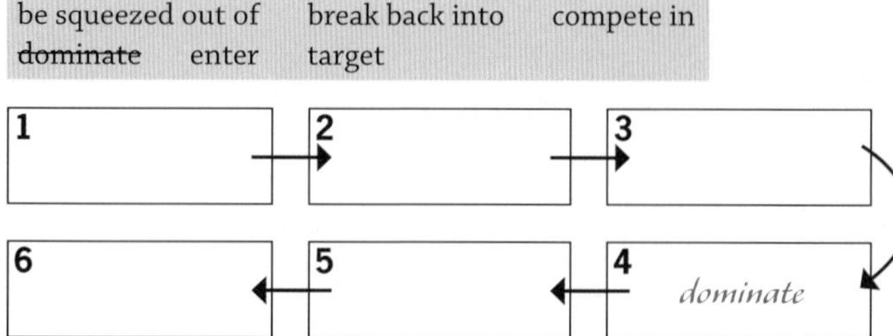

The verbs and verb phrases in the box all form strong collocations with 'the competition'. Put them into the most likely chronological order. One of them has been done for you.

come up against	destroy	fight back against
~~outclass~~	succumb to	take on

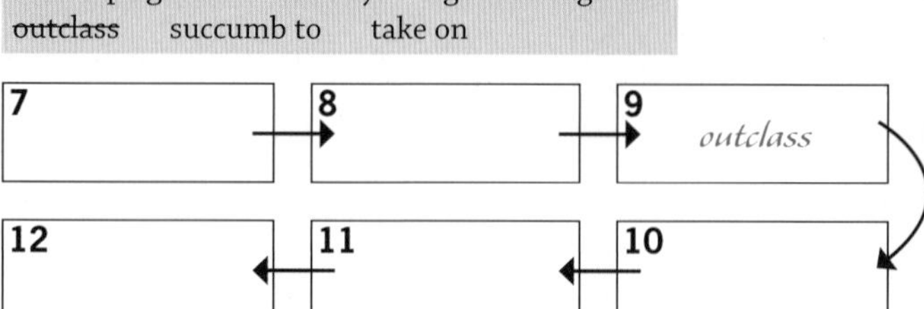

Grammar

Articles

Complete the text with *a*, *an*, *the* or zero article Ø, as necessary.

They say 'All's fair in (1) __________ love and (2) __________ war'. And when it comes to getting (3) __________ good deal, (4) __________ same is true of (5) __________ business. For (6) __________ example, in 1803, (7) __________ half of what is now (8) __________ USA was actually bought from (9) __________ French for three cents (10) __________ acre! How were they able to get such (11) __________ bargain? At (12) __________ time, (13) __________ Emperor Napoleon was preparing to go to (14) __________ war with (15) __________ Britain and was desperate to sell.

The **indefinite article** is used:

- before a singular countable noun when it is unspecified and mentioned for the first time. *I need **a** holiday.*
- before singular countable nouns in exclamations. *What **a** day!; It was such **a** nuisance!*
- before the names of professions. *She's **an** engineer.*
- before a singular countable noun where a plural could be used to mean the same thing. *There's no such thing as **a** free lunch = There's no such thing as free lunches.*
- to mean per when talking about prices, speed, rates, etc. *€3 **a** kilo; three times **a** day.*

The **definite article** is used:

- before a noun that has been mentioned before. *I used to have two BMWs and a Lotus, but I had to sell **the** Lotus.*
- before a noun that is later specified in the same sentence. ***The** guy I met in Rio runs his own business.*
- when it is clear from the context what we are referring to. *I'll drop you off at **the** hotel.*
- when the thing referred to is unique. ***The** human race.*
- before an adjective referring to a group. ***The** Dutch.*

The **zero article** is used:

- before mass or abstract nouns. *Greed is good.*
- before the names of most countries. Exceptions include: the USA, the UK and the Netherlands.
- in certain fixed expressions. *Go to war.*

Phrase bank: Decision-making

Listed below are six key things you need to do in a decision-making meeting. Match each to three things you might say. The first one has been done for you as an example.

1	Encourage collaboration	*b*		
2	Comment on options			
3	Consider pros and cons			
4	Advise caution			
5	Check agreement			
6	Commit to a decision			

a That's a big plus, as far as I'm concerned. But let's look at some of the minuses.

b Okay; I'd like everybody's input on this.

c We need to take our time on this.

d I don't see we have any option but to go ahead.

e So is that unanimous then?

f I think I'm going to have to go with my gut instinct on this one.

g To be honest, I'm in two minds about this.

h Okay, that's the upside. But what about the downside?

i This requires careful consideration.

j I take it we're all in agreement on this?

k Let's put our heads together and see what we can come up with.

l I'm not wholly in favour of this, but what alternative do we have?

m Okay, we've weighed up the advantages and disadvantages.

n Does anybody have any objections to that?

o So that's decided then.

p Let's pool our ideas on this.

q I don't want us rushing into things.

r Okay, so we're going to go with Marc's idea.

11

Stress

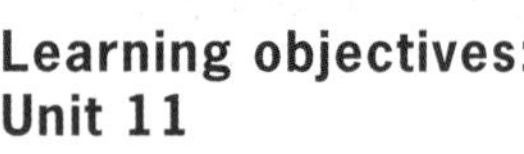

Learning objectives: Unit 11

People skills Analyzing attitudes to stress in the workplace; Identifying techniques for managing stress; Fluency: Helping a staff member in a stressful situation
Reading Article on helping colleagues manage stress
Listening Talk on stress management; Eight managers counselling their staff

1 Look at the cartoon and answer the questions.

a How would you describe the woman's behaviour in the cartoon?
b How does the man feel about the woman and her problem?
c What are their attitudes to stress?

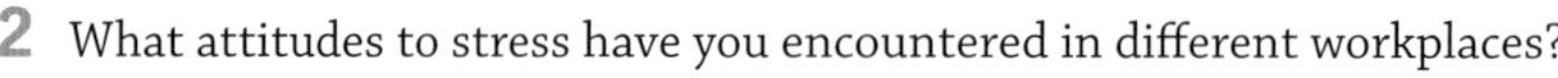

2 What attitudes to stress have you encountered in different workplaces?

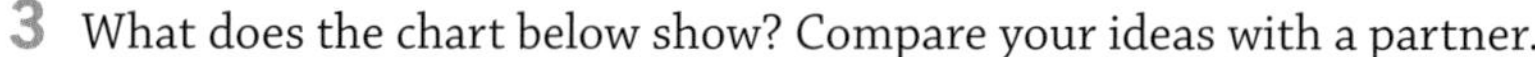

3 What does the chart below show? Compare your ideas with a partner.

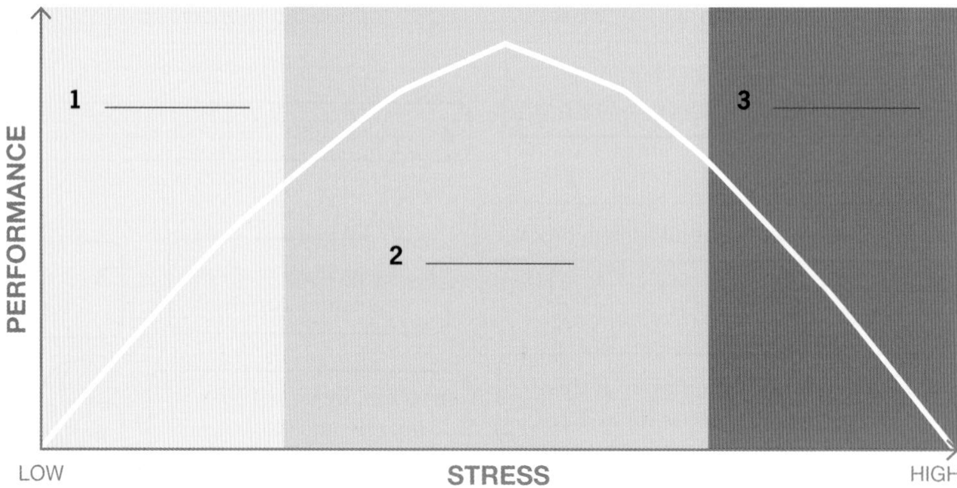

a

b

c

4 2.36 Listen to an extract from a talk about stress management and label the three coloured areas on the chart.

5 2.36 Listen again and match the work environments in the photos on the left to the levels of stress on the chart.

6 The speaker mentions 'the symptoms of distress' – what do you think they are? Consider the effects on the body, the mind and on behaviour. Compare your ideas with a partner.

7 How do you manage your own stress? Do you have any techniques or tips that would help colleagues or team members to manage their stress?

8 Read the article quickly and match the headings in the box to the paragraphs.

Ease the strain | Facilitate change | Identify the source | Share feelings

Helping colleagues manage stress

Stress is contagious; if not handled carefully, a colleague's distress can quickly ruin your own day. Following a four-step action plan will help keep the whole office on track.

1 ______________

First, encourage your stressed-out colleague to talk or even cry; expressing their emotions will provide temporary relief. Don't be judgemental and don't be tempted to force your advice on them; if their frustration is directed at you personally, resist the urge to defend yourself. Simply empathize and help them not to feel guilty about the way they feel.

2 ______________

Next, ask neutral, open questions to elicit the cause of their distress. Very often a minor annoyance will prove to be the tip of a much bigger iceberg. But don't probe, and don't ask leading questions. Don't minimize the problem, but try to help your colleague keep things in perspective.

3 ______________

Ask yourself what you can do to take the pressure off. Can you give your colleague more time, or shift some tasks to someone else? A quiet word with other people who are a source of pressure, or small improvements to the work environment, can help overcome that 'out of control' feeling.

4 ______________

Use counselling techniques like echoing, summarizing and asking hypothetical questions to help your colleague find their own solutions. Don't provide your own answers to their problems; help them take control of their life by making changes or simply learning to live with the problem.

9 Reread the article. How many of the points you discussed in 7 are mentioned?

10 According to the article, you should not do the following things. Why?

- force your advice on colleagues
- defend yourself
- probe
- ask leading questions
- minimize the problem
- provide answers

11 2.37 Listen to eight managers counselling staff members who are suffering from stress. Decide if each manager is doing things right (✓) or wrong (✗). Then match the manager to the advice from the article (a–h) that they are following or need to follow.

a ask what you can do to take the pressure off
b don't probe, and don't ask leading questions
c encourage colleagues to express their emotions
d don't provide your own answers
e use counselling techniques like echoing, etc
f help them not to feel guilty
g don't minimize the problem
h resist the urge to defend yourself

Manager	✓ / ✗	Advice
1 Mark		
2 Jacky		
3 Corey		
4 Brett		
5 Jo		
6 Perry		
7 Chris		
8 Georgie		

12 2.37 Complete the useful expressions you heard in 11. Then listen again and check.

1 It's ______________ normal.
2 It's better to get it off your ______________.
3 I understand how you ______________.
4 Would it ______________ if …
5 It could ______________ to anyone.
6 There's no need to feel ______________ about it.
7 What would ______________ if you didn't …
8 How ______________ a problem would that be?

13 Work with a partner to practise helping a staff member in a stressful situation. Speaker A see page 118. Speaker B see page 136.

MANAGEMENT SCENARIO

Pitch and persuade

Learning objectives: Management scenario C

Business communication skills Identifying effective pitching techniques; Using Cialdini's six principles of influence; Fluency: Pitching a new project
Reading Article on building donor circles
In company in action
C1: A failed pitch;
C2: An effective pitch

1 Who is the most persuasive person you know? How do they get people to do what they want them to do?

2 Read the article below that Cassie sent to her boss, Peter, and mark the statements *T* (true), *F* (false) or *D* (doesn't say).

Peter - thought you might find this useful for the E. India project.
Cass.

Use social media to build donor circles

In today's difficult giving environment, the best place to look for new funding is with your current donors. Put their loyalty and social media contacts to work for your organization.

Forget about mass mailshots and advertising campaigns; new donors are no longer recruited in batches of hundreds or thousands but through small circles of friends, one at a time. Many of your loyal donors are active social media users. Invite them to leverage their willingness to promote your cause by recruiting new supporters from their own circles of friends. Give them the tools to build new donor circles from among their Facebook friends and Twitter followers and organize events to promote your projects. Soon your new supporters will go on to build their own donor circles.

The power of social media lies in its almost unlimited numbers of connections. When you build high-quality relationships with your followers, your donor circles can multiply indefinitely.

a Cassie tells Peter he should use social media to raise money for a project in India. ☐
b Investing in media campaigns and direct mailing is the best way to recruit large numbers of supporters. ☐
c Existing supporters are happy to tell their friends about a good cause via social media. ☐
d Developing donor circles costs the organization nothing. ☐

In company in action

3 Now watch video C1 to see Peter Neubauer, Marketing Manager at Blue Rock, pitching a new fundraising strategy to Sue Jensen, his CEO. Which of the following are mentioned?

a three-day conference	☐	an important interview	☐
a budget cut	☐	an urgent decision	☐
recruiting new staff	☐	waste water treatment	☐
return on investment	☐	a precedent for non-profit organizations	☐

4 Watch video C1 again and answer the questions.

a Why doesn't Sue want to schedule a presentation after the conference call?
b What is the goal of the Eastern India project?
c Why is Sue uncomfortable with the concept of multi-level marketing?
d What major costs does Peter's strategy involve?
e What two reasons does Sue give for saying no?

5 Peter makes a number of strategic and tactical mistakes. Match the following phrases to the errors they illustrate.

1 Couldn't Cassie deal with it?
2 My presentation is in three parts ...
3 So why didn't you say so?
4 I've been there, I know what it's like.
5 Sorry Peter, you've lost me there.
6 No, you don't understand.

a forgetting that a pitch is much shorter than a presentation
b not seeing an opportunity for reciprocity
c using jargon
d losing Sue's sympathy by rejecting her objection too directly
e not adapting the pitch to the audience, giving too much detail
f not explaining the need for new funding

6 Work with a partner. Discuss how Peter could improve his pitch. Brainstorm a list of dos and don'ts for pitching and persuading.

7 Complete the emails below with words from the boxes. The first box is for 1–6 and the second box is for a–f. Compare Emma's advice with your own dos and don'ts.

details	discussion	jargon
overview	specific	structure

Authority	Consistency	Liking
Reciprocity	Scarcity	Social proof

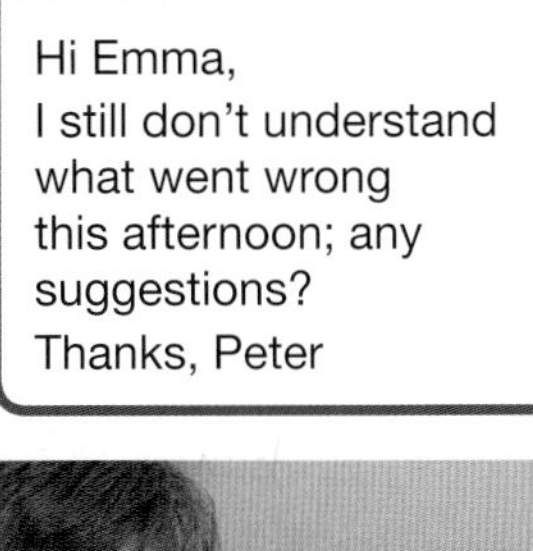
Hi Emma,
I still don't understand what went wrong this afternoon; any suggestions?
Thanks, Peter

Peter,
Sue really put you on the spot, didn't she? For what it's worth, here are a few thoughts.
As you know, an elevator pitch isn't the same thing as a presentation. You don't have time for 1) __________, your goal is just to give a high-level 2) __________ and get your audience interested enough to start a 3) __________. So you have to have a very clear, simple 4) __________ – e.g. (i) a reason to listen, (ii) the objective, (iii) the problem, (iv) the solution, (v) the benefits, (vi) a call for action.
Secondly, be passionate, be lean, be 5) __________, and be sincere. Show that you believe in what you're doing, don't use 6) __________, keep it clear and simple, and show that you really want that agreement.
Finally, have you ever heard of Cialdini's six principles of influence?

a __________ – give something first, then people are more likely to return the favour.
b __________ – it's easier to persuade people if there is mutual like and respect
c __________ – people more often agree if they think they won't get another chance.
d __________ – having the appropriate credentials makes you more persuasive.
e __________ – a logical sequence of arguments builds pressure to agree.
f __________ – show that others are already doing it and people will follow their example.

Hope this helps; as you know, Sue always likes to give people a second chance!
Good luck, Emma

In company in action

8 Now watch video C2 to see Peter make a second pitch. Which points in Emma's advice do the following phrases illustrate?

a Leave them with me. I'll deal with them.
b Did you know 68% of social media users will ...
c This was Cassie's idea, so she should take the credit.
d I know exactly what you mean.
e This strategy is already being used very successfully by high-profile nonprofits like ...
f I've put all the details in this handout.
g If we wait till everybody's doing it, it won't be so effective.
h That's why I'm asking you to give the go-ahead ...

9 After making an unexpected profit, your company has allocated a budget of $1M for an exceptional project to benefit employees. Among the suggestions are building a gym, setting up a day-care centre for young children, or funding MBA courses. Prepare a two-minute pitch to defend one of these projects or your own idea. Make your pitch and answer the group's questions. Hold a vote to decide who gets the go-ahead.

When you have finished, use the checklists on page 127 to help you evaluate your performance.

12 Emailing

The beautiful part of writing is that you don't have to get it right the first time, unlike, say, a brain surgeon. You can always do it better.

Robert Cormier, author

Do you prefer to email or to call colleagues?

Learning objectives: Unit 12

Business communication skills Discussing how to deal with emails; Correcting errors in an email; Shortening and simplifying an email; Adding the personal touch to an email; Choosing an appropriate email style; Fluency: Writing and answering emails
Reading Extracts on emailing
Listening Podcast: what your emails say about your career prospects; Radio programme: The biggest email blunders ever made
Vocabulary Prepositional phrases
Grammar Future forms
Phrase bank Emailing

1 Read the extracts below from web and press articles and discuss the questions with a partner.

2 Make a list of your three top tips for dealing with emails. Compare your list with the rest of your group.

a According to the Electronic Messaging Association, around seven trillion emails are sent annually. How many of them end up in your inbox? And how do you deal with the following problem?

When everybody has email and anybody can send you email, how do you decide whose messages you're going to read and respond to first and whose you're going to send to the trash unread? *Tom Peters in Fast Company magazine*

b Is email a time-saver or does it distract you from more important business? Are you anything like the typical workers mentioned below?

As Clive Thompson pointed out in *The New York Times magazine*, after a worker has been interrupted with a message, it generally takes nearly half an hour for him to return to his original task. According to researchers, 40% of workers moved on to completely new tasks after being interrupted, leaving their old task behind, neglected and unfinished. *SEND, The Essential Guide to Email for Office and Home*

c Are you ignoring your email more these days? Does this company's idea sound like it could work?

Signs are that the first rush of enthusiasm for email may be waning. One big company in the computing industry is considering banning emails in the afternoon. It found that its people had stopped talking to one another. *Stuart Crainer in A Freethinker's A–Z of the New World of Business*

d Have you ever sent an angry email or hidden behind an email when you had bad news to deliver? How do you feel about the advice below?

Rule number one: never send an email when you're mad. And if you want to know if you're mad, just take two fingers, close your eyes and touch your eyelids. If they're hot, researchers say you're mad and you should put it in the draft pile and send it later. One of the things I've learned is that email is for saying 'yes', email is for answering or asking questions. If you say 'no', if you criticize, if you attack, please, do it in person – or, worst-case, do it over the phone.
Tim Sanders, Better Life Media

e The Institute of Management puts working with computers amongst 'The Top Ten Stress Factors at Work'. Have you ever resorted to any of the following?

A survey by Mori reveals that three quarters of computer users shout and swear at their machines. A similar study by IT support company Sosmatic shows that 43% of them have slapped, smacked and even kicked their computer. The mouse is the most abused piece of equipment, receiving 31.5% of the punishment, followed by the monitor, the printer, the hard drive and the keyboard. Over a year such outbursts of 'computer rage' can cost companies up to £25,000 in lost earnings and damaged hardware.

Writing emails

1 Read the article below. Is it easy or difficult to understand?

> Aoccdrnig to rsceearh at Cmabrigde Uinervtisy, it deosn't mttaer in what oredr the ltteers in a wrod are. The olny iprmoatnt tihng is taht the frist and lsat ltteres are in the rghit pclae. The rset can be a toatl mses and you can sltil raed it wouthit a porbelm. This is bcuseae the huamn mnid deos not raed ervey lteter by istlef, but the wrod as a wlohe.

2 2.38 Listen to a podcast explaining what the kind of email you send says about your career prospects. Match the person to the email type.

a high-flier
b born leader
c corporate loser
d time-waster
e poor team player
f office joker

1 reply to all
2 filled with emoticons
3 prefer face mail
4 bcc to boss
5 neatly paragraphed
6 short phrases

3 If Professor Owens's research is right, are you writing the kind of emails that will get you promoted?

4 Look at the email below and the one on page 76. From what Professor Owens said in the podcast you just listened to, which do you think was written by a junior manager?

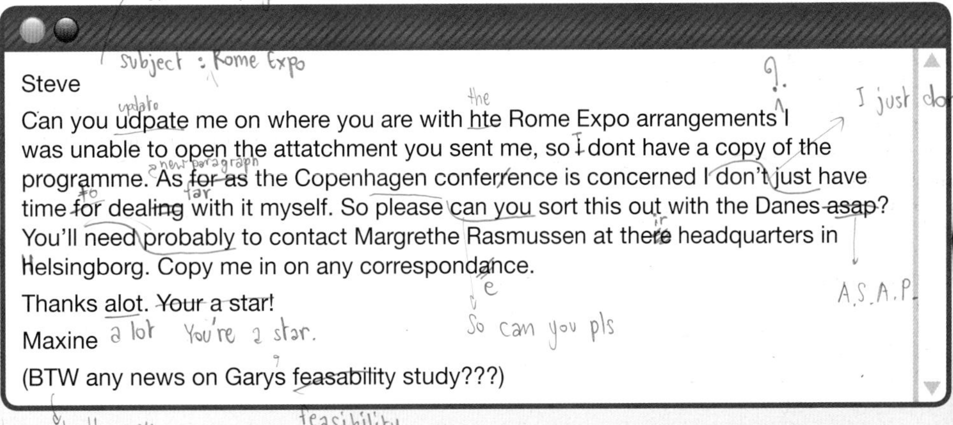

Steve

Can you udpate me on where you are with hte Rome Expo arrangements I was unable to open the attatchment you sent me, so I dont have a copy of the programme. As for as the Copenhagen conferrence is concerned I don't just have time for dealing with it myself. So please can you sort this out with the Danes asap? You'll need probably to contact Margrethe Rasmussen at there headquarters in Helsingborg. Copy me in on any correspondance.

Thanks alot. Your a star!

Maxine

(BTW any news on Garys feasability study???)

5 Correct the grammar, spelling and punctuation mistakes in the first email above. There are 18. Break up the text into short paragraphs and add a suitable subject line.

6 Read the following statements about the emails and decide if you agree (*A*) or disagree (*D*).

The mistakes in the first email are mainly language errors or typos. ☐
Emails like this create a bad impression. ☐
Mistakes don't matter as long as the message is clear and the tone friendly. ☐
I would be more tolerant if I knew the writer was not a native speaker. ☐

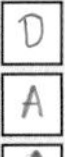

Glossary

asap /ˌeɪ es eɪ ˈpiː/ (abbrev) as soon as possible. In AmE, asap is often pronounced /ˈeɪsæp/

BTW (abbrev) by the way: used in emails and text messages for adding additional information

FYI (abbrev) for your information: used in emails and text messages as a way of introducing a useful piece of information

KR (abbrev) kind regards: used in emails and text messages for an informal closing greeting

7 Make the second email below shorter and simpler by deleting as many words as you can without changing the basic message or sounding too direct.

> Dear Stephen
>
> I do realize that you must be very busy at the moment with all the arrangements for our exhibition stand at the Rome Expo in two weeks' time, but, if you have a spare moment sometime over the next few days, could you possibly just have a quick look at the first draft of my report on the ComTech feasibility study, which I've been working very hard on since we last spoke? As I'm sure Maxine has already told you, it was actually due last week and I know that she needs it quite urgently, but there are just a couple of points I need to check with you, if that's okay, before I submit the final report – see attachment.
>
> FYI, I don't know if anyone has spoken to you about it yet, but it looks like I'm probably going to be coming to Copenhagen with you, Fiona and Michael in September after all. You'll remember from my CV when you interviewed me for this position that I studied German and Danish at university and, as a matter of fact, I still speak pretty good Danish, which might just come in handy ;-) although I'm quite sure most of the Danes we'll be meeting at the conference will have no problem whatsoever with English!
>
> KR
>
> Gary

8 Now make the shortened second email friendlier by adding a few personal touches. Use some or all of the following information to personalize it in your own way.

Stephen:

- has just become a father for the first time
- has put in for a promotion
- is under a lot of pressure because three people in his department are off sick
- has never been to Denmark (Gary knows it well)
- is a keen squash player (so is Gary).

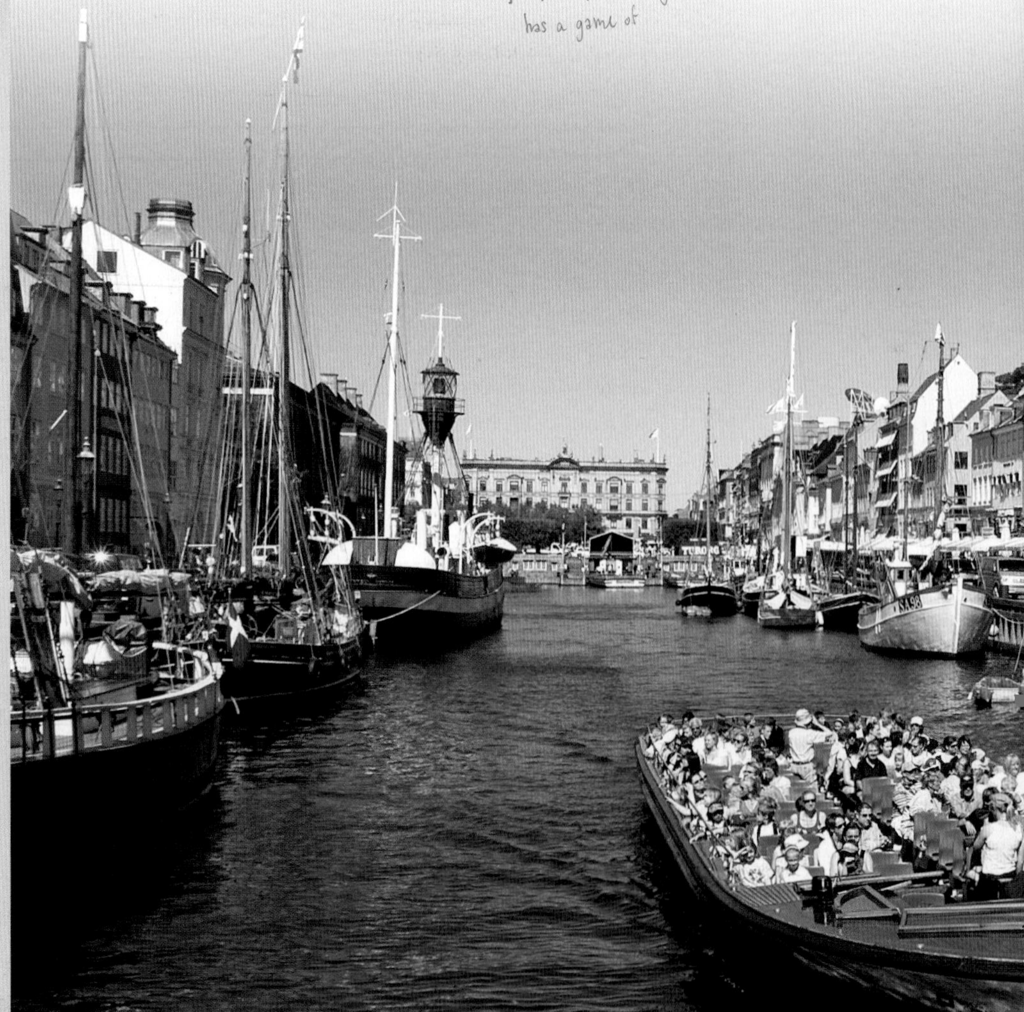

Email style

1 How you write an email largely depends on who you are writing to. If you are writing to a business contact for the first time or you don't know the person, a formal style is generally used.

Read through the email below and underline the best option. This is the first time Simon Allen has contacted Timothy Green.

Dear (1) Timothy Green / Mr Green

(2) I hope everything's fine / I trust you are well.

(3) I would like to congratulate you on an excellent presentation / Just to say you did a fantastic presentation. The product demonstration was extremely (4) well received / went down really well.

However, (5) I'll tell you something I really didn't like / there is one aspect which concerns me. As it stands, the packaging design (6) may be problematic / would really cause a lot of problems. (7) How about changing the design? / Would you consider changing the design? (8) Let's meet next week and see what other ideas we can come up with / Could we meet next week to discuss some alternative ideas?

(9) BTW, I need you to take a look at the Singapore report. / Also, I would be grateful if you could read over the Singapore report. In particular it is rather urgent to get the cost breakdown figures from the report. Would it be possible for you to (10) provide me the information by Wednesday 10 am? / send me the cost breakdown from the report ASAP?

(11) For any questions don't hesitate to contact Sandra Taylor in accounts. / Should you have any questions, please do not hesitate to contact Sandra Taylor in accounts.

(12) Yours sincerely / Best wishes

Simon Allen

Director of Marketing

2 Write a short email in reply to the one above using the prompts below. Remember to use an appropriate style.

glad / enjoyed / presentation / also pleased / response / product demo // disappointed / hear / not keen / design // thought / quite stylish // let / know / free / discuss / alternatives // around / most / next week // happy / go through / report // costing / ready / within / few days // may need / check / few things / Sandra // happen / have / extension number? / thanks

The biggest email blunders ever made

1 Work with a partner and discuss the following questions.

a There are an estimated 100,000 computer viruses out there in cyberspace. Have any of them found you yet?

b What kind of things do people use their office computers for which are not strictly business? Have you ever been tempted to do any of these things yourself?

c Have you ever sent an email and later regretted it? How dangerous is it to send business emails (even internally) without considering the possible implications?

2 **2.39** Listen to the story of some of the biggest email blunders ever made and number the following in the order they are mentioned.

Netscape	☐	Merrill Lynch	☐
Dow Chemical	☐	Cerner	☐
the Love Bug	☐	Western Provident	☐
AOL	☐	Norwich Union	☐
Microsoft®	☐	The Pentagon	☐

3 Work with a partner. Without listening again, can you remember:

a how much the Love Bug cost computer networks worldwide?

b how much the two insurance companies settled out of court for?

c how an English schoolgirl got a hold of US military communications to the UK?

d how many people lost their jobs at Dow Chemical?

e whose stock fell by 28%?

f how much Merrill Lynch had to pay out because of Blodget's email?

g which executives regretted sending emails in the Microsoft antitrust trial?

4 **2.39** Listen again to see if you were correct.

You've got mail!

1 Work with a partner to practise exchanging emails.

Stage 1

Write an email (maximum 150 words) to a real colleague on one of the subjects below. Use the suggested phrases to help you, but change and add anything you need to.

Subject: Change of plan

I was/we were originally hoping to …, but I'm afraid that won't be possible now because …, so what I'm/we're planning to do is …

Sorry it's a bit short notice, but do you think you'll be able to … or is that going to be a problem? I'll wait to hear from you.

Subject: Update please

Sorry to be a pain about this, but I'm still waiting for … Can you let me know how much longer it's likely to be? Do you think you'll have it finished by … because …?

If you anticipate any problems, let me know. I'll … tomorrow to see how you're doing. Cheers!

Subject: Urgent request

I've got an important meeting/presentation coming up on … and I'm going to need … Can I leave it to you to …? I expect I'll also be needing …

I know you're probably up to your neck in work at the moment, but if you can get … to me before next …, it'll be a real help. Thanks.

Subject: Can you do me a favour?

I've had an email/phone call from someone called …, who wants … Can I leave this one with you? I'm sure you'll know a lot more about it than I do. But keep me in the loop.

BTW a few of us may be … on … Are you going to be around? Fancy joining us? Should be fun.

Stage 2

Exchange your emails from Stage 1 with your partner. You are standing in for the person they emailed while that person is off sick / on holiday / on maternity or paternity leave / away on a long business trip (you decide which). Write a reply (maximum 100 words) explaining the situation and asking for clarification or any details you need. Mention that you are new to the department.

Stage 3

Exchange replies and continue the correspondence as long as necessary to complete your business.

2 Give your partner your impressions of the emails they wrote in 1.

- Do they sound friendly but businesslike?
- Is the email written in an appropriate style?
- Have they kept their messages short and to-the-point?
- Have they made any important spelling, punctuation or grammar mistakes?

12 Emailing

Vocabulary

Prepositional phrases

1 In each box write the preposition that precedes the words and phrases below.

a [ ] present first least first glance the very most any rate the latest the same time best

b [ ] the whole average the contrary second thoughts reflection the one hand the other hand no account

c [ ] practice other words theory the circumstances general short particular effect some respects any case

d [ ] a result a general rule a matter of fact a last resort

e [ ] to now to a point

f [ ] the top of my head

2 Complete the meeting extracts using some of the phrases in 1.

a **A** Well, I haven't had time to study them in detail but, at ______ ______, I'd say these figures were quite encouraging.

B Yes, on ______ ______, they're pretty much in line with what we were expecting. In fact, in ______ ______, they're even better.

b **A** Have you been in touch with New York yet?

B As ______ ______ ______ ______, I have.

A And are they in favour of this new initiative?

B One or two of them aren't, but in ______, yes.

A Well, that's something at ______ ______.

c **A** I'm going to authorize this budget increase, but on ______ ______ is this project to go over budget again.

B Yes, okay.

A By the way, how much are the admin costs on this?

B I couldn't tell you off ______ ______ ______ ______ ______, but it shouldn't be more than 30% of the budget at ______ ______ ______.

A 30%! On ______ ______, I think we'd better look at this whole budget again.

d **A** This idea of yours is fine in ______, but in ______, I don't think it'll work.

B But you were all for it when we spoke about it last time!

A On ______ ______, I was as sceptical then as I am now. In ______ ______, even if I supported you, this strategy would only save us a few thousand pounds at ______.

3 Underline the other seven prepositional phrases in 2.

Grammar

Future forms

1 Present tenses for the future

Match the verbs in **bold** to their main function below.

Our train **leaves** (1) at six. So our taxi**'s coming** (2) at quarter to.

I**'m not working** (3) this Saturday! It**'s** (4) my wedding anniversary for goodness' sake!

an arrangement	[ ]	an indisputable fact	[ ]
a refusal	[ ]	a schedule or timetable	[ ]

2 *will*

Match the remarks on the left to the way they were later reported.

a I**'ll** help you. He promised to be there.
b You**'ll** regret it. He suddenly had an idea.
c I**'ll** be there. He offered to help me.
d I**'ll** try it this way. He refused to do it.
e I **won't** do it! He warned me about it.

3 *will be doing*

In each pair of sentences below tick the one you are more likely to hear.

a We**'ll land** at Heathrow in about 15 minutes.
b We**'ll be landing** at Heathrow in about 15 minutes.
c **Will** you **go** past the chemist's this morning?
d **Will** you **be going** past the chemist's this morning?
e Give me five minutes and I**'ll call** you back.
f Give me five minutes and I**'ll be calling** you back.
g By the way, I **won't attend** the meeting.
h By the way, I **won't be attending** the meeting.

4 Match the sentences (a–d) to what was said next (1–4).

a I don't think I'll go. [ ]
b I don't think I'll be going. [ ]
c Will you go to the post office this afternoon? [ ]
d Will you be going to the post office this afternoon? [ ]

1 At least that's what they've told me.
2 If you're not too busy, that is.
3 And if so, could you post this for me?
4 I certainly don't want to.

5 Lexical future

In English there are a lot of *be* (+ word) *to* expressions to talk about future intentions and expectations.

a We're to
b We're due to
c We're about to
d We're hoping to
e We're aiming to
f We're planning to
g We're intending to
h We're going to

meet them to discuss the matter.

Which of the sentences above refer to:

1 something which will happen very soon?
2 something which has been formally arranged?
3 something which other people are expecting?
4 something which has already been decided?
5 something we'd like to happen, but it may not?

6 Future in the past

Put the sentences (a–d) into the past and match them to what was said next (1–4).

a We're going to fly Lufthansa.
b We're meeting at three.
c I'm just about to leave.
d I think we'll have problems.

1 Can it wait till the morning?
2 But something's come up.
3 But there's been a change of plan.
4 But I never expected this!

7 Past in the future

Tick the sentences which refer to the future.

a They won't have heard the news.
b I'll have missed my chance by then.
c You'll have seen our advertisements, I suppose.
d Another month and I'll have been working here for ten years.

The **Present Continuous** and *be to* are frequently used to talk about fixed arrangements.

The **Present Simple** is often used either to talk about schedules and timetables or to refer to the future after words like *if, when, as soon as, before*, etc.

There's a range of expressions including *be going to* and *be hoping to* which are used to talk about plans and intentions.

Both *will* and *going to* can be used to make predictions: *will* for opinions and *going to* for more informed predictions.

'll is frequently used to make offers, promises and take initiatives.

The **Future Continuous**, *will be doing*, is used to talk about something which will be in progress or which is part of a routine.

The **Future Perfect**, *will have done* and *will have been doing*, are used to talk about something which will already be completed at a future time. The continuous form usually emphasizes the activity rather than its completion.

Phrase bank: Emailing

1 The following expressions are all useful in emails. Complete them using the prepositions in the boxes.

against at back down in of off on on out through to up with with with with with with with

back + to in + on on + to out + on out + with through + to up + on up + to

a Have a quick look ___ these figures and get ___ me asap.

b Let me know if you need any help ___ the Koreans. And copy me ___ any correspondence ___ them.

c Could you get ___ our suppliers and sort something ___ them? I'll leave the details ___ you, but keep me ___ the loop.

d BTW, you did a great job ___ the presentation. It went ___ really well ___ the Belgians. We'll just have to wait and see what they come ___ to us ___.

e Could you update me ___ where we are ___ the Expo arrangements? I'm a bit ___ of touch. Can I leave it ___ you to contact the speakers?

f I'd like to sound you ___ this new packaging idea. Let's meet ___ to discuss it sometime next week. BTW, I still can't seem to get ___ Monica.

g I haven't had time to read ___ the whole report and I'll probably need to check some of these figures ___ the computer, but leave it ___ me.

h Thanks for your offer ___ a drink. If I can finish this report ___ by 7, I may just take you ___ it! I could certainly do ___ one!

2 Label these business email expressions according to their function using the labels in the box.

Asking for advice Buying time Delegating tasks Requesting information

a ___
I'll leave the details to you.
Would you mind taking this off my hands?

b ___
Can I sound you out on something?
Can you just cross-check the figures for me?

c ___
Give me a week and I'll see what I can come up with.
Leave it with me. I'll sort it out.

d ___
Can you update me on where we are with this?
Keep me in the loop.

13

Making an impact

Speech is power: speech is to persuade, to convert, to compel.

Ralph Waldo Emerson, American writer, philosopher and orator

What was the best presentation you ever attended?

Learning objectives: Unit 13

Business communication skills Identifying effective presentation openings; Identifying rhetorical techniques; Rephrasing to add impact; Identifying ways of closing a presentation; Fluency: Producing a promotional presentation for a new country
Reading Book extract on opening a presentation
Listening Presentation openings; Extracts from political speeches; Closing remarks from four presentations
Vocabulary Metaphor
Grammar Rhetorical techniques
Phrase bank Opening and closing a presentation

1 Look at the Emerson quote. Can you see any techniques he's using to make his statement more powerful? Think about sounds, lists and repetition.

2 How important is it to make an impact right at the beginning of a presentation? Read the book extract. Do you agree with the author?

> **OPENING**
>
> The opener to any business presentation is nearly always important, establishing the tone for the rest of the event. It's that vital moment when you take charge, gaining people's close attention.
>
> People tend to remember openers more than any other part of a presentation, except perhaps for the closing remarks. You waste a wonderful opportunity if you resort to trivia like: 'Good evening, ladies and gentlemen, it's a great pleasure to be here today.'
>
> Adapted from *The Ultimate Business Presentation Book* by Andrew Leigh

3 With a partner, make a list of ways you can attract people's attention when you start a presentation.

4 3.01 Listen to the openings of six business presentations. Do the speakers use any of the techniques you listed in 3? What other techniques do they employ?

5 How effective are the speakers in 4 at capturing your attention?

6 The openers below were all used in 4. Can you remember the first three words of each? Contractions (*I'd, I'm, it's*, etc) count as one word.

a ______ ______ ______ that of the world's 100 biggest economies only 56 are actually countries?

b ______ ______ ______ favourite lawyer jokes is: this guy's having a quiet café latte at a coffee bar when an angry man starts shouting ...

c ______ ______ ______ start off by thanking Dr Jensen, Dr Tan and Dr Martinez for inviting me to speak today.

d ______ ______ ______ was Thomas Edison who said: 'I have not failed. I've just found 10,000 ways that don't work.'

e ______ ______ ______ through the appointments pages the other day and came across this unusual job advertisement.

f ______ ______ ______ about Total Quality, I think of the story of the American steel magnate, Andrew Carnegie.

7 3.01 Listen again and check your answers.

Glossary

charisma /kərɪzmə/
a strong personal quality that makes other people like you and be attracted to you: *A man sadly lacking in charisma.*

Presence and performance

1 For many people the magic ingredient great presenters have is charisma. What's the equivalent word in your language?

2 **3.02–3.05** Listen to extracts from four famous political speeches. Rank them in order of how charismatic they sound. Compare with a partner.

Extract 1 ☐ Extract 2 ☐ Extract 3 ☐ Extract 4 ☐

3 The speakers in 2 used a number of rhetorical techniques. The main ones are listed below. Complete them using the words in the box.

language	opposites	points	questions	sounds	threes	words

The seven rules of rhetoric

1. Repeat ______
   I still have a dream. It is a dream deeply rooted in the American dream.
2. Repeat ______
   We are the people ... who persuaded others to buy British, not by begging them to do so, but because it was best.
3. Use contrasts and ______
   Ask not what your country can do for you – ask what you can do for your country.
4. Group key points in ______
   We must therefore act together as a united people, for national reconciliation, for nation building, for the birth of a new world.
5. Ask rhetorical ______
   What are our chances of success? It depends on what kind of people we are.
6. Accumulate supporting ______
   We are the people who, amongst other things, invented the computer, the refrigerator, the electric motor, the stethoscope, rayon, the steam turbine, stainless steel, the tank ...
7. Use metaphorical ______
   To lead our country out of the valley of darkness.

4 Look at the extracts on page 84 and find more examples of the rhetorical techniques listed in 3.

John F Kennedy

I do not shrink from this responsibility – I welcome it. I do not believe that any of us would exchange places with any other people or any other generation. The energy, the faith, the devotion, which we bring to this endeavour will light our country and all who serve it – and the glow from that fire can truly light the world. And so, my fellow Americans, ask not what your country can do for you – ask what you can do for your country.

I still have a dream. It is a dream deeply rooted in the American dream. I have a dream that one day this nation will rise up and live out the true meaning of its creed: 'We hold these truths to be self-evident; that all men are created equal.' I have a dream that one day on the red hills of Georgia the sons of former slaves and the sons of former slave owners will be able to sit down together at the table of brotherhood … I have a dream that my four little children will one day live in a nation where they will not be judged by the colour of their skin but by the content of their character. I have a dream today.

Martin Luther King

Margaret Thatcher

What are our chances of success? It depends on what kind of people we are. What kind of people are we? We are the people that in the past made Great Britain the workshop of the world, the people who persuaded others to buy British, not by begging them to do so, but because it was best.

We understand it still that there is no easy road to freedom. We know it well that none of us acting alone can achieve success … Let each know that for each the body, the mind and the soul have been freed to fulfil themselves. Never, never and never again shall it be that this beautiful land will again experience the oppression of one by another …

Nelson Mandela

5 **3.06** Look at the following extracts from ineffective business presentations and rephrase them to give them more impact. Then listen and check.

a Cash flow is the main problem we're facing.
What's the _____ _____ _____ facing? The _____ _____ _____ cash flow.

b It's critical to our success, even though it's so risky and problematic.
It's _____ risky, _____ problematic, _____ yet _____ critical to our success.

c It's faster, cheaper, more reliable – that's the most important thing – and easier to use.
It's _____, _____ and _____ _____ _____.
But, above _____, it's more _____.

d We can still be the best, but we can't ever be the biggest again.
Even _____ we can _____ again be the _____, we _____ still _____ _____ _____.

e Fewer jobs are being fought over by more graduates, that's the point.
The point _____, more and _____ graduates _____ _____ over fewer _____ _____ _____.

f We're number one in Latin America now, not just Brazil.
Not _____ _____ we number one in Brazil. We're _____ _____ _____ in Latin America.

g There isn't a company that's ever outperformed us in this market.
In this _____, no _____ has _____ us, not _____ – _____!

h We've had no complaints in over 30 years of business.
Not _____, in over 30 _____ _____ _____, have _____ _____ had a complaint – not a _____ _____!

6 Look carefully at word order and the order of clauses in the rephrased extracts in 5. What information tends to come last?

7 Practise delivering the rephrased extracts to make as big an impact as possible.

8 **3.07** The last few minutes of a presentation are your final chance to make a lasting impression. Listen to the closing remarks of four presentations and number the techniques in the order you hear them. Which is the most effective?

the sum up	☐	the call to action	☐
the famous quotation	☐	the emergency stop	☐

9 Prepare the last 15 seconds of a presentation you have given or may give in the future using one of the techniques in 8. Use the script on page 153 to help you. Present your close to the class.

A new country, a new start

1 Work with a partner and discuss the questions.

1 If you could create your own country, what would it be like?

2 What factors give a country an ideal standard of living?

3 Develop a profile with key features for your new country. Consider the points in the list below.

a location: which continent? landscape?

b climate: how many seasons?

c population: city vs. rural areas?

d mother tongue: one common language or a mix?

e infrastructure: electricity and water? education and transport systems? political parties?

f established / developing industries: overseas trading policies? effect on employment figures?

g cost of living: pay scales? housing? typical outgoings?

h crime rate: police competence? penal system?

i ecology: strategies to deal with environmental change?

j immigration policies: rules and regulations?

k healthcare: private or public?

l family structure: marriage laws? average number of children?

m tourism: attractions? appeal? economic effects?

2 With your partner, prepare a short presentation about your new country based on the profile you have created. Your aim is to persuade your audience that your invented country is the best place to live and work, as well as being an appealing tourist destination.

The rest of your class will rate your presentation on clarity, persuasion and impact on a scale of 1 to 10 using the card below. It is not necessary to cover all of the points listed on the card, but there must be an opening and close. The class will then vote for the country they would like to live in or to visit!

Rating card: clarity, persuasion and impact

	1	2	3	4	5	6	7	8	9	10
introduction	☐	☐	☐	☐	☐	☐	☐	☐	☐	☐
cost of living	☐	☐	☐	☐	☐	☐	☐	☐	☐	☐
infrastructure	☐	☐	☐	☐	☐	☐	☐	☐	☐	☐
housing	☐	☐	☐	☐	☐	☐	☐	☐	☐	☐
crime rate	☐	☐	☐	☐	☐	☐	☐	☐	☐	☐
environment	☐	☐	☐	☐	☐	☐	☐	☐	☐	☐
healthcare	☐	☐	☐	☐	☐	☐	☐	☐	☐	☐
education	☐	☐	☐	☐	☐	☐	☐	☐	☐	☐
family policy	☐	☐	☐	☐	☐	☐	☐	☐	☐	☐
tourism	☐	☐	☐	☐	☐	☐	☐	☐	☐	☐
conclusion	☐	☐	☐	☐	☐	☐	☐	☐	☐	☐

13 Making an impact

Vocabulary

Metaphor

1 Business English is full of metaphor (describing one thing in terms of another). Match the following expressions. Then match them to their metaphorical reference.

a	takeover	recovery	**war**
b	ballpark	debate	**fire**
c	heated	flow	**health**
d	economic	figure	**water**
e	cash	battle	**sport**

2 Complete the sentences using the words in the boxes.

coming growing pooling pouring sowing trickling

Money is liquid

a They're __________ millions of dollars into R&D.

b A small amount of cash has started __________ in.

c We should be __________ our resources – together we'd have sufficient capital to fund new research.

Ideas are plants

d After years of work, our plans are finally __________ to fruition.

e There's __________ support for the project – most of the people we spoke to think it's a good idea.

f They're __________ the seeds of doubt in the mind of the customer and, as a result, we're losing sales.

attack fight goalposts guns idea odds stakes victory

Argument is war

g They shot down my __________ before I'd even had a chance to explain it.

h We came under __________ from the marketing team.

i He didn't put up much of a __________. In fact, he just seemed to give in completely.

j She stuck to her __________ and refused to move an inch.

Competition is sport

k We've scored a significant __________ in the home market.

l The __________ are high – we're risking the future of this company.

m The __________ are against us, but there's still a chance we can succeed.

n We don't know what our objectives are supposed to be because they keep moving the __________.

Grammar

Rhetorical techniques

1 Word repetition

Decide which word in each statement could most effectively be repeated after a short pause and underline it. Read the statements aloud to check. The first one has been done for you.

a This is very important. (*'This is very … very important.'*)

b This is a much better option.

c It's now or never.

d There'll always be a market for quality.

e It is here in Europe that the best opportunities lie.

f And today we start to turn this company around.

Rewrite (a) so that you can repeat the word important.

2 Sound repetition

1 Replace one word in each sentence with a word from the box that starts with the same sound as other words in the sentence.

~~better~~ dynamism past promotion simpler team willing

a It's bigger. It's ~~superior~~ *better*. And it's British.

b I'm not interested in our history or in our present, but in our prospects for the future.

c We'll reach our targets together as a group.

d We need the right product at the right price with the right advertising.

e We have the drive, energy and determination to succeed.

f Are we prepared to work towards that goal?

g The new system is both more secure and significantly easier to install.

2 What sound is being repeated in each of the sentences above?

a __________

b __________

c __________

d __________

e __________

f __________

g __________

What do sentences a, b, d and e all have in common?

____

3 Contrasts and opposites

Complete the sentences using the idea of contrast to help you.

a It's not a question of time; it's a question of money.

b If we don't seize this opportunity, some______ el______ w______.

c Tackling a few minor problems now will save us a whole ______ of ma______ pr______ la______.

d Some people are saying we can't afford to advertise, but I s______ we c______ aff______ n______ to.

e I'm not saying we're certain to succeed: what I a______ s______ is we'll ne______ kn______ unt______ we tr______.

f Three years ago this company was going nowhere; to______ it's num______ o______ in the ind______.

In adverb + adjective phrases it is more effective to repeat the adverb (technique 1).

If you want to repeat an adjective, it is more effective to use an adverb before repeating it (technique 1).

It is more effective to repeat consonants than vowels (technique 2).

Lists of three are especially memorable (technique 2).

In a contrast it is more effective to make your main point second (technique 3).

Asking questions (particularly negative questions) is a more effective way of getting audiences to think than making statements (technique 4).

Talking about 'us' is a more effective way of building rapport than talking about 'you' (technique 4).

Rhetorical questions sound more convincing when you answer them using some of the same words (technique 5).

You can give weight and formality to what you say by sometimes reversing your word order (technique 6).

4 Rhetorical questions

Rephrase the statements as negative questions and change the second person plural to the first person plural.

a This is what you need to be doing.

b You should be learning from your mistakes.

c Deep down, you all know this to be true.

5 Rhetorical questions + repetition

Complete the following using one word from the box in both gaps.

problem	chances	answer	point	advantages	result

a So much for the disadvantages, but what about the ______? Well, the ______ are obvious.

b We're losing control of the company. So what's the ______? Clearly, the ______ is to centralize.

c What are our ______ of success? Well, frankly, our ______ are slim.

d So what's the ______ of offering an unprofitable service? The ______ is it makes us look good.

e So what's the basic ______ with this system? The basic ______ is it's far too complicated!

f Three years of R&D and what's the net ______? The net ______ is a product that doesn't work!

6 Inversion

Rephrase the statements below making any necessary changes in word order.

a This company is not only leaner, it's also greener.
Not only ______.

b We mustn't under any circumstances panic.
Under no circumstances ______.

c We've done better in Mexico than anywhere.
Nowhere ______.

d We'll only be ready to launch after exhaustive tests.
Only after ______.

Phrase bank: Opening and closing a presentation

Label the presentation openings and closes below with the headings in the box.

Is anybody out there?	Let me take you on a journey
Now, here's a funny thing	Oh, and one last thing
This is a true story, by the way	To cut a long story short
Wise words	Would you believe it?

1 ______
Did you know that ...?
Statistics / Studies show that ...

2 ______
One of my favourite stories / jokes about that is ...
Whenever I'm asked about ... I think of the story of ...

3 ______
I'd like to start off by ...
By the end of this morning's talk, ...

4 ______
I think it was ... who said ...
In closing, I'm reminded of the words of ...

5 ______
I was ... the other day and happened to / came across ...
I remember when I was working / living in ...

6 ______
Could you just raise your hand if you've ever ...
Have you ever been in the situation where ...?

7 ______
So how do you sum up ...?
So my central message today is this ...

8 ______
That just about brings me to the end of my presentation, except to say ...
If you take just one thing from today's talk, take this ...

14

Out and about

Take a little of home with you, and leave a little of yourself at home.

Mark McCormack, founder of IMG sports agency

Do you enjoy travelling for work?

Learning objectives: Unit 14

Business communication skills Discussing business travel and packing habits; Identifying ellipsis in conversation; Striking up a conversation; Telling an anecdote; Fluency: Chatting over a business lunch
Reading Extracts from *The Accidental Tourist*
Listening People talking about their worst flying experiences; Conversations over lunch
Vocabulary Storytelling
Grammar Narrative tenses
Phrase bank Sharing anecdotes
In company interviews Units 12–14

1 When packing to go on a business trip, apart from your travel documents, what are the absolute essentials? A good book? Swimming things? A decent hairdryer? An air pillow? Chargers? Adaptors? A travel alarm? An iPad? Compare with a partner.

2 In *The Accidental Tourist*, travel guidebook writer Macon Leary gives advice on how to pack for a trip. Read the extract and discuss the questions.

The business traveller

'The business traveller should bring only what fits in a carry-on bag. Checking your luggage is asking for trouble. Add several travel-size packets of detergent, so you won't fall into the hands of unfamiliar laundries. There are very few necessities in this world which do not come in travel-size packets.

'One suit is plenty if you take along travel-size packets of spot remover. The suit should be medium-gray. Gray not only hides the dirt, but is handy for sudden funerals.

'Always bring a book as protection against strangers. Magazines don't last and newspapers from elsewhere remind you you don't belong. But don't take more than one book. It is a common mistake to overestimate one's potential free time and consequently overpack. In travel, as in most of life, less is invariably more.

'And most importantly, never take along anything on your journey so valuable or dear that its loss would devastate you.'

From *The Accidental Tourist* by Macon Leary

a Do you tend to travel light or do you bring along 'everything but the kitchen sink'?
b Have you ever had any bad experiences with lost luggage or hotel laundries?
c Is grey your colour? Do you dress for comfort or dress to impress?
d What's the best way of avoiding unwanted conversations with strangers?
e Is it important to allow yourself some free time on a business trip?
f Have you ever lost something valuable on a journey? Tell the story.

3 What kind of person is Macon Leary? Tick the correct answers. Would you want to sit next to him on a flight?

a bit paranoid	☐	antisocial	☐	bitter	☐	dull	☐
fussy	☐	gloomy	☐	lonely	☐	outgoing	☐
overserious	☐	practical	☐	private	☐	sarcastic	☐
sociable	☐	well organized	☐	witty	☐		

Glossary

cocoon a warm, safe place

You're my hero I really admire you/your work

4 3.08 Read and listen to an extract from *The Accidental Tourist*, where Macon Leary finds himself sitting next to an overweight man on a plane. What coincidence links the two men?

Traveller I'm sorry I'm so fat. *Name's Lucas Loomis.*

Leary Macon Leary.

Traveller You a Baltimore man?

Leary Yes.

Traveller Me too. *Greatest city on the earth.* One of these seats is not really enough for me. And the stupid thing is, I travel for a living. I demonstrate software to computer stores. What do you do, Mr Leary?

Leary I write travel guidebooks.

Traveller Is that so? What kind?

Leary Well, guides for businessmen – people just like you, I guess.

Traveller 'Accidental Tourist'!

Leary Why, yes.

Traveller Really? Am I right? Well, what do you know? Look at this. Gray suit – just what you recommend, appropriate for all occasions. *See my luggage*? Carry-on. Change of underwear. Clean shirt. Packet of detergent powder.

Leary Oh, good.

Traveller You're my hero. You've improved my trips a hundred per cent. I tell my wife, going with 'The Accidental Tourist' is like going in a cocoon.

Leary Well, this is very nice to hear.

Traveller *Times I've flown clear to Oregon and hardly knew I'd left Baltimore.*

Leary Excellent.

Traveller I see you have your book for protection there. *Didn't work with me, though, did it?*

5 Find expressions in the conversation which mean:

a That's interesting.
b I suppose.
c How did you know that?
d What a coincidence!

6 In natural conversation certain words are sometimes omitted. Look at the six sentences in italics in 4 and decide which three types of word are missing.

7 The following things were said at different times during a business trip. Delete any unnecessary words to make them more conversational.

a **A** Is everything okay with your meal, sir?
B It's delicious. It couldn't be better.

b **A** Do you need anything else, sir?
B I don't think so, thanks.

c **A** Are you ready to start?
B Yeah, I'm just coming.

d **A** Do you mind if I switch the reading light on?
B It doesn't bother me. I think I'll get another coffee. Do you want one?

e **A** I saw you earlier in the fitness centre. Have you been here long?
B No, I just got here yesterday. Are you here on business too?

f **A** Have you got a light?
B Sorry, I don't smoke.

8 What are the advantages of having someone to chat to on a long journey? Do you find it easy to start conversations with people you don't know?

9 Match A to B to make conversation phrases.

	A		**B**
1	You couldn't help me with my bag, ...	**a**	by any chance?
2	Do you mind ...	**b**	for a bit of turbulence, doesn't it?
3	Looks like we're in ...	**c**	help you with that.
4	Sorry about my kids. Let me know if ...	**d**	swapping seats?
5	Is this row 17, ...	**e**	could you?
6	I like your mobile. ...	**f**	Is that one of the new ones?
7	Let me ...	**g**	you're flying on to Caracas.
8	I'll get someone ...	**h**	is that getting in your way?
9	I see ...	**i**	I love Prada!
10	Nice bag. ...	**j**	to come and help you.
11	I'm sorry, ...	**k**	do you know?
12	Are you from Lima, ...	**l**	they're bothering you.

10 Now match these common ways of starting a conversation with a stranger to the phrases in 9.

a make an observation ____________________

b pay a compliment ____________________

c make a request ____________________

d ask for information ____________________

e offer assistance ____________________

f make an apology ____________________

11 Work with a partner to practise holding short conversations with fellow passengers on planes. Speaker A see page 125. Speaker B see page 132.

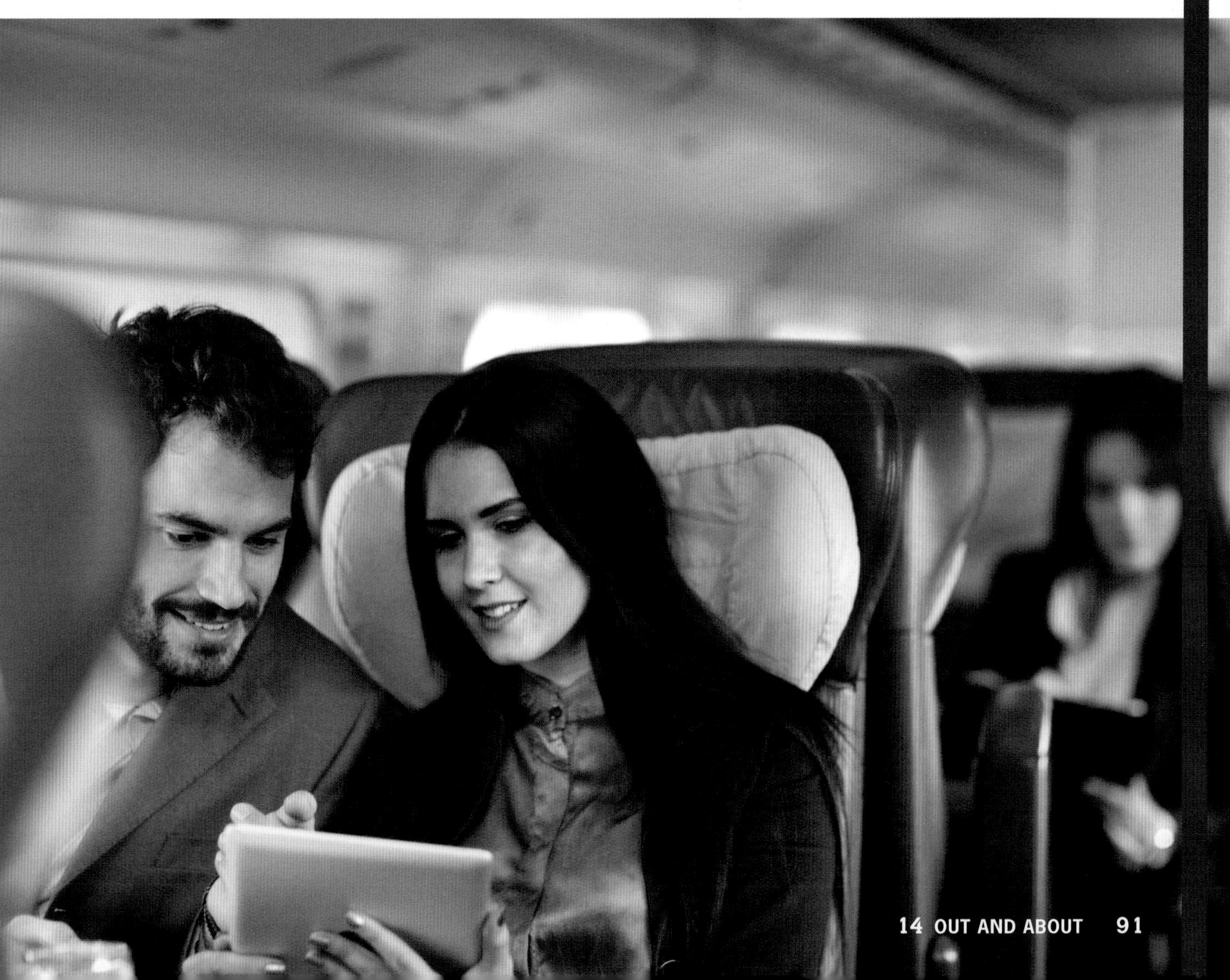

Travellers' tales

1 3.09 Listen to four business people talking about their worst flying experiences and answer the questions.

a What was all the noise about on Emma's flight?
b How might Enrique's flight have ended in disaster?
c What surprised Joe on his flight to London?
d Who got lost on Joe's flight to Frankfurt?
e What was the strange request on Selina's flight in Asia?

2 Read this extract from the first conversation and underline the best grammatical choice.

B After a while, some of the passengers (a) **were starting** / **had been starting** to get nervous, me included!
A I'm not surprised.
B Anyway, eventually, after (b) **we were sitting** / **we'd been sitting** there for about ten minutes with no announcement and the plane still not moving, (c) **I said** / **I'd said** something to one of the stewards and they (d) **went** / **were going** and (e) **opened** / **were opening** the door to see what (f) **went** / **was going** on.
A And what (g) **happened** / **had been happening**?
B The pilot (h) **got** / **had got** in!
A You're joking!
B No, (i) **they'd locked** / **they'd been locking** him out. Seems quite funny now, but it (j) **didn't** / **wasn't doing** at the time.

3 In the extract in 2 how many examples can you find of the:

Past Simple?	☐	Past Continuous?	☐
Past Perfect Simple?	☐	Past Perfect Continuous?	☐

4 According to publisher David Weinberger, 'most of our best conversations are about stories.' How useful is it in business to be able to tell a good story? Do you agree that the best ones are usually true?

5 Listed below are the typical stages in a story or anecdote. Add the expressions in the box to the correct place in the list. They were all in the conversations in 1.

(a) And the strange thing was ... (b) And then, to top it all, ...
(c) Anyway, to cut a long story short, ... (d) But that was nothing compared to ...
(e) Did I ever tell you about the time I was ...? (f) I ended up ...
(g) Seems quite funny now, but it didn't at the time. (h) This was around the time of ...
(i) Way back in (1985) it was. (j) You should have heard/seen ...!

Opener
I'll never forget the time I was ... ☐
Context
It's quite a few years ago now, but I can still remember it. ☐ ☐
Emphasis
You're not going to believe this, but ... ☐ ☐ ☐ ☐
Close
Anyway, in the end ... ☐ ☐ ☐

6 Tick which one of the closes could also come straight after an opener.

7 Match the following to make six things you might say while listening to someone telling a story. They were all in the conversations in 1.

a	You're	goodness!	**d**	So, what	terrifying!
b	I don't	joking!	**e**	Sounds	happened?
c	Oh, my	believe it!	**f**	I see	what you mean.

8 Tell the story of your worst (or best) travel experience to the rest of the class.

The business lunch

1 What's the most expensive meal you've ever had? Was it worth the money? Who was paying? Was it on expenses? Tell a partner about it.

2 Read the information below. Does it shock or amuse you?

Out to lunch

In 1997 a London banker made the headlines when he was sacked for taking a five-hour lunch break – from 11.30am to 4.30pm!

He won back his job after an industrial tribunal ruled that he had been unfairly dismissed. The court decided that five hours is not an excessive amount of time to conduct business over a meal.

Do you agree with the court ruling?

This one's on me

One of the world's most expensive business lunches ever was held in a top London restaurant back in 2002. Luxury truffles were flown halfway around the world, to form part of a specialist main course prepared exclusively for a group of six diners. In addition, the dessert was prepared using gold leaf. The food and drink bill totalled a staggering £44,000!

How could so huge a bill be justified?

3 **3.10** You are in a noisy restaurant with a group of colleagues and have to keep going outside to answer your mobile. Each time you come back in, the topic of conversation has changed. Listen and see how quickly you can guess what it is.

4 **3.10** Listen again and note down key words and phrases that helped you decide. Compare with a partner and then check in the listening script on page 154.

5 Work in groups. Use the chart below to practise chatting over lunch with business contacts. Start off by talking about what you've just ordered and then keep changing the subject as indicated until your meal arrives – it seems to be taking a long time! Try not to interrupt each other too abruptly, but keep the conversation moving.

Anyway, ... Before I forget, ... By the way, ... Incidentally, ... On the subject of ... So, talking of ... That reminds me ... To change the subject for a moment ...

Where on earth's our waiter? Ah, at last!

the meal you've just ordered

the best place you've ever eaten in

Why is the food taking so long?

I wonder what's happened to our order?

a problem you're having at work

your plans for the weekend

Couldn't they at least bring the drinks?

the best/worst film you've seen lately

a recent scandal in the news

your holiday plans

the food and drink you've finally been served

14 Out and about

Vocabulary

Storytelling

Descriptive power

1 When describing things in a story or anecdote, try to avoid overusing (*not*) *very* + neutral adjective. Replace the dull descriptions in **bold** with more interesting alternatives from the box.

absolutely ancient	absolutely delighted	absolutely fabulous	absolutely filthy	absolutely hilarious	drop-dead gorgeous	quite inedible	really fascinating	~~totally pointless~~	utterly astonished	utterly furious	utterly miserable

totally pointless

- **a** The meeting was ~~**not very useful**~~.
- **b** It was a **very interesting** book.
- **c** They were **very happy** about the idea.
- **d** The food was **not very good**.
- **e** The weather was **very bad**.
- **f** Their boss was **very good-looking**.
- **g** Her apartment was **very nice**.
- **h** I was **very surprised**.
- **i** The whole thing was **very funny**.
- **j** The PCs they were using were **very old**.
- **k** He looked **very angry**.
- **l** The hotel was **not very clean**.

2 If you do use neutral adjectives, try using a more interesting adverb to describe them. Match the following pairs of adverbs to a suitable adjective from the box.

beautiful	dangerous	difficult	disappointing	enjoyable	expensive	funny	quiet

- **a** hysterically / hilariously
- **b** stunningly / breathtakingly
- **c** outrageously / prohibitively
- **d** immensely / thoroughly
- **e** bitterly / terribly
- **f** deathly / blissfully
- **g** highly / downright
- **h** exceedingly / fiendishly

The art of exaggeration

3 Complete the conversation below using the words and phrases in the boxes.

1–5	I'm telling you	is literally	like something out of	~~you'll never guess~~	you should have seen

6–10	I'm not exaggerating	out of this world	talk about	you'll never believe	me tell you

(In a restaurant)

A Did I tell you about my trip to Sweden?

B No, I don't think so. On business, were you?

A Yeah, but (1) *you'll never guess* the hotel the Swedes had booked us into.

B Somewhere posh, was it?

A No, not exactly. It's called The Ice Hotel. Have you heard of it?

B No, I don't think so.

A Well, (2) ______________ this place. (3) ______________ it was (4) ______________ a James Bond movie! Right in the middle of nowhere. And completely built out of snow and ice!

B What? You mean the walls were made of ice?

A Walls, ceilings, doors, tables, beds, chandeliers, the lot! The whole thing (5) ______________ made of ice!

B But, hang on. That's not possible, is it? I mean, it would just melt!

A It does. They have to rebuild it from top to bottom every summer.

B You're joking.

A No, it's true. But in the winter it's minus nine or something.

B So how come you didn't freeze to death?

A We nearly did. Let (6) ______________, it was like an igloo in there. It's incredible! They even make their glasses out of ice so you don't need any in your drink.

B Now, you're having me on.

A No, it's true. (7) ______________. All the glasses are made of ice.

B Amazing! But it doesn't sound like the sort of place I'd want to stay in.

A Actually, it wasn't that bad once you got used to it. And it was great at night, lying in bed under a reindeer skin, looking up at the Aurora Borealis lighting up the midnight sky. (8) ______________ spectacular; it really was (9) ______________! And, (10) ______________ who we bumped into in the bar one night.

B Who?

A Naomi Campbell and Kate Moss!

B Oh, come on! You mean the models?

A Yeah, apparently, it's really popular with all the celebs. It's where the cool people go, you might say.

B Yeah, very funny!

Grammar

Narrative tenses

Read the story about Pepsi A.M. and underline the best grammatical choices.

The Story of Pepsi A.M.

In the late 1980s Pepsi (1) **thought / was thinking** it (2) **identified / had identified** a lucrative gap in the highly competitive soft drinks market: breakfast cola. Although it (3) **wasn't conducting / hadn't conducted** very thorough market research, it (4) **seemed / was seeming** that a lot of young consumers (5) **switched / were switching** from coffee to cola for breakfast. Pepsi's R&D department promptly (6) **went away / were going away** and (7) **came up with / had come up with** Pepsi A.M., a breakfast cola 'with all the sugar and twice the caffeine'!

But what the company (8) **wasn't realizing / hadn't realized** was that the Pepsi drinkers (9) **were / were being** perfectly happy with the normal brand. Pepsi A.M., on the other hand, (10) **sounded / was sounding** like something you would only drink in the morning. Six months after its launch it obviously (11) **didn't sell / wasn't selling**.

Marketing experts (12) **were / had been** quick to point out the company's mistake. What (13) **had it thought of? / had it been thinking of?** At a cost of millions, it (14) **had developed / had been developing** a product nobody actually (15) **needed! / was needing!**

Pepsi A.M. (16) **was / had been** immediately withdrawn.

You use the **Past Simple** to talk about the main events in a story or to give factual information about the past.

You use the **Past Continuous** to talk about the things happening at the same time as these main events. Events in the **Past Continuous** are often interrupted by those in the **Past Simple**.

You use the **Past Perfect Simple** and the **Past Perfect Continuous** to look back from the time of the story to an earlier time, but the **Past Perfect Continuous** usually emphasizes the activity rather than its completion. For this reason, it is not normally used with 'state' verbs like *be, know, seem, understand, mean* and *like*.

Phrase bank: Sharing anecdotes

1 All the following phrases and expressions can be used to share anecdotes. Add them to the chart according to their function.

OPENER	CONTEXT
EMPHASIS	**CLOSE**

a You're not going to believe this, but ...
b Anyway, to cut a long story short ...
c Did I ever tell you about the time I was ...?
d So, in the end, what happened was ...
e It's quite a few years ago now.
f I'll never forget the time I was ...
g Talking of ..., that reminds me of the time I ...
h You should have heard/seen ...!
i And then to top it all, ...
j This was around the time of ...
k And you'll never guess who/what/where ...
l Seems quite funny now, but it didn't at the time.
m And the strange/funny/silly thing was ...

Reactions

2 Switch the endings in **bold** below to make 14 common reactions to anecdotes. The first two have been done for you.

a I'm not **awful**! ← (f)
b I can **blame you**!
c How **serious**!
d What a **goodness**!
e You're **you**!
f Sounds **surprised**! ← (a)
g You can't be **odd**!
h I don't **imagine**!
i Wow, that's **really**?
j Oh, I see what **happened**?
k Were you **amazing**!
l So, what **you mean**!
m Oh, my **nightmare**!
n Lucky **joking, right**?

15 Delegation

Learning objectives: Unit 15

People skills Identifying information needed for delegation; Discussing management styles; Fluency: Effective delegation and appropriate management styles
Reading Blog post on delegation
Listening Presentation on management styles; Three managers delegating tasks

1 How do you think the woman in the cartoon feels about her new project? What feelings do you think the manager and the woman have about each other?

2 What information do you need to specify when you delegate a task to someone? Compare your ideas with a partner.

"This is a major project of utmost importance, but it has no budget, no guidelines, no support staff, and it's due in 15 minutes. At last, here's your chance to really impress everyone!"

3 Read the blog post quickly and match the headings in the box to the paragraphs.

Check Deadline Method Objective Means

DELEGATION: provide a clear action plan

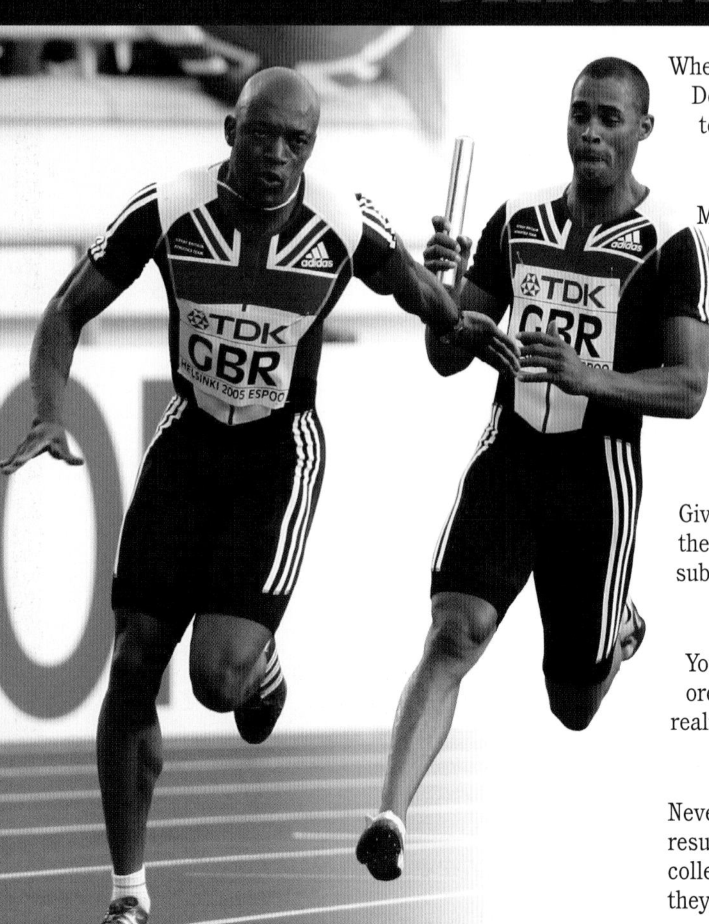

When assigning tasks to your staff, always give them a clear action plan. Depending on your team's skills, experience and autonomy, you will nee to specify some or all of the following points:

1 ________

Make sure your people know exactly what they are supposed to achieve and, most importantly, why. Nobody likes working in the dark!

2 ________

Explain clearly how you would like the job done, or, if you are leaving the choice to one of your staffers, what options are available. There's always a best way to do things, but your folks may not agree on what it is.

3 ________

Give your co-workers clear guidance as to what tools they can use, the budget available and what help they can expect from you, from their subordinates and from their peers.

4 ________

Your associates will need to know exactly how much time is available in order to plan their work and deliver on time. Make sure the timeframe is realistic; avoid the temptation to 'move the goalposts' at a later date.

5 ________

Never, ever delegate a task to a team member without evaluating the results and giving them appropriate feedback. Nothing damages a colleague's motivation more than knowing it makes no difference whether they do a job well, badly or not at all.

4 Reread the blog post. How many of the points you discussed in 2 are mentioned?

5 Underline all the words in the text that mean 'employee(s)'. Which ones are used in your company, by your suppliers or by your customers? How do you prefer to refer to your colleagues? How do you like your manager to think of you?

6 3.11 Write the headings from the blog post in 3 in the left-hand column of the table. Then listen to three managers delegating tasks. Which points does each manager specify? If they omit some points, why is that?

	Manager 1 / Daniel	Manager 2 / Gina	Manager 3 / Pete
1			
2			
3			
4			
5			

7 What is the difference between the four management styles in the box below? Which stage on the timeline of staff development is each style likely to be most suitable for?

Coaching Delegating Directing Supporting

one month six months one year two years

8 3.12 Listen to part of a presentation about management styles and complete the diagram below. Then listen again and check your answers to 7.

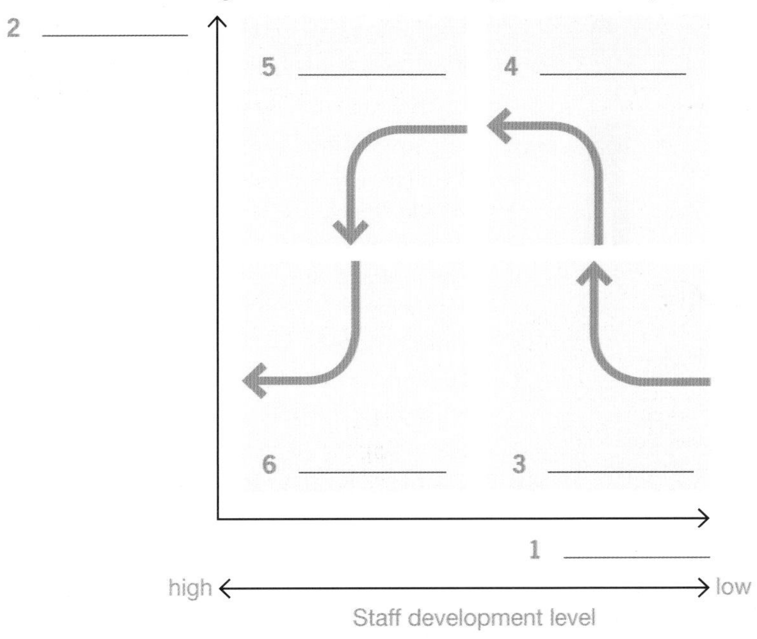

9 3.11 Listen again to the three managers in 6. Which management styles are they using?

10 Which style(s) do you feel most comfortable with when working with a superior? Which do you prefer when working with subordinates? Give examples.

11 Work with a partner to practise delegating tasks. In each situation, decide which management style is appropriate and which points in the action plan need to be specified. Speaker A look at page 119. Speaker B look at page 132. When you have finished, use the checklist on page 137 to help you evaluate your performance.

MANAGEMENT SCENARIO

D

Change champion

Learning objectives: Management scenario D

Business communication skills Discussing implementing change successfully; Identifying the stages for managing change; Fluency: Meetings to implement change

Reading PowerPoint slide on managing change

In company in action
D1: Imposing changes;
D2: Managing change

1 Give examples of how you or other people have made successful changes in lifestyle or organization of work.

2 Match the stages in the change staircase in the cartoon to people's needs (a–h) at each stage.

People need:

a to be shown that the change is feasible.
b to understand why they should change and what the benefits are.
c an incentive to start the process.
d to understand the process and the tools that are available to help them.
e to be motivated.
f to be congratulated and to celebrate their achievement to reinforce good habits.
g to be motivated to continue to follow the new process.
h to be to be encouraged and accompanied.

3 Format the email from CEO Sue Jensen to staff at Blue Rock with all necessary punctuation and spacing.

to all staff re travel and entertainment as from the first of next month several changes will be introduced to our travel policy and expense claims procedures as in the past all travel must be approved by senior management however our travel bureau's contract has been terminated and staff should make their own bookings and arrangements please note that from now on only economy-class travel will be reimbursed hotel accommodation should no longer exceed a three-star rating or local equivalent staff are also reminded to use public transport in preference to taxis whenever possible and to obtain separate receipts for all meals and other necessary expenses finally when entertaining visitors or local contacts you will now need to provide a justification statement and a guest list containing names titles and occupations of every guest I know I can count on you all to ensure these changes are implemented as smoothly as possible Sue Jensen CEO Blue Rock

4 Read the email again and answer the questions.

a What four changes are being introduced?
b Which three things have not changed?
c What is the situation in your own organization regarding travel and entertaining clients?
d What objections might Blue Rock staff have to the changes?

In company in action

5 Now watch video D1 to see Sue talking to Jack Wright from Operations and number the problems in the order they are mentioned.

booking flights	☐	a computer problem	☐	admin time	☐
imposing changes	☐	public transport	☐	company credit cards	☐

6 What do the following phrases tell us about Sue and Jack's attitudes and feelings?

pretty risky   What's not to like about it?   that's not exactly the message that comes across   don't take my word for it   they soon get used to it

7 Complete the PowerPoint slide on Managing Change with the words in the box.

benefits   champions   communicate   need   resources

5 steps to Managing Change

1. explain the ______
help people to understand why change is necessary
2. explain the ______
show people why the change is in their interest
3. recruit change ______
identify and train key people to lead the change
4. provide tools and ______
make sure people have everything they need to make the change
5. continue to ______
celebrate success, monitor and consolidate the change

8 Look at Sue's email and what she said in the video and compare them with the PowerPoint slide. What mistakes has she made? What advice would you give her?

In company in action 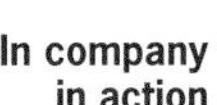

9 Now watch video D2 to see Sue talking to Ed Ryan. In addition to the five steps to Managing Change, what additional piece of advice does Ed give?

10 Watch the video again and answer the questions.

a What does Ed mean by 'more wes' and 'fewer yous'?
b Why does Sue want to make changes?
c What is Ed's solution to the problem with booking flights online?
d Why does Ed suggest holding regular meetings?

11 Match each phrase below to the relevant step 1–5 in Managing Change in 7.

circulating the figures   the people with the most air miles   virtual credit card numbers   more control over when and how they travel   get people on your side

12 With a partner rewrite the email in 3 in a more collaborative style. Explain the need for change and the benefits; invite key Blue Rock staff to a meeting to decide how to implement change, what tools and resources they will need, and how the organization can continue to communicate about the change.

13 Work in small groups to hold meetings about changes in your company. Speaker A see page 134. Speaker B see page 136. When you have finished, use the checklist on page 124 to help you evaluate your performance.

16 Teleconferencing

Teleconferencing is so rational, it will never succeed.

John Naisbitt, Megatrends

What's the best thing about teleconferencing? And the worst?

Learning objectives: Unit 16

Business communication skills Discussing potential uses of tele- and videoconferencing facilities; Discussing action in a crisis; Completing the minutes of a teleconference; Roleplay: Holding a teleconference
Reading Website extract: Business benefits of *TelePresence*; Emails about a film shoot
Listening An unexpected phone call; An emergency teleconference
Vocabulary Teleconferencing, Personnel and production
Grammar Reporting
Phrase bank Teleconferencing

1 Is business travel a perk or a pain? With today's sophisticated telecommunications, how much of it is really necessary? Are business trips being cut back from company budgets?

2 George Mackintosh is the serial entrepreneur who set up Geonconference, at one time Europe's fastest-growing teleconferencing company. Do you agree with what he says?

Videoconferencing is never going to eliminate the need for at least one face-to-face meeting. If you are doing business with someone for the first time, I don't dispute the fact that you need to meet them, look them in the eye and shake their hand. After that it is likely you are going to be speaking to them on the phone or by email. Videoconferencing allows you to have a more personalized relationship.

3 Read the web page below, which presents Cisco's TelePresence videoconferencing system, and answer the questions.

a What is the 'paradox' the web page describes?

b How does TelePresence solve this problem?

TelePresence

Business benefits

We live in a world of paradox. Technology has allowed us to establish economically advantageous business operations worldwide. However, to excel in today's fast-moving business environment, you have to interact and collaborate with co-workers, partners, and customers all over the world at a moment's notice. You need to continuously innovate and transform your business model to maintain competitive edge. And you need to plan ahead to respond rapidly to unexpected issues that affect business continuity.

At the same time, much of business is still done based on the quality of your relationships with the people with whom you interact most often. To build and maintain these critical relationships, you often need to travel, which translates to lost time and reduced productivity, not to mention valuable time spent away from home and family.

All of this points to the need for a technological solution that allows the same type of face-to-face business interactions, without the constant need for global travel. That's where the concept of Cisco TelePresence comes in. It allows for real-time, face-to-face communication and collaboration over the network with colleagues, prospects and partners, even if they're in opposite hemispheres.

4 Find two-word phrases in the web page which mean:

a how your business works
b an advantage you have over your competitors
c making sure your business can still operate even in a crisis

5 **3.13** Now listen to a short commercial for TelePresence. Cisco recommends the system for the following kinds of meeting. Which do you think it would be best suited to? Would you use it?

- design team meetings
- in-company executive meetings
- product demonstrations
- sales presentations
- consultations with vendors, suppliers and clients
- job interviews
- project meetings

6 Which types of meetings above have you experienced? Have you used teleconferencing equipment for them?

Trouble at the plant

1 **3.14** Peter Devlin is CEO of the European division of Oriflamme, a manufacturer of candles and home fragrance products. Currently on a business trip to Vancouver with his marketing director Monica Brookes, Peter was woken at 2 am by an unexpected phone call from his plant manager in Hamburg. Listen to the conversation and answer the questions.

a What has happened at the Hamburg plant?
b Why didn't Max have any alternative?
c What happened last time there was a similar disaster?
d What does Peter suggest doing now?

2 Complete the phrasal verbs in the following sentences from 1 with the correct preposition. Use the synonyms in brackets to help you.

a We're going to have to shut ____________ the Hamburg plant immediately. (close)
b Otherwise, the whole thing could go ____________! (explode)
c We'll have container lorries backed ____________ from Hamburg to Lübeck. (queueing)

3 You also heard the following idiomatic expressions in 1. Can you remember the missing words? The first two letters are given. Use the definitions in brackets to help you.

a Who on ea____________ can that be? (I have no idea who this is.)
b All he____________'s broken loose here. (Everything's in chaos here.)
c Everything grinds to a ha____________. (Everything comes to a complete stop.)
d There's not a mo____________ to lose. (We must act immediately.)
e I'm sorry to get you up at this unearthly ho____________ ... (I don't like to disturb you so late/early.)

4 Work with a partner. List the implications of a crisis like the one above.

5 Now match the words below to produce some implications. Did you include them in your list in 4?

a	a backlog of	bottleneck
b	a production	hazard
c	a safety	productivity
d	a fall in	orders
e	a damaged	man-hours
f	adverse	reputation
g	lost	deliveries
h	delayed	publicity

6 Work with a partner to discuss what immediate action Oriflamme should take to avoid the implications in 5.

7 3.15–3.17 Listen to three extracts from Oriflamme's emergency teleconference to decide what action to take. Answer the questions.

Extract 1

a Who hasn't been able to join the teleconference?
b Where are Peter and Monica?
c How long will it take to fix the problem at the plant?

Extract 2

a What state is the plant in?
b Why can't the orders be met completely?
c Describe Monica's response to Peter's suggestion that they buy products from their competitors to sell on to their customers 'to cover the shortfall'.

- enthusiastic ☐
- negative ☐
- positive ☐
- hostile ☐
- lukewarm ☐
- cool ☐

Extract 3

a Why may Handelsmann be prepared to help?
b Is there still a safety hazard at the plant?
c What arrangement does Peter make with Otto?

8 The minutes below were taken by Françoise Fleurie directly after the teleconference. Complete them using the verbs in the box.

Points 1 and 2
assure authorized confirmed ensure estimated informed keep
Points 3 and 4
agreed follow mentioned Okay'd opposed pointed proposed reach report smooth

Hamburg Plant Shutdown: Minutes of the teleconference

Date: 12th March

Participants: Peter Devlin, Monica Brookes, Max Schiller, Otto Manser, Françoise Fleurie

Apologies: N/A

Next teleconference: 12 pm ET

Point	Details	Action
1 Situation report	PD ________ that a total shutdown of the H'burg plant has been officially ________. OM ________ us that the site had been evacuated in order to conduct safety checks, but was later able to ________ us that the situation has now been brought under control.	OM to ________ PD up to date on any changes in the situation
2 Repairs estimate	MS ________ that repairs will probably take three days to carry out. The main reason given for the delay was the amount of time needed to obtain a replacement heat exchanger (48hrs).	MS to oversee and ________ completion of repairs within three days
3 Production plan	PD ________ rewriting the production plan to give priority to key customers, but OM ________ out that we hold insufficient reserve stocks to fully meet current orders. It was generally ________ that our European plants are too overstretched to transfer goods to H'burg.	OM to ________ a compromise re main customers' orders and ________ back to PD
4 Traded goods	PD's suggestion that traded goods be bought in from another supplier was initially ________ by MB on the grounds that it would damage Oriflamme's reputation. FF ________ the possibility of Handelsmann being able to help us out. This was provisionally ________ by PD.	FF to ________ up the Handelsmann offer and ________ things over with key customers

Desert island blues

The RJK Group is one of the world's leading advertising agencies with an impressive list of blue-chip clients. At the moment RJK (UK)'s top creatives are on location on the remote island of Oamu-Oamu in the South Pacific, filming a commercial for Vivacity, the new shower gel range from French cosmetics and toiletries giant Éternelle. But after eight days on the island, the film shoot is turning into a disaster.

Step 1

Work in groups of three. You are the senior management of RJK (UK). Add your names to the organigram below.

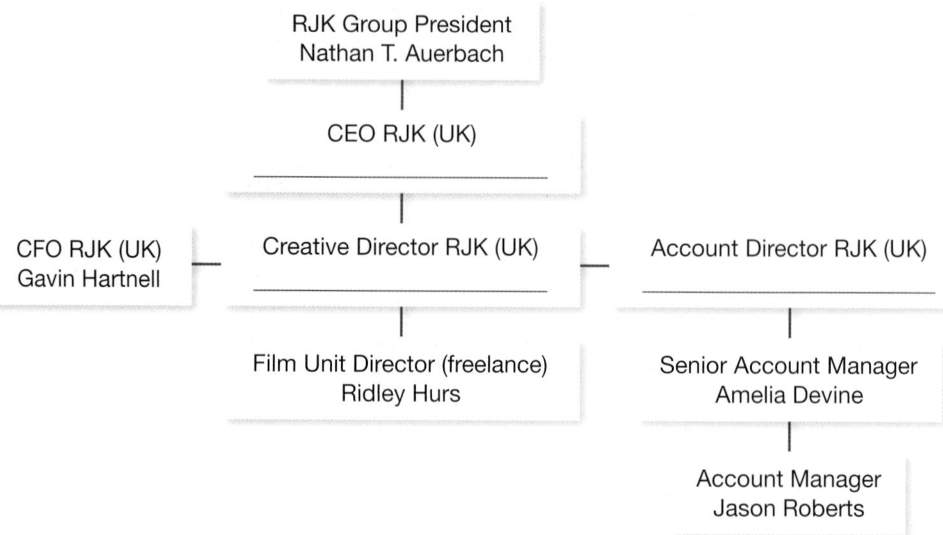

Step 2

You are about to take part in a teleconference to decide what to do about the situation. First check your latest email and make a note of any points you want to bring up.

Speaker A CEO of RJK (UK): You are currently attending an international conference in Milan. Read emails 1 and 2 on page 125.

Speaker B Creative Director, RJK (UK): You are currently in the middle of a pitch for the €15m Heine account. Read emails 3 and 4 on page 133.

Speaker C Account Director, RJK (UK): You are currently on two weeks' holiday in Mauritius. Read emails 5 and 6 on page 135.

Step 3

Hold the teleconference using the agenda below. The CEO should chair the meeting. Report what you have learned from your email and try to commit to a definite course of action on which you all agree. The final decision, however, is the CEO's.

Agenda: Éternelle Account – Vivacity Shoot

1. Situation report: Clarification of the situation on location
2. Financial considerations: Éternelle account – budgetary constraints
3. Action plan:
   - Change of location? If so, where?
   - Switch to studio filming? Implications?
   - Change of actress? Contractual problems?
   - How to present change of plan to client?
   - Any other suggestions?

16 Teleconferencing

Vocabulary

Teleconferencing

1 Complete the puzzle using the extracts from the teleconferences in this unit.

- **a** Okay, so we're just _ _ _ t _ _ _ for Otto.
- **b** Let's go _ _ e _ _ and get the meeting started.
- **c** Max, could you first of all just _ _ l _ us in on what's going on?
- **d** Well, Pete, it's difficult to say at the _ _ _ e _ _.
- **e** I'll see what I c _ _ do.
- **f** I'm already _ o _ _ _ _ _ on that.
- **g** Monica, is there any _ _ _ n _ in us buying in traded goods?
- **h** Pete, you know how I f _ _ _ about buying from the competition.
- **i** Just for the time _ e _ _ _.
- **j** What _ _ _ _ r _ _ _ _ _ _ _ do we have?
- **k** Can I _ _ _ e in on that?
- **l** I've already _ _ _ n on to Handelsmann.
- **m** Okay, get back to them and see if we c _ _ hurry things up a bit.
- **n** And get somebody in after-sales to _ i _ _ round all our biggest customers.
- **o** Okay, I'll see to it n _ _.
- **p** Otto, keep me posted if there's any _ _ _ _ g _ in the situation.

Personnel and production

Organizational issues

2 Combine one word from the box on the left with one word from the box on the right to complete each sentence below.

human	incentive
promotion	appraisal
fringe	job

prospects	benefits
scheme	interview
satisfaction	resources

- **a** These days people talk about ________________ rather than personnel.
- **b** Rates of pay, recognition and opportunities for personal growth contribute to overall ________________.
- **c** An ________________ is one way of monitoring employee performance and personal development.
- **d** ________________ include health insurance, a company car and contributory pension plan.
- **e** For hardworking and ambitious young managers there are excellent ________________.
- **f** Many companies operate an ________________ – commissions, bonuses and so on.

Operations management

3 Listed below are some of the terms commonly used in production departments, but the second word in each collocation has been switched with another. Can you switch them back?

raw **goods**	safety **defects**
zero **regulations**	stock **line**
quality **chain**	finished **materials**
assembly **control**	supply **circle**

4 Which of the collocations in 3 refer to:

- **a** unprocessed materials?
- **b** where the factory workers put the products together?
- **c** a group of workers and managers who meet to discuss quality?
- **d** a series of suppliers selling on raw materials and finished components to manufacturers?

Grammar

Reporting

1 Look at some silly things politicians have said and report each, making grammatical changes where necessary, e.g. *have(n't)* ⟶ *had(n't), did(n't)* ⟶ *had(n't) done, I* ⟶ *he, this* ⟶ *that*, etc.

- **a** We have managed to distribute poverty equally. *Vietnamese Foreign Minister, Nguyen Co Thach*
  Mr Thach announced that ________________.
- **b** I have opinions of my own, strong opinions, but I don't always agree with them. *US President George Bush Sr*
  President Bush affirmed that ________________.
- **c** I will not tolerate intolerance. *US Senator Bob Dole*
  Senator Dole insisted that ________________.
- **d** It isn't pollution that is harming the environment – it's the impurities in our air and water that are doing it. *US Vice President Dan Quayle*
  Vice President Quayle pointed out that
  ________________.
- **e** I haven't committed a crime – what I did is fail to comply with the law. *New York City mayor, David Dinkins*
  Mayor Dinkins denied that ________________.

2 Read the meeting extracts and write a summary of each using the words in brackets to help you.

Jon First of all, I'd like to hear your views on this.
(Jon/open/meeting/invite/comments/group)
Jon opened the meeting by inviting comments from the group.

Anna I don't think this training programme is necessary.
Niels Neither do I.
(Anna/question/need/training programme. Niels/be/same opinion)

____

Anna And what about the training budget for this?
Jon I haven't made up my mind about that yet.
(Anna/raise/issue/training budget. Jon/reply/not come/decision)

____

Niels So the board's okay about this?
Jon Absolutely.
(Jon/confirm/project/give/go-ahead)

____

Jon How about bringing in consultants?
Anna I don't think that's a good idea.
(Jon/wonder/if/be/good idea/bring in consultants. Anna/be/against)

____

Niels Anna and I think the situation should be reviewed.
(both Anna/Niels/recommend/review/situation)

____

Niels Well, I'm very much against these spending cuts.
Jon But they won't affect your department, Niels.
Anna Jon's right. These cuts won't affect us.
(there/be/some initial opposition/spending cuts)

____

Anna So, you see, Niels, the new system will actually be an improvement.
Niels Hm, well, on reflection, I suppose you're right.
Jon So do I take it we're now in agreement on this?
(issue/finally/resolve)

____

Jon I think this is an excellent proposal.
Anna So do I.
Niels Me too.
(there/be/unanimous agreement/proposal)

____

In reports:

- it is more important to communicate the basic message than to repeat the exact words that were spoken.
- we tend to use the passive when what was said is more important than who said it. *It was suggested that …*
- long conversations are often summed up in a simple noun phrase. *There was some disagreement …*

Phrase bank: Teleconferencing

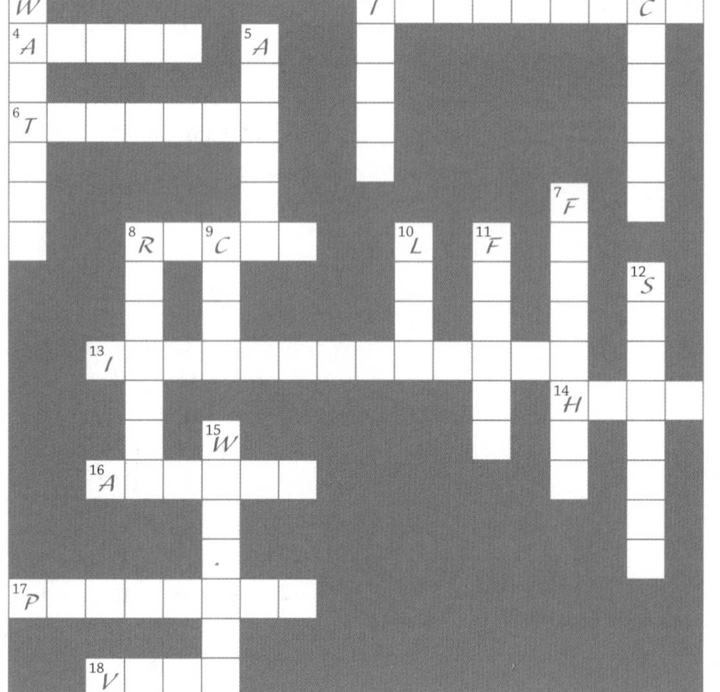

Across

2 Before we start, could we all just ______ ourselves? (9)
4 Okay, let's go ______ and start. (5)
6 Sorry, I had a bit of ______ getting through. (7)
8 So, just to ______ on what we've said so far. (5)
13 Let's try to keep ______ to a minimum. (13)
14 Sorry, I can't ______ you very well. (4)
16 So, are we all ______ on that, then? (6)
17 I suggest we ______ item three until Beatrice can join us. (8)
18 Can we take a quick ______ on that? (4)

Down

1 Looks like we're just ______ for Stefan. (7)
2 Can we keep our ______ quite short? (5)
3 I think that just about ______ everything. (6)
5 Did everyone get a copy of the ______? (6)
7 I'd like to be ______ by 11 if that's okay with everyone. (8)
8 Right, we're ______ short of time, so let's move on. (7)
9 Could I just ______ in here? (4)
10 Elise? Hello? We seem to have ______ Elise. (4)
11 Could everyone in ______ just say 'Yes'? (6)
12 Let's move ______ on to item four. (8)
15 ______ to the meeting, everybody. (7)

17 Negotiating deals

Don't ever slam a door. You might want to go back in.

Don Herold, US negotiator

Are there any business contacts you wish you'd kept in touch with?

Learning objectives: Unit 17

Business communication skills Negotiating a tricky situation; Identifying negotiating tactics; Fluency: Negotiating a contract
Reading Analysis of a negotiation; Article about the music business
Listening Negotiations; People talking about negotiating strategy; Meeting: signing a new band
Vocabulary Negotiations
Grammar Diplomacy and persuasion
Phrase bank Negotiating
In company interviews Units 16–17

1 Work with a partner and answer the questions.

a Are you a good negotiator? Work in groups of three to try out your negotiating skills. Speaker A see page 126. Speaker B see page 127. The third person in the group should observe and take notes on the kind of language the other two use.

b Speakers A and B, did you reach an agreement or did you get into an argument? What was the main problem you faced?

c Try the negotiation again, but this time read the extra information on page 123 first. The observer should again take notes.

d Was the negotiation easier this time? Did you manage to reach a compromise? Find out from the observer if the language used was different in the two negotiations.

2 **3.18** Listen to a management trainer giving feedback to some trainees who have just finished the negotiations in 1. Do you agree with the analysis?

3 Complete the phrases by matching the compound adjectives. Then match each phrase to its definition. You heard all the phrases in 2.

a	a single-	sum game	one which is very direct
b	a long-	win situation	one from which both sides feel they've gained
c	a win-	issue negotiation	one that lasts
d	a one-	term relationship	one where one side wins what the other side loses
e	a zero-	on conflict	one that happens only once
f	a head-	off deal	one where only one topic is being discussed

4 You also heard the following expressions in 2. Can you remember the missing words? The first few letters are given. The definitions in brackets may help you.

a There's little room for man________. (It's difficult to change your position.)
b win at all cos________ (do whatever you have to do to win)
c It simply wasn't worth the hass________. (It was too much trouble.)
d The negotiation ended in dead________. (Neither side was prepared to move.)
e resort to emotional black________ (make people feel guilty to get what you want)
f reach some kind of comp________ (an agreement that partially satisfies both sides)

Negotiating style

1 Work with a partner. Listed below are the eight most common high-pressure tactics negotiators use. One of you should match the first four to their description. The other should match the second four. Then compare notes.

Tactics
1 The shock opener
2 The strictly off-limits ploy
3 The take-it-or-leave-it challenge
4 The I'll-have-to-check-with-head-office ploy
5 The good cop, bad cop approach
6 The once-in-a-lifetime offer
7 The salami technique
8 The last-minute demand

Description
a Make it look as though you are ready to leave the negotiating table if your demands are not met, that you are not prepared to move an inch further.
b Point out at the start that, though you are prepared to negotiate A, B and C; X, Y and Z are definitely not negotiable.
c Having obtained a concession from your opponent, inform them that you need your boss's approval before you can do what they ask in return.
d Make a ridiculous initial demand (or offer), but keep a straight face as you make it. This works particularly well on inexperienced opponents.
e Don't make all your demands right at the start. Make a small demand and get agreement on it before you make the next, and the next …
f Pressurize your opponent by suggesting that the offer you're making is only for a limited period and if they don't act quickly, they'll miss it.
g After the deal has been done, make one modest extra demand in the hope that your opponent will not want to jeopardize the agreement for one small detail.
h One of your team is friendly and flexible, the other unpleasant and unreasonable. Your opponent will want to please Mr/Ms Nice to avoid Mr/Ms Nasty.

2 How might you respond to each of the tactics in 1? Can you see any risks in using them yourself?

3 3.19–3.20 Listen to extracts from two different negotiations. Which tactics in 1 are they trying to use? How successful are they?

Extract 1 ☐ ☐
Extract 2 ☐ ☐

4 Work with a partner. One of you should reconstruct sentences a–j from the negotiation extracts in 3 by putting the bold words in the correct order. The other should reconstruct sentences k–t. When you have finished, check your answers together.

a Okay, so, do **take agreement we're in on I it** volume?
b Wouldn't it be a **idea before talk to good we prices go** any further?
c But in **happy principle taking about you're** 40 cases, right?
d Look, **price back getting to a for** moment.
e Can you give us some **what idea of kind figure were you** thinking of?
f There **seems slight a been have to** misunderstanding.
g With **prices respect simply are your not** competitive.
h I'm afraid that **absolute really bottom our is** line.
i Let's set the price **side moment the issue to one for,** shall we?
j I'll throw **free service 12 parts and months' as in** well.
k Now, I **can't fairer that say than**, now can I?
l What we'd really like to **movement see is more on bit a** price.
m A 6% discount **quite is had not what in we** mind.
n We were **closer hoping something for bit a** to 10%.
o I don't think **stretch far could I as as** that.
p Surely **sort we something out can** here.
q Would **meet willing be you to** us halfway?
r We might **position be a increase to in** our order.
s We'd need to **bit on flexibility see a more** terms of payment.
t I suppose **manoeuvre room there be may some for** there.

5 Look back at the expressions in 4 and answer the following questions.

a Find two phrases which mean 'bad news coming'.

b Explain the use of the word *seems* in f).

c If you change sentences e) and n) into the present tense, does this make them sound more or less negotiable?

d Do the question tags in i) and k) make it easier or more difficult to disagree?

e Does the negative question form in b) make the suggestion:
more persuasive? ☐ more diplomatic? ☐ both? ☐

f Why do you think the speakers use words like *slight, some, a bit* and *quite*?

g What is the overall effect of changing:
wouldn't to *isn't* in b)?
can to *will* in e)?
could to *can* in o)?
would to *are* in q)?
might to *are* in r)?
may to *is* in t)?

6 The following expressions from the negotiations in 3 show strong disapproval, but think twice before using them yourself as they may cause offence. Complete them using the pairs of words in the box.

joke + something	lot + that	other + time	way + earth

a Is this meant to be some kind of __________ or __________?

b There's no __________ on __________ I'm paying you €4!

c Oh, come on! You'll have to do a __________ better than __________.

d Frankly, I think we're wasting each __________'s __________ here.

7 **3.21–3.23** Listen to three experienced negotiators talking about strategy and answer the questions.

Speaker 1 Why isn't win-win a realistic outcome?
How can a friendly attitude be counterproductive?

Speaker 2 Why is silence more powerful than talking?
In what way is listening 'gold'?

Speaker 3 How do you avoid pointless debates?
What are the two most useful phrases in a negotiation?

8 Discuss the meaning of the following idioms with a partner. They were all in 7.

a Give them an inch and they'll take a mile.

b Play your cards close to your chest.

c They can talk till the cows come home.

Negotiating a recording contract

1 What kind of music are you into? Compare your tastes with a partner.

2 Work with a partner to answer the following questions. If you've no idea, just have a guess! Then check your answers in the article.

a Which is the world's wealthiest rock band?
b Who are the world's four most bankable solo performers?
c What is the bestselling album of all time?
d What are the two bestselling singles of all time?
e Which pop song has been recorded in over 2,000 versions?

INSIDE THE MUSIC BUSINESS

1 The world's biggest band

When Mick, Keith, Charlie and Ronnie come on stage to 40,000 adoring fans, they have the satisfaction of knowing that the Rolling Stones are easily the world's wealthiest rock band. Having generated more than $1.5 billion in gross revenues since 1989, two thirds of that earned on tour, they have made more money than even fellow megastars U2, Bruce Springsteen and Sting.

2 Financial acumen

Now firmly established rock legends, the Stones are also a rock-solid business. It was their chief financial advisor, London banker Prince Rupert zu Loewenstein, who was first to see that, whilst concerts make the most money, music rights provide the steadiest income stream. And though the Stones may never have produced a real blockbuster on the scale of Fleetwood Mac's *Rumours* or Pink Floyd's *Dark Side of the Moon*, Jagger and Richards have made over 40 albums and written more than 200 songs. Each time they get airplay, they collect 50% of the royalties. According to *Fortune magazine*, that amounts to $56 million in the past decade. Microsoft® alone paid them $4 million to use 'Start Me Up' in the Windows 95 commercial.

3 Big business

The music business has come a long way since the Stones started out in the 60s. In those days record labels like Motown, Island and Elektra all had their own distinctive sound, and you could have a string of top ten hits but still barely be able to afford the bus fare home from your latest sell-out gig. These days just five major music companies – UMG, Sony, Warner, EMI and BMG – control 75 to 80% of all commercially released recordings and the sums of money involved are huge.

4 Bankability

Today's most profitable solo performers remain Madonna, Elton John, Celine Dion and Garth Brooks. The back catalogues of Sinatra and Elvis also bring in millions. In fact, dead Elvis started out-earning live Elvis in 1988. The version of 'Candle in the Wind' Elton John sang at the funeral of Princess Diana overtook Bing Crosby's 'White Christmas' to become the world's bestselling single of all time and the most recorded pop song ever is The Beatles' 'Yesterday', which exists in over 2,000 different versions. But the real money has always been in albums, not singles. The top seller is Michael Jackson's *Thriller*, which has sold over 100 million units worldwide, more than double the most successful albums of runners-up AC/DC, the Eagles and Backstreet Boys.

5 Rights and rip-offs

With this kind of money at stake, it's not surprising that the relationship between artist and record company can be an uneasy one, with young up-and-coming bands often too dazzled by the prospect of stardom to look closely at the small print in their contracts. Even established performers like Prince and George Michael have had well publicized clashes with their management. Courtney Love went so far as to file a lawsuit against Geffen Records to be released from her contract. And Mariah Carey found herself in the opposite situation, reputedly being paid off to the tune of £19.5 million when Virgin Records decided it didn't want to record her after all.

3 Find words and phrases in the article which mean:

a money earned before tax and costs (paragraph 1)
b the most regular source of money (paragraph 2)
c highly successful album, book or film (paragraph 2)
d money paid to artists each time their work is sold or performed (paragraph 2)
e a series of bestselling records (paragraph 3)
f a musical performance to which all the tickets are sold (paragraph 3)
g earning more than (paragraph 4)
h likely to become popular soon (paragraph 5)
i excited at the chance of becoming stars (paragraph 5)
j the details in a contract – often limiting your rights (paragraph 5)
k angry disagreements (paragraph 5)

4 **3.24** A major record label is considering signing a new band. Listen to an extract from a meeting between their A&R people (talent scouts) and senior management.

a Why does Kate think they have to sign the band quickly?
b What are the band's strengths?
c Why isn't Ronnie as impressed as Kate?
d Why does Ronnie sound more enthusiastic at the end of the meeting?

5 Work in two teams to negotiate a recording contract between the record company and the up-and-coming rock band you heard about in 4.

Team A You are representatives from the band The Penitents and their managers. The high-profile record company Starburst is interested in signing your band. See page 126 for your negotiating objectives.

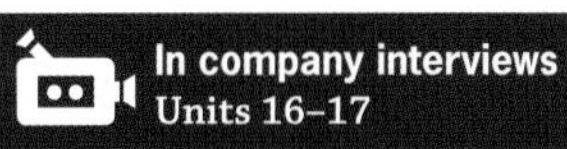

Team B You are executives from the record company Starburst and their lawyers. You are interested in signing the promising new band The Penitents. See page 137 for your negotiating objectives.

17 Negotiating deals

Vocabulary

Negotiations

Sounding out your opponent

1 Complete the questions using the prepositions in the box.

about	at	for	of	towards	with

What sort of …

a figure were you thinking ________?
b terms would you be happy ________?
c discount were you hoping ________?
d delivery time are we talking ________?
e timescale are we looking ________?
f deadline are we working ________?

Discussing terms

2 These are all key points you may want to discuss in a negotiation. Write in the missing vowels.

pr _ c _	c _ ns _ gnm _ nts
d _ sc _ _ nt	m _ _ nt _ n _ nc _
cr _ d _ t	d _ l _ v _ ry t _ m _
v _ l _ m _	p _ ym _ nt t _ rms
tr _ nsp _ rt _ t _ _ n	sp _ r _ p _ rts
p _ ck _ g _ ng	_ xch _ ng _ r _ t _
d _ c _ m _ nt _ t _ _ n	_ ft _ r-s _ l _ s s _ rv _ c _
g _ _ r _ nt _ _	p _ n _ lty cl _ _ s _ s

3 Complete the negotiator's proposal using the words and phrases in 1. Which one is not needed?

Well, on a repeat order of this (1) ________ – 20,000 units – we'd be able to offer you what I think you'll agree is a very generous (2) ________ of 17%. I think you'd also find our (3) ________ extremely favourable – 120 days' (4) ________, of course – and we'd cover any fluctuations in the (5) ________ between the dollar and the euro.

We'd also be prepared to include in our quoted (6) ________ all (7) ________ costs. That is to say, we'd handle the shipping charges, insurance and all the necessary (8) ________ to save you doing the paperwork yourself. We would have to use the same carrier for each delivery, however, which means the (9) ________ would be 14 days. I hope that's acceptable to you.

Now, all our products come with a three-year (10) ________ which includes full (11) ________ and (12) ________. There's also a free 24-hour customer helpline, so your customers would be getting excellent (13) ________.

I think we could also be fairly flexible on (14) ________ if you decided to increase or reduce your order from time to time.

So, that just leaves the question of (15) ________. We normally use styrofoam containers …

Negotiating procedure

4 Complete the phases of a negotiation using the nouns in the box.

atmosphere	breakthrough	champagne	concessions		
deadlock	details	interests	options	phase	position
procedure	proposals	strategy	table	time-out	

1 create a good ________	6 make counter ________	11 return to the negotiating ________
2 agree on a basic ________	7 trade ________	12 discuss the ________
3 state your opening ________	8 reach a ________	13 make the final ________
4 explore each other's ________	9 call for a ________	14 work out the ________
5 enter the bargaining ________	10 rethink your ________	15 crack open the ________

Grammar

Diplomacy and persuasion

Look at the negotiation extracts. Make the direct remarks more diplomatic and persuasive using the words in brackets to help you.

Negotiation 1

A This is still too expensive.
(afraid/would still/a little out of/price range)
I'm afraid that would still be a little out of our price range.

B Well, how much do you want to pay?
(what sort/figure/did/in mind)

A $12 per unit.
(were thinking/somewhere/the region of/$12 per unit)

B I can't go as low as that.
(be honest/not/a position/quite/low/this stage)

Negotiation 2

A You said we'd get 90 days' free credit.
(were promised/90 days' free credit)

B Yes, but you said you'd be placing a larger order.
(respect/was understood/rather larger)

A Look, this is getting us nowhere. We want free credit.
(doesn't seem/getting/very far/afraid/must insist/ free credit)

B Well, I can't offer you that unless you increase your order.
(unfortunately/unable/offer/you're prepared/slightly)

Negotiation 3

A We need a commitment from you today.
(had/hoping/some kind)

B Impossible! We're still unhappy about these service charges.
(this point/might/a bit difficult/not entirely/service charges)

A But you said you were okay about those!
(was assumed)

B Not at all. Look, I think we should go over these figures again.
(afraid/shouldn't we/figures/again)

Modal verbs (*would/might/could*, etc) are often used to soften the verb.
Modifiers are common (*a little difficult*).
Continuous forms keep your options open (*We were wondering; We had been hoping*).
Introductory softeners (*I'm afraid*) warn that bad news is coming!
Negative adjectives like *expensive* are often avoided.
seem is common (*We don't seem to agree.*)
There's a lot of **approximation** (*sort of*).
Qualifying phrases are common (*at the moment*).
Alternatives are preferred to *can't* and *won't*.
The passive sounds less like an accusation (not *You promised us* …, but *We were promised* …).
Suggestions are often phrased as negative questions (*Wouldn't it be better to* …?).

Phrase bank: Negotiating

The following negotiation expressions are grouped according to their function. Alternate letters are missing from key words. Complete them.
Then circle the appropriate heading for each.

Agreement / Probing

a Can you give us some i_e_ of delivery times?
b What k_n_ of figure were you thinking of?
c We were hoping for something a bit c_o_e_ to $3,000.

Agreement / Flexibility

d So, in p_i_c_p_e, you're happy with the proposal, right?
e So, do I take we're in a_r_e_e_t on payment in installments?

Probing / Compromise

f Would you be w_l_i_g to meet us halfway?
g Surely, we can s_r_ something out here.

Flexibility / Agreement

h I suppose there may be some room for m_n_e_v_e there.
i I don't think I could s_r_t_h as far as that.
j We might be in a p_s_t_o_ to increase our offer.
k What we'd really like to see is a bit more m_v_m_n_ on price.
l We'd need to see a little more f_e_i_i_i_y in terms of interest rates.

Miscommunication / Concessions

m Okay, I'll t_r_w in free service and maintenance as well.
n I can't say f_i_e_ than that, now can I?

Compromise / Rejection

o 3% is not quite what we had in m_n_.
p I'm afraid that really is our absolute bottom l_n_.
q With r_s_e_t, your terms are simply not competitive.

Probing / Refocusing

r Look, g_t_i_g back to price for a moment.
s Let's set the issue of discounts to one s_d_ for the moment.

Miscommunication / Flexibility

t There seems to have been a slight m_s_n_e_s_a_d_n_.
u I think we may be talking at c_o_s-p_r_o_e_ here.

18 Mediation

Learning objectives: Unit 18

People skills Discussing the qualities of a good mediator; Identifying the stages of mediation; Fluency: Mediating between colleagues
Reading Article about causes of conflict at work
Listening Poor and positive mediation

1 How would you define the relationship between the two men in the cartoon? What is the woman's role and how is she trying to achieve this?

2 What are the qualities of a good mediator?

3 What sort of things can cause conflict in the workplace? Compare your thoughts with a partner.

4 Skim read the article below. Does it mention any of the types of conflict you discussed in 3?

8 Causes of Conflict at Work

You arrive at the office expecting a relatively hassle-free day. Your schedule is light, you have nothing urgent to deal with and everything seems to be running smoothly. Then the problems start. Two members of your team are at each other's throats over their shared office space and another colleague is clearly leaving it till the very last minute to write the report you need by tomorrow morning. And, to top it all, you get an email informing you that your department's budget has been slashed and you now have a whole new set of team objectives to satisfy. Welcome to work!

According to psychologists Art Bell and Brett Hart, there are eight classic causes of conflict in the office. How many of the following sound familiar?

1 Conflicting needs

This might just be a case of competing over limited resources – office supplies or the use of a meeting room. Or it may be something deeper, such as when one person needs more personal recognition than another. Either way, there's friction.

2 Conflicting styles

People obviously have different ways of working. Some require order, while others thrive on chaos. Some are team players, while others work best alone. Expect these people to collaborate and you're heading for a personality clash.

3 Conflicting perceptions

Two people may view the same incident in two totally different ways. As far as I'm concerned, you went ahead and made a decision without consulting me first. You thought you were doing me a favour by saving me time. Now we're heading for a confrontation.

4 Conflicting goals

You think we're supposed to be expanding our customer base. I think we're in the business of improving the quality of our service. Asking us to work on the same team is a recipe for disaster!

5 Conflicting pressures

A common cause of conflict when you're relying on other people to help you do your job. I need you to send someone to fix my computer, but you need your whole IT team to attend a training session!

6 Conflicting roles

I was called in to help you with a crippling workload. You think you can manage just fine without me and don't appreciate the interference.

7 Different personal values

Your boss asks you to do something you disapprove of ethically. But, if you refuse, you'll lose her trust and have to face the consequences!

8 Unpredictable policies

Whenever company policy is changed without warning or is inconsistent, there will be negative reactions. Poor communication is always a major cause of irritation.

In all cases, it sounds like a job for ... the mediator!

5 Work with a partner. Check you know what the underlined words and phrases in the article mean. Try to work out the meaning of any you don't know from the context.

6 Reread the article. Have you found yourself in any of the situations it describes? If so, share your story. How did you resolve the issue?

7 3.25 Listen to a manager trying to resolve a dispute between two of his team members and answer the questions below.

a Which two of the eight causes of conflict do you think are the main ones here?
b Whose side (if anybody's) are you on? Can you see any possible solutions?
c What is the manager doing wrong? Which of the qualities you discussed in 2 does he lack?

8 Complete the stages of a mediation session using the verbs in the box.

describes encourages generates gets holds identifies imposes
listens opens prevents sets speaks writes

1 The mediator ________ the meeting, ________ the process and ________ the ground rules.
2 Each party ________ in turn. The mediator ________ carefully and ________ interruption.
3 The mediator ________ the main issues and ________ alternatives if they can.
4 If necessary, the mediator ________ one-on-one meetings with each party.
5 The mediator ________ the parties to reach an agreement, but ________ nothing on them.
6 The mediator ________ up what's been agreed and ________ the parties to sign up to it.

9 Match the sentences below to the stages in 8 that you would you expect to hear them.

a Okay, so clearly this issue is important to you. ☐
b Remember, this is entirely your decision. ☐
c First of all, I'm completely impartial in all this. ☐
d Do you think you could both live with that? ☐
e Okay, let's talk about this a bit more in private. ☐
f It's just a suggestion, but how about this? ☐
g So, if you'd just like to check what you've agreed. ☐
h Here's one option you might like to consider. ☐
i Hang on, Ian! You'll get your chance in a minute. ☐
j As I understand it, you're unhappy about this. ☐
k Everything you say is totally confidential. ☐
l It looks like there's some common ground here. ☐

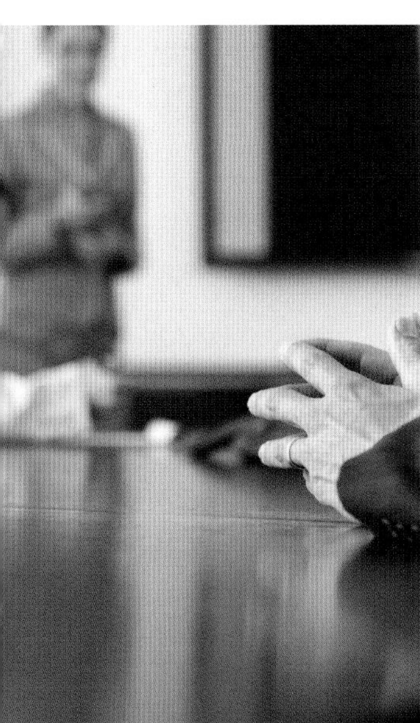

10 3.26 After their disastrous first meeting, James decides to bring in a mediator to try and help resolve the conflict between Henri and Elena. Listen and make a note of what the main issues are for each person. How would you rate the mediator out of ten?

11 Are you in a better position now to find a solution to the conflict? If so, what would you do?

12 3.27 Listen to what is agreed at the meeting and compare it with your ideas in 11.

13 Work in groups of three to practise your mediation skills. See page 126.

MANAGEMENT SCENARIO

Moral quarrel

Learning objectives: Management scenario E

Business communication skills
Staying assertive in meetings; Mediating to resolve a conflict; Fluency: A conference call mediation
Reading PowerPoint slide on assertiveness
In company in action
E1: A failed mediation;
E2: A successful conference call

1 Give a man a fish and you feed him for a day. Teach a man to fish and you feed him for a lifetime. – *Chinese proverb.*

Should international assistance focus on immediate aid or long-term development?

2 Complete the minutes below using the verbs in the box and answer the questions.

agreed announced congratulated emphasized urged

Date: April 2 **Time:** 11.00 **Chair:** Charles Ojara

Venue: Sheraton Hotel, Kampala **Attendees:** Amos Jeffah, Ed Ryan

Item	Discussion	Action
Village wells project	AJ (1) ________ Blue Rock on achieving the Q1 target of 30 new wells. ER (2) ________ that the objective for Q2 had been raised by 20%.	
Educating Engineers	CO (3) ________ Blue Rock to invest in this project. He (4) ________ that supporting national education policies was critical to continued cooperation on local water projects. ER (5) ________ to sponsor three African students on water resources engineering courses at universities in the UK, to be confirmed by Blue Rock headquarters.	ER by April 16

Next meeting: April 16 11.00

a Who represented Blue Rock at the meeting?

b What could happen if Blue Rock does not sponsor African students in the UK?

c What action does Ed need to take?

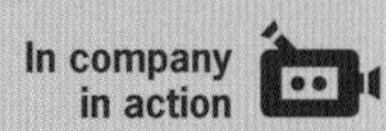

3 Now watch video E1 to see a discussion at Blue Rock's head office in London about sponsoring African engineering students. Who is in favour of the proposal and who is against it? Complete the table.

	Cassie Sugden, Marketing	Ed Ryan, Operations	Peter Neubauer, Marketing	Jack Wright, Operations	Emma Lambert, Operations
For		✓			
Against					
Neutral					

4 Watch the video again and circle the best answers.

1 Emma steps in to mediate because she has been (a) invited (b) disturbed (c) interested.

2 Her language is (a) passive (b) assertive (c) aggressive.

3 She tries to control the meeting by (a) listening (b) dominating (c) staying calm.

4 Emma is (a) subjective (b) impartial (c) uncommitted.

5 She takes disagreement (a) personally (b) professionally (c) passively.

6 Emma's attempt to mediate is (a) inconclusive (b) a success (c) a failure.

5 Put Emma's words in the correct order. How could she reformulate these sentences to make them less aggressive and more assertive?

a a bit Can down keep noise the you?
b asked I Jack, not Peter, you.
c do help, Look, me not or to to try want you?
d all collecting donations have I'll on out street the you!
e as be considered corruption could Don't realize that you?
f and are being totally Ed unprofessional You!

6 Match the beginnings (1–6) with the endings (a–f) in this slide on assertiveness.

Assertiveness tips

1 Assertive, not passive or aggressive:
2 'I' not 'you';
3 'I'd like' not 'you can't /shouldn't';
4 Description, not judgement;
5 Specific, not general;
6 Incentives, not threats;

a give concrete examples not broad generalisations
b build mutual respect not dominance or submission
c describe benefits rather than imposing conditions
d make constructive suggestions not negative vetos
e describe your own feelings rather than others' behaviour
f stick to facts rather than opinions

7 Referring to the tips in 6, give examples from the video of how Ed, Jack, Cassie and Peter were not assertive enough.

In company in action

8 Now watch video E2 to see how CEO Sue Jensen mediates and tick the items you see or hear.

The mediator:

describes the process	☐	sets the ground rules	☐
has each party speak in turn	☐	listens carefully	☐
prevents interruption	☐	identifies the main issues	☐
generates alternatives	☐	holds one-on-one meetings	☐
encourages agreement	☐	imposes nothing	☐
writes up what's been agreed	☐	gets the parties to sign an agreement	☐

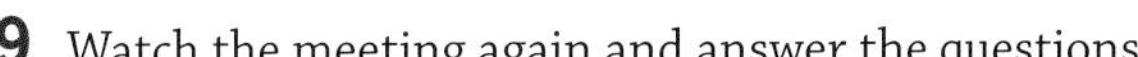

9 Watch the meeting again and answer the questions.

a Why was the meeting held by conference call?
b How does Sue set up the meeting?
c How does she deal with aggressive behaviour from the participants? Give examples.
d What compromise does Emma suggest?
e What three things do they agree to do at the end of the meeting?
f Do you think the conference call makes mediation more difficult, or easier? Why?

10 Complete the gaps in these phrases from the video. Which assertiveness tips in 6 do they refer to?

a Let's stay ____________ please, Ed; tell us about the benefits rather than negatives, okay?
b I'd like us to ____________ this ____________ together …
c … let's leave ____________ aside for the moment, all right?
d … can you be more ____________?
e Let's not get too ____________ here, okay?

11 Work in groups of three or more to simulate a meeting or conference call. Speaker A (mediator) see page 134, Speaker B see page 138, Speaker C see page 128.

When you have finished, use the checklists on page 132 to help you evaluate your performance.

Additional material

01 Business or pleasure?

Corporate entertainment (p7, ex4)

Group A

British Grand Prix, Silverstone
(100 km from central London)

Engines roar, tyres squeal and sparks fly as $2 million supercars accelerate from 0 to 250 kph in under seven seconds. 200,000 spectators descend on Silverstone for this fabulous sporting occasion that attracts a worldwide TV audience of 350 million. From your trackside seat you'll soak up all the atmosphere of one of the most glamorous and spectacular events in the motor racing calendar. VIP treatment; breathtaking action!

VIP box and hospitality tent: €1,500 per person

Banquet on board the Royal Yacht Britannia, Edinburgh
(600 km from London)

Dinner on board Britannia at her permanent berth in Scotland's capital is a once-in-a-lifetime experience – oysters and aperitifs, tables decorated with ice sculptures, waiters in white gloves and music played on the very piano Princess Diana used to practise on. You'll be seated in the state dining room where the Queen once entertained world leaders like Boris Yeltsin, Bill Clinton and Nelson Mandela. Why not really roll out the red carpet for your guests and make your corporate hospitality event a truly 'royal' occasion?

Five-course dinner, military band, fireworks: €800 per person

02 Information exchange

Breaking the bad news (p17, ex1)

Speaker A

Proposal: Work environment

- A lot of staff (35%) complaining about feeling tired and stressed
- Board thinks one of main causes may be poor work environment
- Feng shui expert called in – recommendations include radical changes to office layout
- Reception area to be turned into a water garden to create positive 'chi' (energy)
- Internal walls to be removed to improve 'channels of communication'
- Desks ideally to be moved during the year to remain 'in harmony with the seasons'

Scenario A

(p23, ex9)

Speaker A

You work for a well-established and respectable business with a proud reputation for technical innovation. The company has a rather hierarchical organization: managers have reserved parking spaces and separate tables in the canteen. Relations are rather formal – first names are only used between colleagues at the same level. Most people work in small individual or shared offices. Information is communicated on a need-to-know basis.

The company employs a majority of men, mostly engineers, and only a few women, mainly administrative assistants. Your business is very technical: customers' and suppliers' attitudes are very conventional. The dress code is formal – customers frequently visit the office and expect high standards.

In your company, time is money. Punctuality and efficiency are valued highly. Everybody, including management, has to clock in and out. Humorous emails or remarks are discouraged as a waste of time. Criticizing the company, its products or its staff, even humorously, is discouraged. Staff do not socialize much; romantic relationships between staff are actively discouraged.

In your business, work is stressful and staff turnover is high. However, people are generally happy because the company is successful and they are well-paid; bonuses are also awarded for exceptional individual achievement. You would like to keep as many of the positive aspects of your culture as possible in the new organization.

11 Stress

(p71, ex13)

Speaker A

1 You are Speaker B's manager. Speaker B is suffering from stress. Try to:
- help them express their feelings
- identify the source of stress
- find ways to relieve pressure
- find ways to adapt to their situation.

2 Speaker B is your manager. You are suffering from stress because you have financial problems. Your mortgage payments have just gone up, your car is getting old and unreliable, your children's school/university fees are rising and your household bills are growing. Your expenses are constantly increasing but your income remains the same and there seem to be no prospects of promotion.

Talk to your manager about the problem.

02 Information exchange

Buzzword bingo (p14, ex5)

Choose a bingo card from the selection below.

04329		
think outside the box	mindset	core competencies
proactive	empowerment	drill down
paradigm shift	the big picture	the next level

04330		
ramp up	drill down	core competencies
the big picture	mindset	proactive
think outside the box	bottom line	paradigm shift

04331		
benchmark	ramp up	empowerment
synergize	mindset	bottom line
proactive	the next level	buy-in

04332		
the next level	the big picture	benchmark
buy-in	ramp up	bottom line
scope out	customer-centric	paradigm shift

04333		
mindset	benchmark	drill down
synergize	proactive	reality check
core competencies	bottom line	paradigm shift

04334		
bottom line	ramp up	reality check
buy-in	empowerment	the big picture
core competencies	drill down	synergize

02 Information exchange

Queries and comments (p15, ex2)

Speaker A

1 Read out the following report to your partner. There are seven discrepancies in it (marked in bold). Can your partner spot them? If not, keep reading. Apologize for or justify any discrepancies your partner points out. If you lose your place in the text, ask your partner: 'Where was I?'

Report: World Trade Fair

Our exhibition stand at the World Trade Fair in Munich was very successful again this year, attracting visitors from all over **Munich**. Although this was **our first appearance** at the Fair, our people did a great job and handed out **nearly three** brochures.

We met a group of Austrian business people at the **Frankfurt** Hilton, where we were staying, and arranged a formal meeting with them by the **pool**. They were very interested in our products and said they would email us as soon as they got back to **Australia**.

Apparently, next year the Fair is being held outside Europe for the first time – **Paris** here we come!

2 Now listen to your partner reading out a report. There are also seven discrepancies in it. Can you spot them? Remain polite no matter how confused your partner seems!

Useful language

Sorry, I thought you said ...
Hold on, didn't you just say ...?
Wait a minute. You just said ..., didn't you?

15 Delegation

(p97, ex11)

Speaker A

1 You are Speaker B's manager. You need them to buy some new equipment for the office (you decide what and why). Speaker B is new in the job; last time they were given a task to do they got it all wrong, so make sure you give very clear instructions.
2 Speaker B is your manager and has a task to delegate to you. You are a very experienced member of the team; you prefer to get on with the job without too much interference from your manager. You tend to get annoyed if your manager underestimates your abilities.
3 You are Speaker B's manager. You need to delegate a task to them (you decide what and why). Speaker B has been in your team for two or three years; they are able to be autonomous and use initiative, but tend not to finish work on time if you don't check up on them.
4 Speaker B is your manager and has a task to delegate to you. You are new in your job and very keen to show what you can do and make a good impression.

04 Voice and visuals

Giving feedback (p26, ex1)

Speaker A: Boss

You are a senior partner in a major management consultancy. You have just attended a presentation by one of your best consultants to an important Taiwanese client. Unfortunately, the presentation was an absolute disaster from start to finish.

You forced a smile during the presentation but are now going to tell Speaker B exactly what you thought of their performance. Base your criticisms on the following information. Try to end on a positive note by making some suggestions for future presentations.

- Speaker B was wearing a T-shirt and jeans. The Taiwanese must have felt deeply insulted.
- You could hardly hear a word Speaker B said.
- The PowerPoint slides were not working properly – it all looked very unprofessional.
- You have no idea what happened to the DVD you were expecting to see.
- You nearly died when they cracked a joke about China. The Taiwanese left the room in silence, clearly not amused.

Useful language

Why did/didn't you ...?
You should(n't) have ...
Couldn't you at least have ...?
Don't you think it would have been a good idea to ...?
Well, anyway, in future I suggest you ...
And next time – if there is a next time – just make sure you ...

05 Problems on the phone

Dealing with a chatterbox (p32, ex5)

Speaker A

If you don't know Speaker B well, swap lists of the following with them before you start your telephone conversation:

- your partner's name, job and main interest
- your children's names, ages and main interests
- when and where you went on your last holiday
- your own main interest
- your favourite sport (spectator or player?)
- the name of a close colleague
- a problem you've been having at work recently

You are director of the purchasing department for Mi Casa, a large chain of furniture stores in Mexico. You like to get in touch with your suppliers from time to time – not necessarily to do business, just to maintain the relationship. It's 10 am on Friday morning, most of your week's work is done and the weekend is fast approaching. Phone Speaker B, the sales director of Möbelkunst, a designer furniture manufacturer in Berlin, for a little chat.

Keep the conversation going by asking lots of questions (using Speaker B's list as a starting point). You don't really want to do any business today, but Möbelkunst's stylish chairs, tables and lamps have been very popular with your customers who love the bright colours and modern designs. If the terms were right, you might want to increase your order – even double it – for a trial period.

Scenario A

(p23, ex9)

Speaker B

You work for a creative and informal high tech company: most of the staff are recently qualified engineers. New employees are instructed to use first names with everybody, from the most junior intern right up to the President. Everybody except top management works in large open-plan offices. Once a month the CEO organizes a tea party where everybody is invited to give their opinions and chat about any subject they like.

The company has an equal opportunities policy: over half of managers are women. The dress code is very informal – management want people to feel as comfortable as possible. Staff can arrive and leave when they want as long as they meet their objectives. However, meetings rarely start or finish on time and there is a chronic difficulty to deliver projects on time.

Because work is stressful, staff are encouraged to organize informal, fun events. The social committee organizes frequent parties, sports, cultural and social events. Overall, people are happy because their work is satisfying; even if pay is lower than average for engineering companies and bonuses depend on corporate results. Very few people choose to leave the company. You would like to keep as many of the positive aspects of your culture as possible in the new organization.

05 Problems on the phone

Tackling problems (p34, ex7)

Speaker A

At the end of each conversation, give Speaker B a score out of ten for (a) helpfulness and (b) assertiveness.

1. You are having problems with your computer – it either won't do something you want it to or it's just done something you definitely didn't want it to (you decide which). Phone Speaker B and see if they can give you any advice. If not, ask them who you should phone instead.
2. Speaker B, your boss, will phone you with a problem. It's 6 pm and you are just on your way out of the office when the phone rings. You've arranged to go out with a few colleagues this evening (you decide when and where). This is the fifth time this month your boss has held you up right at the end of the day.

3 You have just been promoted and Speaker B is now your boss. You particularly like your great new office (you decide why), which is exactly what you need to do your new job (you decide why). Someone told you today that a colleague from an overseas division of your company may be coming to work at your division for a few months and you are waiting for your boss to phone and give you the details.

4 Speaker B is usually a star member of your team, but at the moment they are a month behind with an important report and you are under pressure from head office to get it completed on schedule (within the next two weeks). You think the best idea is to bring someone else in (you decide who) to help get the report finished in time and team present the final results to senior management with Speaker B. Phone and make your suggestion as tactfully but forcefully as you can.

10 Making decisions

Crisis management (p67, ex5)

Coke products banned in Belgium

Associated Press

BRUSSELS, Belgium (AP) – Stores across Belgium removed all beverages of the Coca-Cola Co. from their shelves today, complying with a ban prompted by the hospitalizations of people who got sick after drinking Coke products.

For a second consecutive day, poison alert centers across Belgium received hundreds of phone calls from people seeking information. Some callers said they too had become nauseous after drinking Coke or Coca-Cola brands.

On Monday, Health Minister Luc Van den Bossche banned all sales of Coke and Coca-Cola brands such as Fanta, Sprite, Aquarius, Bonaqua and Minute Maid fruit juices.

'We are hard at work trying to find the cause of the problems,' said Maureen O'Sullivan, a spokeswoman for Coca-Cola in Belgium. 'We are also implementing a total recall of our products.'

The ban was imposed after nearly 50 people, most of them young people, were hospitalized on Monday suffering from nausea after drinking Coke products. Eight remained in the hospital today.

Strategy meeting agenda

Client: Coca-Cola Co.

- Should there be an immediate product recall in spite of the lack of solid evidence?
- In the absence of any proof of contamination, should Coca-Cola appeal to the four European governments to lift their ban? Or even threaten legal action against them?
- Should any decision be postponed until the final results of the tests become available? Or will this just give the competition time to increase its market share?
- How should the company persuade the public that there's no real threat?
- Should there be an official apology? Or would that look like an admission of guilt?
- Should Coca-Cola put the blame firmly on its Belgian bottling plant and their shippers, whilst exporting Coke directly to Europe from the USA?
- What kind of public relations exercise would restore confidence in the world's number one brand?

Step 4

Each group should present its recommendations to the class.

Step 5

2.35 Listen to the final part of the case and find out what really happened. How do your recommendations compare with the action Coca-Cola actually took?

06 Leading meetings

(p41, ex6)

Meeting 1

Should genetic tests decide job prospects?

What if you were faced, at a job interview, with a test that would tell whether you could expect to develop Alzheimer's or Parkinson's disease? What if you were turned down because of that tiny bit of your DNA?

This scary scenario is coming closer to reality with the development of a technology that will allow employers to carry out genetic tests and get the results in the time it takes to stroll to the canteen and have a cup of coffee.

Would it be ethical? Would it be legal? Would it be acceptable to recruiters, let alone society at large? The moral debate lags behind the scientific advances. A technology that will identify DNA electronically has been developed by Dr John Clarkson and his colleagues at the company Molecular Sensing. They plan to miniaturize it and build a hand-held device that will produce results in less than 30 minutes.

Adapted from *The Sunday Times*

Meeting 2

Employers spy on workers

Big Brother is watching. And it's increasingly likely to be your boss.

She might be recording the casual conversations between you and your co-worker, or tracking emails on your company computer, or watching the goings-on in the staff lounge.

Sounds like an invasion of your privacy? Think again. Most employee monitoring in the workplace is perfectly legal, and it happens more than most people realise.

Two-thirds of US businesses eavesdrop on their employees in some fashion – on the phone, via videotape and through email and Internet files – according to a survey by the American Management Association International.

In fact, employers can trace everything from deleted emails and voice mails to the exact computer keys a worker strikes. Special software can follow employees' paths across the Internet and high tech employee badges even let bosses track their workers' movements within an office building.

Adapted from *Knight Ridder Newspapers*

Meeting 3

Creative way to better management

From Chopin to Schubert and jazz to jive, music, along with theatre, film, drawing and painting, is now widely used in UK business schools to help executives improve their management skills.

It may all be great fun, but does it work? Opinion is divided. Strongly against is David Norburn, director of Imperial College Management School, London. He says that after a few drinks he could probably make a case for any human activity having managerial relevance. 'Weber's clarinet concerto and emotion; jazz and chaos theory; sex and timing.'

His argument is that when executives and MBAs invest time in business school programmes they want rigorous and relevant training.

But staff at many of the UK's leading business schools, such as Patricia Hodgins at the London Business School, disagree. 'The key to creativity is being relaxed and being able to think laterally. Using arts, music and theatre helps us to find that.'

Adapted from *The Financial Times*

02 Information exchange

The language of meetings (p16, ex1)

Eight of these nouns will complete the extracts:

answer fact idea issue opinion option point position problem question situation view

08 Promoting your ideas

Audience analysis (p49, ex1)

Exercise 1 answers

USA – Extract 3	UK – Extract 5
Germany – Extract 1	France – Extract 6
Japan – Extract 4	Kuwait – Extract 2

Scenario B

(p47, ex7)

Speaker A

Giving feedback on presentations

Do ...

- Get permission to give feedback. Even if you are the presenter's boss, make sure they are ready to hear your feedback here and now.
- Invite the presenter to give feedback first. This helps you to be positive when they are overly critical, and to identify which weaknesses they are already correcting and which ones they really need help with.
- Start with the positives. Find things to be positive about in order to build confidence and trust.
- Be specific and constructive. Go on to point out specific problems; make suggestions as to how the presenter can improve. Try to agree on a specific action plan.
- Use questions and indirect language.
- Encourage the presenter to find their own solutions rather than telling them what to do.

09 Relationship-building

Are you an effective networker? (p55, ex2)

Questionnaire analysis

How you network in specific situations will, of course, be influenced by many factors, but, in general, the most effective strategy will be: 1a, 2c, 3b, 4b, 5c and 6c.

1c, 2b, 5b and 6a could be risky.

3a and 4c might be unfair to other people.

1b, 3c, 4a and 5a may show a certain lack of assertiveness.

09 Relationship-building

Getting out of the office (p58, ex4)

Speaker A

Situation 1

Background: You're an IT security specialist. You're playing golf with Speaker B, the IT director of a major insurance company and one of your best customers. It's a beautiful spring morning.

Situation: You're playing really well today. Although Speaker B is a much better golfer than you, you were actually a shot ahead on the 16th hole, but you've just dropped two shots on the 17th. Damn! It was looking as though you might even beat them for a change.

Hidden agenda: You've heard a rumour that Speaker B may be looking to engage another IT security consultancy. You've always got on well with them, but you know your company's fees are not the most competitive. When they invited you to play golf with them today, you saw it as your chance to find out what's going on.

Speaker B will start.

Situation 2

Background: You're a sales director for an international sports goods company. You're playing tennis with Speaker B, a new member of your sales team. When you started playing it was a warm summer afternoon, but it's just clouded over and looks like it might even rain.

Situation: You pride yourself on being an excellent tennis player, but Speaker B, who you haven't played before, is totally destroying you – 6–2 in the first set and 4–1 up in the second. This hasn't put you in a very good mood, especially as your company's marketing director, who's playing on the next court, seems to be thoroughly enjoying your humiliating defeat!

Hidden agenda: Although Speaker B joined you with excellent qualifications and a good track record in sales, they don't seem to be fitting in very well. The other sales personnel complain that they're not much of a team-player and that they act superior to the rest of the staff. In fact, Speaker B is creating something of a morale problem. The only good thing about them is that, if they always play this well, you'll have no trouble beating marketing at the annual interdepartmental match!

You start: There's something I've been meaning to talk to you about …

17 Negotiating deals

(p107, ex1)

Extra information

You and the other speaker are ex-neighbours and very good friends. Your kids even used to play together. You both moved to different areas of the city about six months ago and meant to keep in touch, but, what with work and settling into new homes, you just haven't had the time.

09 Relationship-building

A dinner invitation (p60)

Host: Ulterior motive

You're considering promoting your guest to a more senior post (you decide what) at your company's subsidiary in Melbourne. You are very impressed with your guest's work record and general management ability, but you haven't made up your mind yet about the promotion. So, drop a few hints during the evening and see what the reaction is. Don't be too specific at this stage and be ready to change the subject if things don't go according to plan!

Scenario A

(p23, ex9)

Meetings checklist	Yes	No
Was the meeting well structured?		
Was the objective achieved in the time allowed?		
Were all participants able to express their ideas and opinions?		
Were all participants satisfied with the outcome?		
Did participants use appropriately direct/blunt or indirect/vague language?		
Did participants query discrepancies?		
Did participants reformulate to check understanding?		
Did participants express disagreement tactfully?		

Cultural sensitivity checklist	Yes	No
Were participants aware of their own culture and differences with others?		
Did participants suspend judgement of other cultures?		
Did participants identify and share common values, beliefs, goals and attitudes?		
Did participants respect differences and resist the temptation to make converts?		
Did participants use language sensitively and prefer 'we' to 'I' or 'you'?		
Were participants objective and positive in spite of difficulties?		

10 Making decisions

Worst-case scenarios (p63, ex3)

5 While staying in a hotel in Paris, you wake up to find the whole place is on fire. Your way down is blocked and you end up on the roof. Do you:

a take a long run-up and jump onto the next building (a distance of four and a half metres)?
b jump six floors down and land on your back in a truck packed with soft insulation materials?
c leap well away from the building to clear obstructions and land in the truck?

6 On a business trip to Amsterdam your taxi skids on a patch of oil and plunges off the road and into a canal. In seconds you are half-underwater. Do you:

a force open the door and swim to safety (taking the driver with you)?
b wind down the window fully to let the water in?
c wind the window up to trap air inside the car in case you sink?

7 You agree to do a parachute jump for charity with a group of friends. But as you free-fall from 14000 feet at 120 mph both your parachute and emergency chute fail to open. Do you:

a keep struggling with your emergency chute? It must work!
b grab hold of the nearest member of the group before they open their chute?
c take valuable time to attach yourself to the chest straps of another parachutist?

8 Whilst snorkelling off the Great Barrier Reef in north-eastern Australia, you suddenly see a large shark swimming swiftly towards you from the depths. Do you:

a try to attack the shark's eyes?
b punch the shark on the nose?
c splash about and make a noise to frighten it away?

07 Coaching

(p45, ex10)

Work in groups of three and take turns to be the coach, the coachee and the observer.

Coach: Using the GROW model, listen, ask lots of questions and try to help your coachee identify their goals and develop a realistic plan of action within a timeframe they are comfortable with. Resist the temptation to give them advice unless you can see they are 'stuck'. If you do offer advice, make it clear that is what you are doing, but try not to influence the coachee too much. Show empathy and understanding, but remain neutral.

Coachee: Decide on a topic for the coaching conversation you're about to have. Topics you could discuss include communication skills, learning English for business, new work responsibilities, time management, stress and workload, career development, strategies for building your professional network, personality clashes at work, leadership and motivation issues. Try to focus on one specific aspect of the issue.

Observer: Watch the coaching session, but do not say anything. Take notes on how well the coach helps the coachee to deal with their own issues. Do they use the GROW model? Are they empathetic? Do they stick to a neutral coaching approach or move into a mentor role too much? How does the coachee respond? What is the outcome of the session? At the end of the meeting give both of your partners some brief feedback.

Scenario D

(p99, ex13)

Meetings checklist	Yes	No
Was the meeting well chaired?		
Was the objective clear?		
Were all participants able to express their ideas and opinions?		
Did participants listen carefully to each other?		
Did participants use appropriate disagreement strategies?		
Was the objective achieved?		

Change management checklist	Yes	No
Did participants explain the need for change?		
Did participants explain the benefits of the change?		
Did participants (plan to) recruit change champions?		
Did participants plan to provide tools and resources to facilitate the change?		
Did participants plan to continue to communicate about the change?		

14 Out and about

In-flight conversations (p91, ex11)

Speaker A

Hold short conversations with a fellow passenger, Speaker B, on three different international flights.

Use the information below to get you started, but invent any extra information you need to keep the conversation going for a minute or two.

1 **Flight BA1311 from Dubai to London Heathrow, business class (9pm)**

- You are an engineer travelling back from Dubai, where you have been working for Royal Dutch Shell (Emirates) for the last five years, to take up a senior position at Head Office in London.
- Your three-year-old son is accompanying you on the flight, but your partner won't be joining you in the UK for another couple of weeks.
- You're not looking forward to the flight much because your son is quite a hyperactive child and you can never sleep on planes anyway.
- Try to start a conversation with the person sitting next to you, Speaker B. They seem to be playing with their hand-held computer at the moment.

2 **Flight AF6001 from Paris to Rio de Janeiro, economy class (3am)**

- You are a product manager for Pfizer Pharmaceuticals on your way from a project meeting in Paris to another meeting in Rio.
- You have an appointment with a group of Brazilian research chemists with whom you are collaborating on a new kind of miracle travel sickness pill, which, if all goes well, could be on the market in six months.
- So far your journey has been a nightmare. Your original flight was cancelled due to bad weather and the only seat you could get was in economy class on the red-eye (a night flight, on which you do not get enough sleep) leaving at two-thirty in the morning.
- To top it all, it looks like it's going to be a bumpy flight. You can't sleep, so you might as well try and read your book, a crime novel you picked up in the airport called *The Pentangle* by A. J. Bell. Seems quite good.

3 **Flight LH1706 from Los Angeles to Munich, first class (2pm)**

- You are a film producer for Touchstone Pictures flying from a meeting with Oscar winning actor Al Pacino in Los Angeles to a casting meeting in Munich.
- You are looking for a German- and English-speaking actor to play the part of an environmental activist in your latest film and would prefer to choose an unknown rather than a big box office star.
- You've just enjoyed your in-flight meal, when you notice that the passenger sitting next to you looks perfect for the part! You can't believe your eyes, but remind yourself they are probably a business executive with no acting ability whatsoever.
- At the moment they are watching the in-flight movie on their headphones, but try to find an excuse to get talking to them.

16 Teleconferencing

Desert island blues (p104)

CEO of RJK (UK)

1 

email

I'm becoming increasingly concerned about the costs we're running up on the Éternelle account. I think we're in serious danger of exceeding our budget.

As you know, the Éternelle marketing people were extremely unhappy when we came in €250,000 over budget last time, and it was for this reason that they insisted at the planning stage on a ceiling of €2.5m for the Vivacity campaign.

I've been looking at the figures and we're well past the €2m mark already. The main problem is this two-day film shoot on Oamu-Oamu which has already cost us €1m. The Hollywood actress the client insisted on using is costing us €100,000 a day! What on earth is going on there?

I estimate that with post-production costs, we could run €500,000–€700,000 over budget on this one.

We desperately need to talk.

Gavin Hartnell, Chief Financial Officer, RJK (UK)

2

email

I'm hearing rumours of a budget overrun on the Vivacity campaign. Please tell me I'm imagining things!

I had lunch with Éternelle's new head of marketing, Thierry DuPont, and he sounded pretty annoyed with what he called our 'endless production hold-ups'. He even said they may be forced to postpone the Vivacity launch.

I'm sure I don't need to remind you that Éternelle is by far this company's biggest European client (worth €10m annually) and that the loss of their account would have a drastic effect on both Group turnover and our reputation in the industry.

Your creative director must be in contact with our team on Oamu-Oamu. Are they still having weather problems or what?

I'm counting on you to sort this one out. Don't let me down.

Nathan T. Auerbach, RJK Group President

17 Negotiating deals
(p107, ex1)

Speaker A

It's 6 pm on Christmas Eve and you're still at the office. You've been so busy lately, you've hardly had a moment to spend with your family. You even had to miss your young son's first match for the school football team last week to attend an important meeting. Apparently, you were the only parent not there.

Fortunately, you have a chance to put things right. You know there's something kids are all going mad for this Christmas – the Z-Cube Gaming System. At $189, it's a little more than you were planning to spend, but it would be great to see the look on your son's face when he opens it. After phoning seven stores without success, you finally find one that has three left. You try to reserve one, but the shop assistant says 'Sorry, only my boss can do that and she's not here. But if you hurry, you should be okay. We're open till 6.30.'

You fly out of the office and into a taxi. You get to the store just before it closes. To your horror, you see there's only one Z-Cube left. It has a big label on the box saying 'LAST ONE'. But as you head for it, you see another person with the same idea (Speaker B) coming in the other direction. You both reach the box at the same time and grab opposite ends ...

17 Negotiating deals
The recording contract (p111, ex5)

Team A: The Penitents (band and management)

Obviously, you are delighted that a record company as high-profile as Starburst is interested in signing your band. If the deal goes through, you stand to make a lot of money. You are aware, however, that relatively unknown artists are vulnerable to exploitation by the big labels and should take this into account in your dealings with them.

Read your negotiating objectives below and then work with your team to plan your overall strategy. In particular, make sure you know which of your objectives are:

a tradeables (things you'll concede to get what you really want in return)

b ideals (things you'd really like to get, but not if it costs you the deal)

c essentials (things you absolutely have to get or the deal's off)

1 **Band line-up** The four members of the band – the lead singer and rhythm guitarist, lead guitarist, bass guitarist and drummer – all met at college in Dublin and have played together through good times and bad for five years. You've heard a rumour that Starburst Records may want to make changes to the line-up – perhaps sacking the drummer, who is also the band's female backing vocalist.

2 **Term** You'd like a three-year commitment from Starburst. It can often take several albums before band members make a profit, so you'd like them to commission at least two albums during that time. If, after three years, the contract is terminated, you'd prefer to keep the rights to all the songs you have recorded – otherwise you would have to pay Starburst a fee to perform or re-record your old material.

3 **Royalties** You think a 15% royalty on net receipts from album sales would be fair. If the band's current popularity does not last, you'd like to make as much as money as possible before the bubble bursts.

4 **Deductions** You expect Starburst to cover all the costs of packaging and promotion, including any TV advertising. Accessing marketing power is one of the advantages of signing to a major label.

5 **Advances** You are more interested in a good long-term relationship with Starburst than instant cash. Nevertheless, a $200,000 non-repayable advance would allow band members to cover living costs, purchase of equipment and stage costumes, etc.

6 **Territory** You're happy for Starburst to have 'universal rights' to your material globally, provided the terms are right. Otherwise, you'd like to be able to approach other labels in the States and Asia.

7 **Touring** Touring is an essential part of building a band, especially in the early stages of its development. But some of the band members have other jobs and family commitments. They wouldn't want to take on more than 20 weeks' touring (not consecutively) in the first year unless the financial rewards were high – say, 50% of ticket sales.

8 **Songwriting** The lead singer, Rick Harlow, writes all the band's songs. He says he wants the usual 50:50 split with the music publisher on fees for airplay on radio and TV and other public performances.

18 Mediation
(p115, ex13)

Work in groups of three: two colleagues and a mediator. Take turns to be the mediator in *some or all* of the following situations. Spend at least five minutes preparing for the situation as a group before you begin. Change anything you need to make the situation as realistic and relevant for you as possible.

As the mediator, make sure you follow the procedure you looked at in 8 and try to remain impartial throughout the session. Keep order, encourage both parties to speak one at a time, identify the main issues and phrase any ideas of your own as suggestions. You can hold a maximum of one three-minute private session with each party. Write down whatever is agreed and get both parties to sign up to it before you close the meeting. If an agreement cannot be reached, ask the parties if they think a further session would be a good idea.

Situation 1: A simple dispute

You are two colleagues working on a six-month project together (jointly decide what the project is).

Speaker A

You like to have regular weekly meetings to discuss progress and you generally dislike email (you decide why).

Speaker B

You prefer to deal with issues by email as they arise and you generally dislike meetings (you decide why).

At the moment, neither of you is able to get on with the project efficiently because of the other's work-style (you decide what problems you've been having). Meet with your mediator to try and sort things out.

Situation 2: A more complicated dispute

You are unit managers of two separate work teams (jointly decide what line of business you are in). Owing to a reduced budget (you decide why it has been reduced), only one of your teams will be able to receive training this quarter. You both think your team should be the one to get the training. Meet with your mediator to try and sort things out.

Speaker A

Your team has had no training for nine months (you decide why you need it now).

Speaker B

Although your team has had regular training, you have just acquired a lot of new recruits, who urgently need training (you decide precisely why).

Situation 3: A very complex dispute

You are the area managers for two different branches of the company you work for (you decide what your company does). Rationalization has meant that Speaker A's team has been relocated to the offices of Speaker B. This has obviously caused all kinds of problems concerning space-sharing and resource allocation (you decide precisely how these problems are affecting you). At the moment there's a very bad atmosphere in office. Meet with your mediator to try and sort things out.

Speaker A

You are the manager of the team that relocated. The team has lost some of its original members, who didn't want to move, and so you now have to train up new staff. You are also worried that you may lose your job if senior management decide it would be better to have just one person manage both teams.

Speaker B

You are the manager of the team which has not moved. You don't like the idea of two separate teams 'under one roof' and would like to see a lot more integration. As the manager of the larger team (and with a higher turnover), you think you should be managing both teams, with the other manager as your deputy.

17 Negotiating deals
(p107, ex1)

Speaker B

It's Christmas Eve and you and your family are placing the last few presents under the tree. Your partner turns to you and whispers how excited your young son is: 'Thank goodness you bought him that new gaming system back in November. Apparently, the stores have completely sold out, and it's all he's talked about for months. You remembered to get him the blue one, didn't you?'

You feel a sudden surge of panic. Oh, no ... the Z-Cube Gaming System! How could you have forgotten? You meant to get one months ago, but you've been so busy it completely slipped your mind. You mumble something to your partner about going out to get some better lights for the tree and spend the next three hours searching every store in town. But nobody has one. One shop offers to order it for you, but it will take at least a fortnight ... = 2 weeks

In desperation, you try a tiny shop in a side street. It's just about to close as you walk in. To your relief, you see they have one Z-Cube left – and it's a blue one. You can't believe your luck. It has a big label on the box saying 'LAST ONE'. But as you head for it, you see another person with the same idea (Speaker A) coming in the other direction. You both reach the box at the same time and grab opposite ends ...

Scenario C
(p73, ex9)

Pitching checklist	Yes	No
Was the pitch short and to the point?		
Did the pitch provide a high-level overview to encourage discussion?		
Was the structure clear and simple?		
Was the pitcher passionate, lean, specific and sincere?		
Did the pitcher avoid jargon?		
Was the pitch successful?		

Influencing checklist	Yes	No
Did the pitcher use reciprocity to persuade the audience?		
Was there mutual like and respect between the pitcher and the audience?		
Did the pitcher refer to scarcity to support their proposal?		
Did the pitcher provide proof of their authority on their subject?		
Were the pitcher's arguments consistent and logical?		
Did the pitcher provide proof that other people are already adopting their solution?		

05 Problems on the phone

Dealing with a chatterbox (p32, ex5)

Speaker B

If you don't know Speaker A well, swap lists of the following with them before you start your telephone conversation:

- your partner's name, job and main interest
- your children's names, ages and main interests
- when and where you went on your last holiday
- your own main interest
- your favourite sport (spectator or player?)
- the name of a close colleague
- a problem you've been having at work recently

You are the sales director of Möbelkunst, a designer furniture manufacturer in Berlin. Your stylish products are getting rave reviews in the press, but business in Germany has not been good lately. Fortunately, you have recently won some very big overseas orders – one of them with Mi Casa, a large chain of furniture stores in Mexico. The only problem is Speaker A, Mi Casa's director of purchasing, who seems to like phoning you rather too often for no particular reason.

It's 5 pm on Friday afternoon. You would normally be getting ready to go home soon, but today there's been a crisis to deal with – your factory in Potsdam has just turned out 1,000 leather sofas in bright pink (rather than dark red) by mistake. You're still trying to sort a solution out with your plant manager. The last thing you need now is any interruptions.

Scenario E

(p117, ex11)

Speaker C

You are in charge of International Marketing for a company that sells high quality tea all over the world. Recently, sales have decreased due to competition from cheaper brands, so you have decided to invest in reinforcing your upmarket image and justifying your higher prices.

You have just negotiated a deal with a top film star (choose a name) to star in a campaign of TV commercials and magazine ads endorsing your product.

However, you are furious with the Sales team (Speaker B). Without consulting you, they have agreed to give large discounts to all the major supermarket chains. This low value, high volume policy will not only reduce your margins and damage the product's image. It will also mean you will not be able to pay for the air time and media space you have ordered. You will also have to cancel the contract with the film star, who will probably demand compensation. You feel that Sales' poor results are responsible for the company's difficulties and you are determined to force Sales to cancel the discounts and support your advertising campaign. Invent any other details as necessary.

02 Information exchange

Queries and comments (p15, ex2)

Speaker B

1 Listen to your partner reading out a report. There are seven discrepancies in it. Can you spot them? Remain polite no matter how confused your partner seems!

2 Read out the following report to your partner. There are also seven discrepancies in it (marked in bold). Can they spot them? If not, keep reading. Apologize for or justify any discrepancies your partner points out. If you lose your place in the text, ask your partner: 'Where was I?'

Report: Korean negotiations

We held our first meeting with the Koreans two months ago at their headquarters in **Osaka**. Since then we've had **12 weeks** of tough negotiations. There were some cultural difficulties at first. Of course, we've never done business in the **Middle East** before.

They were very positive about our products, although they weren't happy with **the design**, **performance**, **price and maintenance costs**. Initially, they were demanding a discount on orders of over 10,000 units of 17%, but we finally managed to beat them down to **18**.

We haven't heard anything from them so far, but the email they sent **this morning** looks promising – an initial order of **a dozen units**.

Useful language

Sorry, I thought you said ...
Hold on, didn't you just say ...?
Wait a minute. You just said ..., didn't you?

02 Information exchange

Breaking the bad news (p17, ex1)

Speaker B

Proposal: Travel budget

- Board deeply concerned about cost of business travel (nearly $13m last year)
- Insist on 60% cut in travel budget
- Propose three main courses of action (see below)
- All flights from now on to be economy class or on low-budget carriers (no exceptions) – preferably on cheapest early morning and late night flights
- Motels and two-star hotels for everyone in future – room-sharing wherever possible
- Meal allowance to be reduced to $20 a day (no alcoholic drinks)

01 Business or pleasure?

Corporate entertainment (p7, ex4)

Group B

All England Lawn Tennis Championships, Wimbledon (11 km from central London)

Experience the nail-biting climax to the world's premier international tennis tournament as the true giants of the game clash in the men's Wimbledon final. All the tradition of strawberries and cream combines with 225 km-an-hour serves and awesome cross-court shots to make what many consider to be the greatest sporting event on Earth. Game, set and match!

Men's final, lunch, music: €4,000 per person

London Eye and Private Tour of Tate Modern, central London

Your evening begins 130 metres above London in your very own capsule on the London Eye. A waiter serves a choice of drinks. On a clear day you can see for 25 miles – all the way to Windsor Castle. You are then transferred to the Tate Modern for a private tour of one of the world's most cutting-edge contemporary art galleries, followed by a superb dinner in the tasteful surroundings of the OXO Tower Restaurant overlooking the Thames. High altitude; high culture!

London Eye, tour of Tate Modern, dinner: €500 per person (minimum 20)

Scenario B

(p47, ex7)

Speaker B

Giving feedback on presentations.

Don't ...

- Extrapolate or get off topic. Avoid the temptation to criticize behaviour or weaknesses unrelated to the presentation.
- Mix praise and criticism. Avoid saying 'x was good, but y was bad.' This just confuses people and reduces the impact of both praise and criticism. Encourage the presenter first for what they did well, then deal with the problems separately and specifically.
- Forget that people are human beings, not machines. Adapt your feedback to each person's intellectual, emotional and physical state. Evaluate how much criticism the presenter can accept without becoming negative.
- Say 'you'. Use the third person to be objective ('it wasn't very clear' rather than 'you didn't explain) or the first person to be collaborative ('how can we simplify this?' rather than 'you have to simplify this').
- Damage confidence and motivation. The coach's role is to build skills, not to destroy them.

03 Rapport

(p21, ex10)

Speaker B

Situation 1

You are a consultant. You are meeting Speaker A to discuss how to reduce administrative costs in their company.

1 Make a list of ways the company could reduce its administrative costs, e.g. downsizing, outsourcing, teleworking, eliminating paper, investing in technology, etc.

2 Hold a meeting with Speaker A to get agreement for as many measures as possible. You will need to build rapport in order to get agreement for your ideas; try to adapt to Speaker A's communication style in terms of posture, gestures, facial expressions, breathing, voice, speech rate and key words and phrases.

Situation 2

You are meeting Speaker A, a consultant, to discuss how to improve staff motivation in your company.

1 Choose one of the following communication styles:

- You are very self-confident and energetic; you speak loudly and fluently and make expansive gestures.
- You are very reserved and tense; you speak quietly and hesitantly and your body language is defensive.
- You are nervous and laugh a lot; you speak quickly in a high voice and you are constantly changing your position and posture.
- You are extremely relaxed and comfortable; you smile and nod your head a lot; you speak slowly in a deep voice.

2 Hold a meeting with Speaker A. Disagree systematically with their ideas. Wait until you consider that they have adapted well to your communication style before giving your agreement.

05 Problems on the phone

Tackling problems (p34, ex7)

Speaker B

At the end of each conversation, give Speaker A a score out of ten for (a) helpfulness and (b) assertiveness.

1 Speaker A will phone you with a problem. You are very busy at the moment (you decide what you're doing) but try to give them some advice. If you can't, suggest someone they could phone who might be able to help.

2 You are Speaker A's boss. It's 6 pm and you still have a mountain of papers on your desk to go through before the morning (you decide what sort of papers they are). Phone Speaker A and ask them if they'd mind staying on for an hour or so to help you out. Be diplomatic but don't take no for an answer – unless they can suggest someone else.

3 Speaker A has just been promoted and you are now their boss. But a colleague from an overseas division of your company (you decide who) is going to spend the next three months working on an international project in your division and they need to be provided with a suitable office. Speaker A's office would be ideal (you decide why). Phone them and try to get their agreement without causing any bad feeling.

4 You have been working on an important report for nine months. Because of a lot of unforeseen difficulties and complications (you decide what) you are a month behind schedule and now need six, rather than two, more weeks to finish it. On completion of the report you are due to present your findings to senior management and you think they will be impressed. Much to your annoyance, however, you think your boss, Speaker A, is going to try to speed things up by bringing in someone else to help you finish the job and take half the credit for all your hard work.

06 Leading meetings

(p41, ex6)

Speaker A

Meeting 1: Genetic profiling (chair)

You have been asked by head office to chair a meeting on the possible introduction of genetic testing for job applicants at all levels. Your company already insists on a medical when people apply for a job, as well as psychometric tests and checks on possible criminal records. Now they think a genetic profile would help to reduce the risk of employing or promoting people with potentially serious diseases and mental health problems. The test would probably be voluntary – this hasn't been fully discussed with the legal department yet – but refusal to undergo it may affect a candidate's chance of employment or promotion.

You have read that vulnerability to stress, alcoholism and strokes – the three main causes of people being off work for prolonged periods – are all to some extent genetically inherited, but the idea of genetic testing does seem quite drastic and is bound to provoke a certain amount of hostility.

Leader's brief: Open the meeting, inform those present of HQ's proposal, make sure everyone gets a chance to speak and no one dominates. Try to avoid digressions and keep the meeting short. Give your own opinion only after everyone else has spoken and try to reach a decision on what recommendations to make to HQ.

Meeting 2: Employee surveillance (in favour)

You have heard a rumour that head office is planning to introduce a system of checking up on employees using PC monitoring software and closed circuit television (CCTV). You are about to attend a meeting to discuss the subject. At the moment you are firmly in favour of the idea, but listen to what the other participants have to say before finally making up your mind. You are sure that huge amounts of company time and money are being wasted by employees accessing gaming and adult websites during working hours. You've even heard some of the male staff joking about it. An article you read in Business Week claims that employees who play computer games whilst at work cost US firms $100 billion a year – or 2% of GDP. You also remember the famous case of Chevron, who, by failing to monitor computer use, ended up being sued by four female employees who had suffered sexual harassment through the internal email system. The company finally had to pay out $2.2 million in compensation.

Hidden agenda: You've heard that a junior manager in your department, who seems to have his sights set on your job, spends hours in private chatrooms on company time. In order to catch such people, you think the computer surveillance should be covert.

Meeting 3: Alternative management training (against)

You have heard a rumour that head office is planning to introduce a series of alternative management training courses for all levels of staff. You are about to attend a meeting to discuss the subject. At the moment you are not keen on the idea, but listen to what the other participants have to say before finally making up your mind. Frankly, you don't believe that 'fads' like this represent very good value for money. A friend of yours works for a firm that sent him and his colleagues to a Benedictine monastery to learn about 'Morality in the Workplace'. Predictably, it was thought to be a complete waste of time. You've also heard about weird courses offered by drama groups, orchestras, circuses, the army and even the prison service where executives spent a week in jail to build team spirit.

Hidden agenda: You have a close friend who is in charge of in-company training at a prestigious business school in the United States. If your company booked a course, you personally might get some kind of 'thank you'.

08 Promoting your ideas

Pitching your idea (p52)

Team 1

Standing Task Chair

The Standing Task Chair supports the body in a standing position which promotes a yoga-style, healthy working posture.

Designed for use with standing desks, the Standing Task Chair supports the body in three remarkable ways. The user sits on the seat and rests the knees against a cushion. A platform maintains the feet at an angled position. The seat is completely adjustable, and will pivot to allow more freedom of movement.

iPhone Pocket Tripod

The Pocket Tripod for iPhones can be folded flat and conveniently put away inside a wallet or pocket. Easily folded back out, it can be set up to support the iPhone in a number of positions.

The Pocket Tripod is only 3 mm thick – about the same thickness as two credit cards. It can be set up with the phone in either landscape or portrait mode – and can be easily tilted to almost any angle. Compared to most portable stands, the Pocket Tripod gives smooth, 90° sweeps of tilt adjustment. This lets the photographer have precise aim when using the phone's camera. This is true flexibility!

09 Relationship-building

A dinner invitation (p60)

Guest: Ulterior motive

You've secretly applied for and been shortlisted for a better job (you decide what) at another company in San Francisco. You've been fairly happy in your current job and you don't want to upset your host, so break the news gently at some point during the evening and try to see if they'll write you a good reference. Be careful what you say and be ready to change the subject if things don't go according to plan!

09 Relationship-building

Getting out of the office (p58, ex4)

Speaker B

Situation 1

Background: You're playing golf with Speaker A, an IT security specialist. As IT director for a major insurance company, you frequently engage their services. It's a beautiful spring morning.

Situation: Your game is a bit off today. Although you're a better player than Speaker A and usually beat them, they were actually a shot ahead on the 16th hole. Then they were very unlucky to drop two shots on the 17th, putting you back in the lead.

Hidden agenda: You've always got on well with Speaker A and rate them very highly as an IT expert. However, the consultancy they work for charges extremely high fees – higher than any of their competitors. You invited Speaker A to play golf because you've been considering offering them a permanent job within your company, but don't mention this straightaway. They seem to have something on their mind – or perhaps it's just that they don't like losing!

You start: Oh, bad luck! Looks like it's all down to the last hole ...

Situation 2

Background: You work in the sales department of an international sports goods company. You're playing tennis with Speaker A, the sales director. When you started playing it was a warm summer afternoon, but it's just clouded over and looks like it might even rain.

Situation: You were warned that your boss takes tennis very seriously and doesn't like losing, but, even though you're not really trying very hard, you beat them 6-2 in the first set and you're 4-1 up in the second. You should probably lose a few games to make them feel better, but you've noticed the head of marketing is watching you from the next court and you'd like to impress them.

Hidden agenda: You've only been in the sales department for a few months, but already you hate it. Direct contact with customers all day is just not you and you don't get on with the rest of the team, who are all very competitive. You studied strategic marketing at university and that's what you really want to do, but there were no vacancies when you applied to the company, so you took the job in sales to gain experience. Big mistake. You keep meaning to talk to your boss about your problems, but now doesn't seem like a great moment!

Speaker A will start.

Scenario E
(p117, ex11)

Mediation checklist	Yes	No
Did the mediator:		
describe the process and set the ground rules?		
have each party speak in turn?		
listen carefully and prevent interruptions?		
identify the main issues?		
generate alternatives?		
hold one-on-one meetings if necessary?		
encourage agreement but impose nothing?		
write up what was agreed and get the parties to sign up to it?		

Assertiveness checklist	Yes	No
Did participants behave and speak assertively rather than passively or aggressively?		
Did participants use 'I' to describe their feelings rather than 'you' to criticize others?		
Did participants use 'I'd like' rather than 'you can't /shouldn't'?		
Did participants describe facts rather than imposing judgements and opinions?		
Did participants give specific examples rather than making generalizations?		
Did participants offer incentives rather than making threats?		

14 Out and about

In-flight conversations (p91, ex11)

Speaker B

Hold short conversations with a fellow passenger, Speaker A, on three different international flights.

Use the information below to get you started, but invent any extra information you need to keep the conversation going for a minute or two.

1 **Flight BA1311 from Dubai to London Heathrow, business class (9pm)**

- You are the senior partner in a small software company specialising in computer-assisted engineering applications for the oil industry.
- You are travelling back home from a series of meetings with potential clients in Dubai. It's been an exhausting trip and not as successful as you would have liked.
- Frankly, you'd just like to skip dinner and try and get some sleep. First, however, you think you'll update your client files on your Blackberry.
- You are not pleased to see that the person sitting next to you, Speaker A, has a young child with them. There goes your relaxing flight!

2 **Flight AF6001 from Paris to Rio de Janeiro, economy class (3am)**

- You are a financial speculator who specialises in medical, pharmaceutical and biotech stocks.
- You are coming back from a meeting in Paris to Rio where you live with your American partner, the crime novelist A. J. Bell.
- Due to the cancellation of your business class Varig flight, you've ended up in economy class on an early morning Air France flight instead. And you are already regretting this – there's barely room to move and the plane seems to be experiencing some turbulence. You've never been a great flyer and are starting to feel a bit sick.
- Perhaps talking to the person sitting next to you would take your mind off it. But they seem to be reading a book. Actually, the book looks quite familiar ...

3 **Flight LH1706 from Los Angeles to Munich, first class (2pm)**

- You are a highly paid German-English interpreter based in Munich and travelling back from LA, where you've been assisting at the American launch of the new BMW sports car.
- When you arrived for your business class flight this morning, you were delighted to find that it was overbooked and that you had been upgraded to first class.
- You've had quite an exciting, if stressful, week in LA and are now thoroughly enjoying the flight home. You've had an excellent lunch and have just tuned into the in-flight movie on your personal video screen.
- You've already seen the film, but don't mind seeing it again as it stars your favourite actor, Al Pacino. And anyway, the person sitting next to you looks like some big-shot multimillionaire business type.

15 Delegation

(p97, ex11)

Speaker B

1 Speaker A is your manager and has a task to delegate to you. You are new in your job; last time someone delegated a task to you it wasn't clear what they wanted and it ended badly. Make sure you know exactly what you have to do and how you have to do it this time.

2 You are Speaker A's manager. You need them to organize an event (you decide what and why). Speaker A is a very experienced member of the team and has often done this type of task before. Make sure you leave room for them to use their skills and initiative.

3 Speaker A is your manager and has a task to delegate to you. You have been a member of the team for two or three years and are confident in your ability to do the job. However, your manager is not always very clear about what they want and when they want it, so make sure you get enough information about the task.

4 You are Speaker A's manager. You need to delegate a task to them (you decide what and why). Speaker B is new in the job; they are very enthusiastic but a little too optimistic about their skills and abilities in your opinion.

Scenario B
(p47, ex10)

Presentations checklist	Yes	No
Was the objective clearly stated?		
Was the presentation clearly structured and signposted?		
Was the presentation the right length; not too short, not too long?		
Was the presenter's body language appropriate?		
Was the presenter's voice comfortable and pleasant to listen to?		
If the presenter used visual aids, were they clear and helpful?		
Did the presenter invite and answer questions?		
Overall, was the presentation interesting and convincing?		

Coaching checklist	Yes	No
Did the coach get your permission to give feedback?		
Did the coach invite you to give feedback first?		
Did the coach start with the positives?		
Was the feedback specific and constructive?		
Did the coach use questions and indirect language to help you find solutions?		
Did the coach encourage and motivate you?		

02 Information exchange
Breaking the bad news (p17, ex1)
Speaker C

Proposal: Language training

- Board keen to market products more internationally
- English now language of international business but many staff (65%) already speak it
- In board's view, Chinese is business language of the future
- Mandarin, however, is one of world's most difficult languages
- Therefore, compulsory Chinese lessons (in employees' own time) to start immediately
- All new managerial staff to be obliged to accept 12-month transfer to new subsidiary in Beijing

16 Teleconferencing
Desert island blues (p104)
Creative Director of RJK (UK)

email

Well, we've had eight days of incessant rain, two cameras damaged in transit and now the electricity generator's broken down. Whose idea was it to use a real desert island for the shoot?

Flying Sandra in and out from Fiji every day is proving totally impractical. Didn't I say using a big Hollywood star was asking for trouble? She came down with some kind of tropical fever two days ago and hasn't come out of her hotel room since. So far we've only got about 15% of the commercial in the can.

To keep costs down the crew are staying on Oamu-Oamu until we're finished. Today is the first fine day, but there's still no sign of Sandra, so we're just getting some footage of the island.

I strongly suggest we either fly out a replacement or seriously consider filming the whole thing in a studio in Britain.

Ridley Hurst, Film Unit Director

4

email

No doubt you've already heard from Ridley. The good news is that Sandra's PA tells me she may be well enough for filming tomorrow. My suggestion is that we forget Oamu-Oamu and find a nice secluded spot here in Fiji. I'm sure that would suit Sandra much better if she's still not feeling too well. I've sent some of the team out scouting the beaches for possible locations.

The bad news is that the animal handler's gone missing. You remember that we wanted to use real animals on this shoot instead of adding them digitally later? Well, now I'm left here with 36 African parrots and a rather lethal-looking python.

Ridley seems to think we'd be better off doing the whole thing in a studio, but I think it would be a shame to pack up and leave now we're all here. Might be rather hard to explain the unnecessary expense to the client, too. Are we insured for this?

Amelia Devine, Senior Account Manager, RJK (UK)

Scenario D
(p99, ex13)

Speaker A

Meeting 1

Lead a meeting with Speaker B to explain one of the following proposed changes:

- Moving the office to a new location.
- Outsourcing production to a low-cost country.
- A four-day week in return for a salary reduction of 15%.
- Your own idea.

Explain your proposals and try to get a commitment to support the change from the other participants.

Meeting 2

Listen to B's proposals; ask any questions and raise any objections you can think of.

06 Leading meetings
(p41, ex6)

Speaker C

Meeting 1: Genetic profiling (in favour)

You have heard a rumour that head office is planning to introduce genetic testing for future job applicants. You are about to attend a meeting to discuss the subject. At the moment you are basically in favour of the idea, but listen to what the other participants have to say before finally making up your mind. You know that 350 million working days are lost each year in the EU alone through illness – stress being the cause of 41 million of those. UK companies lose £13 billion annually because of employees going off sick. If people with potential social problems (such as alcoholism or drug abuse) could be screened out at the job application stage, it would make for a healthier workforce and could save the firm millions.

Hidden agenda: Your department has been particularly affected by people taking sick leave. At the moment you are trying to cope without three of your key managers – one of them, you suspect, has a drink problem.

Meeting 2: Employee surveillance (against)

You have heard a rumour that head office is planning to introduce a system of checking up on employees using PC monitoring software and closed circuit television (CCTV). You are about to attend a meeting to discuss the subject. At the moment you are very much against the idea, but listen to what the other participants have to say before finally making up your mind. You firmly believe that a good work atmosphere is built on trust and that such security measures should only be taken when there is strong evidence to suggest that company facilities are being abused. Moreover, you suspect that phone taps, video cameras and PC monitoring may just be the thin end of the wedge. You've heard in some companies workers have also been videotaped in toilets and locker rooms and investigators have even been hired to follow them home. What next? Electronic tagging devices? Implants?

Hidden agenda: You often surf the Internet on your office PC during coffee and lunch breaks (never during working hours, however) and regularly log on to chatroom channels. You see this as valuable networking and not an abuse of company Internet access. Still, if Internet monitoring was introduced, you'd prefer the company to announce the fact and not investigate past use.

Meeting 3: Alternative management training (chair)

You have been asked by head office to chair a meeting on the possible introduction of a series of alternative management training courses. In the past, your firm has sent junior members of staff on practical office skills courses and middle and senior management on executive courses at several top business schools. But the feedback has sometimes been rather negative. As people at all levels in your company require a high degree of creativity, HQ is proposing to hire the services of a number of 'arts and business' companies to help employees 'think outside the box'.

Suggestions so far include: working with a renowned artist to produce a 5m x 30m company mural to be displayed at HQ; putting on a variety show with the help of professional actors with all members of staff taking part in song, dance and comedy routines; choreographing a modern ballet to dramatize the challenges facing the company; and music lessons from professional musicians leading to an end-of-year company jazz session. Many big-name companies have found similar training to be highly enjoyable and successful – why not your company too?

Leader's brief: Open the meeting, inform those present of HQ's proposal, make sure everyone gets a chance to speak and no one dominates. Try to avoid digressions and keep the meeting short. Give your own opinion only after everyone else has spoken and try to reach a decision on what recommendations to make to HQ.

Scenario E
(p117, ex11)

Speaker A

You are the mediator. You have organized a meeting to mediate between Speakers B (Sales) and C (Marketing). Their company sells high-quality tea all over the world, but sales are falling and they have developed opposing strategies to try to rescue the company.

Make sure you remain impartial throughout the session. Keep order, encourage both parties to speak one at a time, identify the main issues and phrase any ideas of your own as suggestions. You can put each party on hold for a maximum of three minutes for a single private session with the other party. Make sure you write down whatever is agreed and get both parties to agree to sign up to it before you close the meeting. If agreement cannot be reached, ask the parties if they think a further session would be a good idea.

08 Promoting your ideas

(p52, ex6)

Team 2

Tag on That

Why not personalize everything from a peanut jar to a bottle of cola with Tag on That? This is a specialty printer than can print on just about any surface.

They're calling this "the world's first affordable Specialty Printer Machine." The Tag on That has a flexible stamp that allows printing on flat, curved or even rough surfaces. The device can also work on cupcakes, sweets or even pieces of cheese. We offer a complete online training program for the system with tips, techniques, ideas and support.

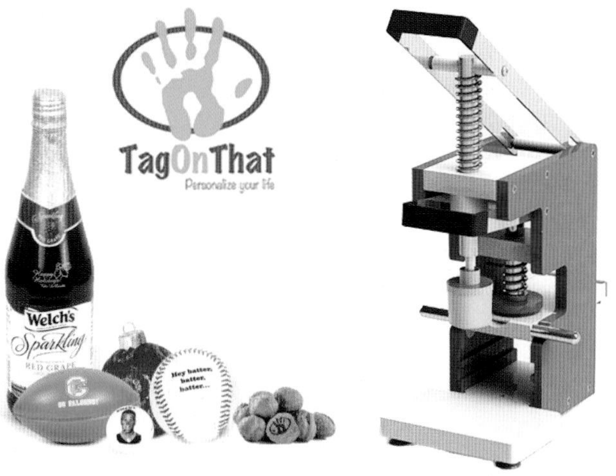

Bulletproof paint extracted from rice

A research chemist has announced a remarkable development – paints made from rice husks that can resist bullets, fire, bacteria or rust.

The main material used to develop all four paints is the nano silica found in the rice husk. The bulletproof paint vest requires less layers than conventional vests, so it is more lightweight. And it can even stop a bullet shot from 2 meters away. Moreover, the flame-resistant paint can protect a surface for up to 6 hours. The antibacterial paint can kill up to 99% of bacteria. Finally, the rustproof paint can keep an object under the ocean rust-free for up to 10 years.

16 Teleconferencing

Desert island blues (p104)

Account Director of RJK (UK)

email

Sorry to bother you on holiday, but we're having major problems with the Vivacity shoot. As you've no doubt heard through the grapevine, we're running six days over schedule owing to bad weather, logistical problems and a leading lady with a fever …

I've been asked to look into alternatives and have come up with the following, which I thought I'd better copy you in on:

1 If we fly the film crew home to do the commercial in a studio, with set building, studio hire and post-production, we could be looking at an extra €750,000. Plus we'd be unlikely to finish on schedule.

2 Finding an A-list actress to replace Sandra at such short notice would be extremely difficult, although there is provision for her replacement, if unable to perform, in the terms of our contract. I did speak to someone at a lookalike agency who said he had 'Sandra's twin' and could let us have her for €5,000 a day.

Jason Roberts, Account Manager, RJK (UK)

6

email

I must say I am very disappointed with the number of delays on the Vivacity project. These problems with the film shoot are just the latest in a series of expensive mistakes. I trust the extra costs will not be coming out of our agreed budget.

Your Group President Nathan Auerbach tried to persuade me over lunch that everything was going well, but now I'm told we may have lost our actress for the commercial. I should emphasize that in France the use of celebrities to endorse products is a proven and powerful advertising technique. Sandra's appearance in the Vivacity commercial was part of the original brief to your agency and any replacement would have to be approved by my marketing department.

I might add that, as RJK's Account Director with overall responsibility for our account, I'm surprised to see you've found time to take a vacation in the middle of this crisis.

Thierry DuPont, Director of Marketing, Éternelle (Europe)

06 Leading meetings
(p41, ex6)

Speaker B

Meeting 1: Genetic profiling (against)

You have heard a rumour that head office is planning to introduce genetic testing for future job applicants. You are about to attend a meeting to discuss the subject. At the moment you are strongly against the idea, but listen to what the other participants have to say before finally making up your mind. One thing you are fairly sure of is that genetic screening without consent would be illegal under civil law. You certainly consider it unethical. Also, since some of the conditions screened for (such as sickle cell disease) affect mostly black people, and others (such as breast and ovarian cancer) solely women, you are concerned that the tests could easily lead to racial and sexual discrimination.

Hidden Agenda: There is a genetically inherited disease that runs in your family. Although you do not have the condition yourself, you are worried that it might show up in a genetic test and that you might be discriminated against if you applied for promotion.

Meeting 2: Employee surveillance (chair)

You have been asked by head office to chair a meeting on the possible introduction of surveillance and electronic security equipment to check up on employees of the company. In your business confidentiality is essential as many of your workers are dealing with highly classified information. Of course, a lot of your company files are encrypted, but leaks still happen. HQ is also concerned about the amount of time employees appear to be spending making personal phone calls and sending private emails. Details of what system to install have not yet been fully discussed, but suggestions include Internet monitoring software, random phone tapping and closed circuit television (CCTV) throughout the building.

You yourself are a little alarmed at the number of unnecessary emails sent back and forth over the company intranet and have overheard staff making international phone calls that were clearly not business. Monitoring Internet access and phone use is common practice in many companies these days and you don't see why anyone would object unless they had something to hide. CCTV seems a bit radical, however.

Leader's brief: Open the meeting, inform those present of HQ's proposal, make sure everyone gets a chance to speak and no one dominates. Try to avoid digressions and keep the meeting short. Give your own opinion only after everyone else has spoken and try to reach a decision on what recommendations to make to HQ.

Meeting 3: Alternative management training (in favour)

You have heard a rumour that head office is planning to introduce a series of alternative management training courses for all levels of staff. You are about to attend a meeting to discuss the subject. At the moment you are fairly enthusiastic about the idea, but listen to what the other participants have to say before finally making up your mind. You already have an MBA, but have never found what you learnt at business school much use in the real world of business. On the other hand, an ex-colleague of yours went on a course to learn about negotiating technique from an Olympic gold medal-winning judo player and says it was the best business training she's ever had.

Hidden agenda: You have a favourite cousin who runs a company that teaches business people creativity through song, poetry and drama workshops, stand-up comedy and exotic sports like Zen archery and rodeo riding. He's not doing too well at the moment and could do with more clients.

Scenario D
(p99, ex13)

Speaker B

Meeting 1

Listen to Speaker A's proposals; ask any questions and raise any objections you can think of.

Meeting 2

Lead a meeting with Speaker A to explain one of the following proposed changes:

- A merger with your main competitor.
- Introducing teleworking for all staff.
- Two weeks' intensive English training per year for all staff – to be deducted from annual leave.
- Your own idea.

Explain your proposals and try to get a commitment to support the change from the other participants.

11 Stress
(p71, ex13)

Speaker B

1 Speaker A is your manager. You are suffering from stress because your workload and responsibilities are constantly increasing. Several people have left the company and have not been replaced; you work 12 hours a day and haven't had a holiday for more than a year; there is constant pressure to reduce costs and improve productivity, but you are receiving more and more customer complaints. You feel exhausted and unable to produce the results that are required from you.

Talk to your manager about the problem.

2 You are Speaker A's manager. Speaker A is suffering from stress. Try to:

- help them express their feelings
- identify the source of stress
- find ways to relieve pressure
- find ways to adapt to their situation.

15 Delegation
(p97, ex11)

Delegation checklist	Manager's opinion	Employee's opinion
Did the employee receive all the information required to perform the task?		
Did the employee receive unnecessary details about the task?		
Was the management style appropriate for the staff development level?		
Were manager and employee confident that the desired outcome would be achieved?		

17 Negotiating deals
The recording contract (p111, ex5)

Team B: Starburst Records (executives and lawyers)

You are very excited about this band's prospects. The Penitents are musically exceptionally strong with proven songwriting abilities. What's more, they have already generated a lot of media interest. However, the risks with a new signing are always high. Fashions change quickly in your business and you should bear this in mind in your dealings with the band's management.

Read your negotiating objectives below and then work with your team to plan your overall strategy. In particular, make sure you know which of your objectives are:

1 tradeables (things you'll concede to get what you really want in return)
2 ideals (things you'd really like to get, but not if it costs you the deal)
3 essentials (things you absolutely have to get or the deal's off)

1 **Band line-up** Three of the four members of the band – the lead singer/rhythm guitarist, lead guitarist and bass guitarist are exceptionally talented, though the lead guitarist has a reputation for hitting members of the paparazzi and was recently involved in an unpleasant incident aboard an airliner that resulted in his being banned for life. The weak link is the drummer, who simply must be replaced.

2 **Term** You are prepared to offer a one-album deal, but would like to retain an option on at least two subsequent albums, if the first is successful. You'd also like to keep the performing and recording rights to all the songs – otherwise, if you don't renew their contract and they later become successful with a different label, you won't be able to profit from their backlist of songs.

3 **Royalties** You think a 10% royalty on net receipts from album sales would be fair. This might be renegotiable after the album, but you'd like to offset the initial risk of taking on the band by maximizing profits in the early stages.

4 **Deductions** If sales of the first album are good (at least 200,000 units), you may want to run a TV campaign. In this case you would like to deduct the cost of 20% of this from the band's royalties.

5 **Advances** Since advances are normally non-repayable, you'd prefer to offer a relatively modest one on the first album (say $120,000) and promise higher ones on later albums once the band is established.

6 **Territory** As you'll be spending a substantial amount of time and money on promoting The Penitents, you require total 'universal rights' to sell their music globally.

7 **Touring** With a band like The Penitents touring is a key part of building a fan-base. The band is particularly strong live and you would like to capitalize on that. You'd expect them to tour for at least six months in their first year. Your preferred schedule would be: release two singles, record the first album and do the tour. You'd want 70% of the revenue from ticket sales but will pay for hotels, coach travel, clothes and food while on tour.

8 **Songwriting** The standard songwriter-music publisher split on fees for airplay on radio and TV is 50:50. You're quite happy with this arrangement as long as you retain the rights (see item 2).

02 Information exchange
Making things clear (p14, ex1)

1 American
2 Russian
3 German
4 Brazilian
5 French
6 Italian
7 British
8 Chinese
9 Indian
10 Japanese

Scenario E
(p117, ex11)

Speaker B

You are in charge of International Sales for a company that sells high-quality tea all over the world. Recently, sales have decreased due to competition from cheaper brands, so you have decided to defend your market share by temporarily reducing your prices. You have just negotiated a deal with all the major supermarket chains; you have agreed to give a large discount if the supermarkets promote your brand as their 'best buy'.

However, you are furious with the Marketing team (Speaker C.) Without consulting you, they have agreed to pay a top film star (ask Speaker C for their name) to star in a campaign of TV commercials and magazine ads endorsing your product. You consider that this high value, low volume policy is suicidal. It would not only force you to raise prices and cancel the deal with the supermarket chains, but could also lead to job cuts in production and sales if the company continues to lose market share. You feel that Marketing don't understand how price-sensitive the market is; their insistence on maintaining an upmarket image and high prices is the explanation for the company's difficulties. You are determined to force Marketing to cancel the advertising campaign and support your strategy. Invent any other details as necessary.

03 Rapport
(p21, ex10)

Speaker A

Situation 1

You are meeting Speaker B, a consultant, to discuss how to reduce administrative costs in your company.

1 Choose one of the following communication styles:

- You are very self-confident and energetic; you speak loudly and fluently and make expansive gestures.
- You are very reserved and tense; you speak quietly and hesitantly and your body language is defensive.
- You are nervous and laugh a lot; you speak quickly in a high voice and you are constantly changing your position and posture.
- You are extremely relaxed and comfortable; you smile and nod your head a lot; you speak slowly in a deep voice.

2 Hold a meeting with Speaker B. Disagree systematically with their ideas. Wait until you consider that they have adapted well to your communication style before giving your agreement.

Situation 2

You are a consultant. You are meeting Speaker B to discuss how to improve staff motivation in their company.

1 Make a list of ways the company could improve staff motivation, e.g. training and personal development, incentive schemes, bonuses, mentoring and coaching, away days, etc.

2 Hold a meeting with Speaker A to get agreement for as many measures as possible. You will need to build rapport in order to get agreement for your ideas; try to adapt to Speaker B's communication style in terms of posture, gestures, facial expressions, breathing, voice, speech rate and key words and phrases.

04 Voice and visuals
Giving feedback (p26, ex1)

Speaker B: Presenter

You work for a major management consultancy and have just given a presentation to an important Taiwanese client. The presentation didn't go very well and unfortunately your boss was in the audience.

You are meeting your boss now, and are not expecting very good feedback. Make it clear that the disaster wasn't entirely your fault. Defend yourself using the following information, and assure your boss that this will never happen again.

- You've been asking your boss for a new laptop for ages – the one you've got just can't handle PowerPoint properly.
- You've been on the road for four weeks and are completely exhausted – this is your tenth major presentation. To make matters worse, the laundry ruined your best suit and left you with virtually nothing to wear.
- Some of your jokes may not have translated very well, but you were just trying to break the ice.
- You're sure the DVD you were going to use was stolen from your hotel bedroom.
- No one checked the microphone: the amplifier was turned down much too low.

Useful language

How was I supposed to know ...?
It's not my fault. You should have ...
Somebody should have ...
It might have helped if ...
Look, I'm not trying to make excuses, but ...
I can hardly be blamed for ...ing, can I?
Rest assured, it won't happen again.

Listening scripts

01 BUSINESS OR PLEASURE?

 1.01

Speaker 1

Okay, well, now, we don't know a lot about what the team might be interested in. And, this is going to be a mixed group with their partners so it'll be difficult to choose something they'll all like. But, since this is the first visit to Britain for some of them, I suggest we go for something, you know, quintessentially British. The main thing is to make sure nothing can go wrong. Most important, let's plan on something weatherproof! And we definitely need to provide a bit more than just an expensive dinner. What about doing something cultural?

Speaker 2

Hm, I think culture can be tricky. We don't want to drag the group somewhere, only for them to be bored out of their minds. We just need a pleasant setting to be able to socialize. Let's think of a good restaurant where we can relax, enjoy decent food and talk about business. Of course, we need to check if any of the team are vegetarians before we make any bookings.

Speaker 3

Hang on. We'll have plenty of time to talk business in the meetings. This is about making sure we show them a good time. Russians are very people-oriented. This is an opportunity for us to build a good working relationship with them, you know, a bit of team spirit. In some ways it could even be a team-building kind of thing. And, let me tell you, Russians certainly like fine dining!

So top quality catering, sure, but let's offer them something a bit special as well. And keep business out of it!

Speaker 4

Well, I think the main thing is to make the visit as personal as possible. I mean, we could spend a fortune on attending some big event, but that's not very personal, is it? In fact, spending a little less on the event might mean you could afford to do something extra for the team members – I'm not necessarily talking gifts, but something. And, by the way, I happen to know that their project leader, Yuri, spent a year studying in London, so we might think about taking them somewhere else. That means travel expenses, of course, but I'm sure we can keep those within reason.

 1.02

Conversation 1

A Hi, mind if I join you?

B Er, not at all. Be my guest.

A Only if I have to sit through 'Rule Britannia' by the Band of the Royal Scots Dragoon Guards once more, I think I'll scream.

B And I thought you Americans were supposed to like all of that traditional British stuff.

A Yeah, well, you can have too much of a good thing. Thought I'd come out here and enjoy the view. I must say, though, it was an excellent lunch. Fabulous ship too.

B Yes, isn't it? I'm James McRae, by the way. BP, engineering division.

A Hello, James. I'm ...

B Helen Keating. Exxon Mobil.

A Yes, how did you ... oh ... ? Have we met somewhere before?

B We have indeed, but I obviously failed to make much of an impression.

A Wait a minute. It's not like me to forget a face. I know – Riyadh. The Petrochemicals Conference. I thought I recognized you.

B As matter of fact, we had dinner together.

A You're kidding! Now, I think I would have remembered that.

B Well, there were rather a lot of us in the group. At least 40. I don't think we actually spoke.

A Aha. Okay. Yes, it's all coming back to me now. I seem to remember spending most of the evening trying to avoid some annoying little guy called Alan.

B Alan Sullivan. My boss.

A Oops! I'm sorry. I didn't mean to ...

B No problem. He's not my favourite person either. Anyway, Helen, looks like we've got the best part of the Royal Yacht to ourselves this afternoon. How about another drink?

A Okay. Why not?

 1.03

Conversation 2

A So, Mr Ishida, let me freshen your glass.

B Thank you. I'm fine.

A Some more strawberries, then, perhaps?

B Er, not at the moment, thank you.

A I am sorry about this weather. Typical English summer, I'm afraid. The forecast did say we might have showers. But I'm sure it'll blow over in half an hour or so. So, how are you enjoying the match?

B Ah, very entertaining, I'm sure ...

A Good. Splendid ... So, tell me, have you been to one of these big tournaments before? The American Open perhaps?

B Ah, no, I haven't.

A Ah. But I hear you're quite a tennis fan, though.

B Er, not really. In fact, I never watch tennis normally.

A Oh, ... I see. My marketing people must have made a mistake.

B Maybe they meant table tennis. I used to play for my university in Tokyo – many years ago.

A Table tennis! Ah, yes. I understand the Japanese are world table tennis champions, isn't that right?

B As a matter of fact, that's the Chinese.

A Ah, yes, of course ... Erm, so, do you still play?

B Not any more. Much too old for running around now.

A Oh, I'm sure that's not true.

B I assure you it is true, Mr Thompson. Bad heart, you see. Doctor's orders.

A Oh, right. Sorry. Erm, ... I see the Nikkei's looking strong. That must be good news for you.

B Not especially. It makes our exports more expensive.

A The world economy is still really unpredictable, don't you think?

B It may seem that way for now, but I'm still hoping for some stability in the markets.

A Ah, well, I suppose, er ... Oh, look, the rain's stopped! Yes, the players are coming back on. Excellent. So, shall we return to our seats?

C Quiet, please. Nadal to serve. Nadal leads by three games to two and by two sets to love.

1.04

Conversation 1

A Alistair, we've been here nearly three hours! Can't we just make our excuses and go? You know how I hate these things.

B Look, Fiona, I'm not enjoying myself any more than you are, but this is business. Besides, I need to speak to Julian about this Internet advertising idea of his.

A Oh, all right. Where is Julian, anyway? We haven't seen him all evening ...

C Hello! You must be Julian's guests. I don't think we've met. I'm Dan Wilson, Creative Director at JJK Advertising. I work with Julian.

B Ah, pleased to meet you, Mr Wilson. No, we've not met. Julian's mentioned your name, of course. Alistair Hamilton. And this is my wife, Fiona.

C A pleasure to meet you both at last. And please call me Dan.

A We were just wondering what this pile of dirty laundry was doing in the middle of an art gallery.

B Fiona!

C So, you're not a fan of contemporary art then, Fiona – you don't mind me calling you Fiona, do you? Actually, this, er, 'dirty laundry', as you call it, came second in this year's Turner Prize, believe it or not.

A Doesn't surprise me in the least, but, er, still just looks like dirty laundry to me, I'm afraid.

C Well, yes, but I don't think that's what the artist would call it.

A What does he call it, then?

C Erm, I'm not sure. I'll check the catalogue for you ... Here we are – erm, exhibit 12, oh, 'Dirty Laundry'.

A What did I tell you?

C Yes, quite. Erm, Alistair, I wonder if we could have a word? Julian tells me you're not very happy with the new Internet campaign.

B Er, yes. Would you excuse us a moment, Fiona? Dan and I need to talk.

A Oh, don't mind me. There's a heap of broken glass in the room next door I'm just dying to see.

B Er, right. Well, I'll catch you later, then ... Now, look, Dan, the thing is ...

 **1.05**

Conversation 2

A Ricardo! Glad you could make it.

B Hello, Tom. I wouldn't have missed it for the world. It's not every day I get invited to something like this. I hear Webber's out, so it should be a good race.

A Yes, it certainly evens things up a bit with Red Bull down to one car. Talking of races, how's the South African bid going? I heard it was just between you and Swedish Steel now.

B Hm, yes, the negotiations are still going on, but we're hopeful. I don't think the Swedes can beat us on price.

A Well, let me know how it goes. We'd be happy to organize the transportation if you need it. We'd do you a good deal.

B Sure, I'll certainly keep you in mind if we win the contract.

A Great ... Ricardo, there's someone I'd like you to meet.

B Oh, really?

A Yes, but first let me get you something to drink. Can't have you standing there with an empty glass. What can I get you?

B Just mineral water for now, thanks.

A Oh, all right ... Here you go.

B Thanks. So, who's this person you wanted me to meet?

A Ah, yes ... Oh, here she is now. Élise, this is Ricardo Piquet. Ricardo, Élise de Cadenet. Élise is ...

C Hello, Ricardo. Long time no see. What is it, five years?

B Hello, Élise. Must be five at least. You haven't changed a bit.

C Neither have you!

A Ah, I see you two know each other already.

C Ricardo and I go back a long way, Tom.

B Yes, actually, we first met in Monaco – at the Grand Prix, funnily enough ... So, Élise, last I heard you got married.

C That's right. In fact we only just got back from our honeymoon last month. But now it's back to work. It's been really hectic setting up this new business in Biarritz.

A Er, well, I'll leave you two to chat. See you later. Don't forget the race starts at three.

B Yes, see you later, Tom. So, Élise, how about something to drink?

C Mm, sounds good. I'll have whatever you're having.

02 INFORMATION EXCHANGE

 **1.06**

A Okay, people. Let's get the ball rolling. Well, you've all seen the latest figures and I don't need to tell you they're not good. It's clearly time for a reality check, ladies and gentlemen. This division is about to go under if we don't change our attitude and fast. What we need is a complete change of mindset. We need to synergize and take a much more proactive approach to product development. The same tired old ideas simply won't work any more. If we always do what we've always done, then we'll always get what we've always got. And what got us where we are won't get us where we're going.

B I'm sorry?

A What I mean is we need to be thinking outside the box, maximizing our creativity. Yes, that's right. I'm talking about nothing less than a complete paradigm shift in the management of this company.

B What's he talking about?

C I don't know.

A Okay, the bottom line is: if we don't figure out how to turn this operation around, we have no future in this business. So, let's look at the big picture and then see if we can drill down to the details.

D Can I just say something, Daryl?

A Fire away, Kelly.

D Erm, I don't think we're quite with you.

A I'm trying to say that it's very important I get your buy-in on this. What we have to do is establish what our core competencies are and then benchmark ourselves against the current market leader. Right now we're struggling just to compete. If we can only learn from our competitors, then we'll be able to upskill our own people, ramp up product development, and start to take this company to the next level.

C Erm, and you really want our input on this?

A Yes, Nigel. Change begins at the grassroots in an organization. Empowerment – that's what this is all about.

D Daryl?

A Yes, Kelly.

D Have you ever played buzzword bingo?

 **1.07**

A Right. That brings us on to our main business this morning – the new Quasar Online Gaming System. As you already know, the news is not particularly good. In spite of a considerable investment in design and marketing, I'm sorry to report that the project has not been a complete success.

B Not a complete success? What you mean is it's failed – dismally!

A Now let's not overreact, Alan. Certainly, it's failed to meet our original expectations. And, yes, technically speaking, we have run into negative profit ...

B Negative profit! What do you mean negative profit? You mean we've made a loss – an enormous loss if these figures are anything to go by!

C Can we come back to the figures later, Alan, if that's okay? First, let's consider why sales are so disappointing. Now, in my view, it's not the product, but the market. I think there's a general lack of consumer confidence ...

B In other words, sales are falling. Look, I'm sorry, Hannah, but you're just looking for excuses. It's obvious that Quasar is simply not innovative enough for today's market.

A Alan, we leave innovation to companies like Sony and Nintendo. What we do is clone the technology and do it cheaper.

C Alan, you know we've always been a market-driven organization ...

B Market-driven? What you really mean is we've never had an original idea. I say we need to be developing an innovative new product line ...

A What, when the market's so massively oversupplied? I don't think so. Now is not the time to expand, but to consolidate.

B So what you're saying is, let's do nothing.

A No, I'm saying let's consolidate.

B I see. And what will this 'consolidation' mean in terms of our staff? Redundancies, I suppose.

C Well, obviously, there will have to be some restructuring of the department.

B You mean people are going to lose their jobs.

C It's a possibility, yes. And we may also have to consider outsourcing production to cut costs.

B In other words, our assembly plant may be closed down too. I can't believe I'm hearing this!

A Of course, we won't be able to finalize anything today.

B You mean we'll have to hold another meeting! If we've all still got a job by then, that is.

A Yes, well, I'm glad you raised that point, Alan.

B What do you mean?

1.08

Meeting 1

A Right, I'm allowing an hour and a half for this meeting. Kate is going to fill us in on how the appraisals went. That'll take about a quarter of an hour or so. So that only gives us 45 minutes to deal with everything else. We'd better get started.

B Sorry, I thought we had an hour and a half.

A What? Oh, yeah, sorry. We've got 75 minutes, haven't we? Still, there's a lot to get through.

Meeting 2

A Look, it's no good going on about pay rises. We pay nearly twice what most of our competitors do. And I really don't see how people can expect another salary increase this year, when they're already earning three times the average rate.

B Hang on a second. You said we pay twice as much, not three times.

A Hm? Oh, all right, twice as much, then. It's still a lot more than everybody else.

Meeting 3

A You know as well as I do that this project was supposed to take 16 weeks. And this isn't the first time we've run over budget, is it? I mean a 20% overspend is pretty serious. And surely three months was sufficient time to complete the project.

B Just a minute. I thought you said 16 weeks, not three months.

A Okay, okay, that's four months, then. But you've taken nearly six.

Meeting 4

A Frankly, with the Asian economic situation the way it is and both the euro and the dollar going up and down, we're not doing well in the Far East. South America is where we should be concentrating our efforts. As a matter of fact, Brazil is now our second biggest market after China.

B Hold on. Didn't you just say we're not doing well in the Far East?

A Well, I meant apart from China, obviously! China's always been a huge market for tobacco products.

Meeting 5

A I'm sorry, but I don't want us bringing in people from outside the company to sort this problem out. There's a lot of highly confidential information on our intranet. And we should really be able to deal with this ourselves. There's a guy I play golf with who runs his own consultancy. He's offered to help us out.

B Wait a moment. You just said you didn't want to bring in people from outside the company.

A Erm, well, what I mean is I don't want just anybody. This guy's different. I've known him for years.

1.09

A Okay, everyone. It's bad news, I'm afraid. As you may have heard, the latest European sales figures are looking extremely disappointing.

B Are you saying they've fallen short of projections again?

A I'm afraid so. In fact, we may be 30% down. Now, this will be the third quarter in a row we've missed our targets and, frankly, unless things pick up considerably next quarter, we may have to rethink our whole pricing strategy.

C Are you suggesting we introduce price cuts?

A If we still can, Anna. Certainly if we'd done that a year ago, it might have stimulated demand. But do it now and we may end up running at a loss. As you know, we're barely breaking even on some of our product lines as it is.

D Surely you're not saying it's time to phase them out!

A No, no, of course not. At least, not yet. But what I am saying is that we need to keep production costs down somehow if we want to remain competitive.

B Does this mean we should be investing more in new technology?

A If only it was that simple, Erik. But right now we're not really in a position to invest in anything, even if we wanted to. No, I'm afraid the situation calls for more drastic action. It's clearly time for a major restructuring.

D Are you telling us there could be lay-offs?

A I don't see how we can avoid it, James – unless, of course, we can get some of our people to accept reduced hours.

C You mean some kind of job-share scheme?

A Yes, either that or introduce a four-day week – providing the unions don't oppose it. Of course, it's not just a question of costs. It's also a question of product. The fact is, better products are coming onto the market all the time.

D So you're saying we should be spending more on R&D.

A As I've said, capital investment is no longer an option for us. Pour any more money into R&D and we'll simply slide further into debt. And then there are all the problems we've been having with our overseas distributors.

B Does this mean you're thinking of centralizing distribution?

A Well, that's one option, yes. But even if we decided to do that, and it's a big if, it would take time to implement – time we simply don't have. As you know, our share price has fallen to an all-time low of just 85 cents. And I wouldn't be surprised if, by our next meeting, it's fallen even further. The fact is, we're selling old products at inflated prices in a volatile market through inefficient distributors.

D I hope you're not suggesting the situation is hopeless.

A Well, let's put it this way: we've cancelled the summer party!

1.10

a

A Right. Basically, the position is this: the contract is ours if we want it.

B But we're not in a position to take on another project right now, are we?

A I know. Jan, what's your position on this?

b

A Look, it's not just a question of software, Alessandro.

B Of course not. It's also a question of hardware. The entire system needs upgrading.

A But that's out of the question. We can't afford that kind of capital outlay.

c

A Sales are down. One option would obviously be to cut our prices.

B That's no longer an option for us. We're barely breaking even as it is.

A Well, then we've no option but to rethink our whole marketing strategy.

d

A Well, there's no easy answer to this, but how about voluntary redundancy?

B I don't think that's the answer, but maybe we could reduce people's hours.

A That might have been the answer if we didn't already have a strike on our hands!

e

A Now, let's not make a problem out of this. What if we just pulled out of Sudan?

B Well, I've no problem with that, but our partners won't be happy.

A No, but that's not our problem, is it? The political situation is just too unstable.

f

A I'll get straight to the point. We're getting too many customer complaints.

B I agree with you. But the point is we don't have the staff to deal with them.

A That's beside the point. We shouldn't be getting them in the first place!

g

A I'm afraid the situation is serious. And if the press get hold of the story, ...

B Look, we'll deal with that situation if and when it arises. Let's not panic just yet.

A You're right. What this situation calls for is calm and careful planning.

h

A The fact is, we're simply not spending enough on R&D.

B As a matter of fact, we've doubled our R&D budget this year.

C That may be so, but the fact remains we're losing our technological lead.

03 RAPPORT

 1.11

A Come in, sit down. It's, um, Helena, isn't it? Jacob Sanders. I think we already met.

B Erm, thank you. Yes, in Chicago, but it was, erm, several years ago. Did you erm, did you have a good flight?

A Yeah. Well, Helena, you know why I'm here. We want to get this teleworking policy implemented as soon as possible.

B Yes, well ... would you like some coffee or tea?

A No, I'm good to go.

B Erm ... well, as you know, I, erm, I spoke to Harry Stross about the special circumstances here, and ...

A Harry's just transferred to South America, actually. Look, Ellen, um, Helena, I won't beat about the bush, this is a global policy. Head Office don't like exceptions, and it's my job to make sure that we don't have any.

B I understand. Erm, it's just that people here don't really like the idea of working from home. And erm, not having their own office any more. It's quite upsetting for people who've been working here for years and years.

A So which part of the policy is it they don't understand? I mean, it's not as if they were losing their jobs! We just want them to work from home three days a week. Most folks in the States are really happy with it.

B It's just that ...

A I'm sorry?

B Oh, erm, nothing.

 1.12

A Hi Helena, Jacob Sanders.

B Hello.

A I don't know if you remember me, we met in Chicago.

B Yes, of course I remember you! It was the conference with that awful team-building day, wasn't it?

A Yeah; what a disaster that was!

B Anyway, how are you? Did you have a good flight?

A Not too bad, thank you. But I have to say, the Atlantic seems to get wider every time I cross it!

B Yes, it's a long flight, isn't it? Maybe you should consider teleworking!

A Aha, touché! But you know why I'm here, Helena. We want to get this policy implemented as soon as possible.

B Yes. Erm, would you like some coffee or tea?

A Yeah. A cup of coffee would be nice, thank you.

B So, did Harry Stross fill you in on our special circumstances here?

A Yeah. But you know Harry's just transferred to South America, don't you? So I'm taking over where he left off. I won't beat about the bush, Helena; this is a global policy. Head Office don't like exceptions, and it's my job to make sure that we don't have any.

B I understand. And let me reassure you on that point, I'm confident that we can bring people round to the idea. It's just that we're going to need a little more time ...

04 VOICE AND VISUALS

 1.13

Hello, this is Cheng Jing from Nanogen, Taiwan. I just wanted to let you know that your presentation this morning was a tremendous success with everyone here. What a brilliant idea to do the whole thing in such a casual, low-budget and alternative way! Very clever. The board certainly got the message.

Our executives really liked your calm, quiet approach. So please pass on my congratulations to your excellent presenter.

Oh, by the way, the joke about Beijing was greatly enjoyed – even in translation. So, see you at the next strategy meeting. Goodbye now.

 1.14

a There's a whole market in Eastern Europe just there for the taking.

b Quite frankly, the results we've been getting are absolutely incredible.

c Now, I'm sure I don't need to tell you just how crucial this is.

d Net profits are up 97% – yes, 97%.

e Would you believe that so far we've not been able to sell a single unit?

f Miss this deadline and we'll lose the biggest client this company's ever had.

 1.15

a There's a whole market | in Eastern Europe | just there for the taking.

d Net profits | are up ninety-seven per cent | – yes, | ninety- | seven | per cent.

 1.16

a There's a whole market | in Eastern Europe | just there for the taking.

b Quite frankly, | the results we've been getting | are absolutely | incredible.

c Now, I'm sure | I don't need to tell you | just how crucial | this is.

d Net profits | are up ninety-seven per cent | – yes, | ninety- | seven | per cent.

e Would you believe | that so far | we've not been able to sell | a single unit?

f Miss | this | deadline | and we'll lose the biggest client | this company's ever had.

 1.17

A Welcome back to CBN Business. To be or not to be? That is the question for an increasing number of companies putting their staff through drama courses in an attempt to turn them into better public speakers. Jon Heller meets a group of British managers making their theatrical debut.

B 'Next time you are about to make a presentation, take a deep breath and imagine yourself walking on stage – about to give the performance of your life.' That's the advice of William Freeman of Cambridge Associates, one of a new wave of management trainers who believe that presenting is less about PowerPoint and more about acting the part.

At Prospero, a company with similar aims, Tina Packer and Michael Lame have taken the idea one step further and put Shakespeare on the programme. After all, who better to teach managers how to speak effectively and relate to an audience than classically trained actors? Whether you're a platform speaker at the annual conference, a salesperson pitching to a client or just chairing your weekly staff meeting, actors have powerful communication techniques you can learn from. Prospero is certainly in demand, regularly running courses at Columbia Business School, Harvard and MIT.

So what is it that makes someone a brilliant speaker? Richard Olivier, Royal Shakespeare Company director, creative management consultant and son of acting legend Sir Laurence Olivier, thinks it's 'self-belief'. According to Olivier, 'Much of leadership is acting. Not faking it, but taking on a role. Paradoxically, the acting makes it real.'

But what do the trainees think? We questioned a few who'd taken a course in acting like leaders.

C I thought my boss had gone mad at first. I mean, Shakespeare? No way! But, in fact, it's been really inspiring. And a lot of fun!

D Frankly, I was terrified. Me, acting on stage? I don't think so. But I've learned a lot of stuff I never got on those boring presentation courses.

E Well, the actors have been fun to work with. We've had a lot of laughs. I'm not so sure how useful it all is – you know, in a business context. But, hey, it got us out of the office for a couple of days, so I'm not complaining.

F Well, this really isn't my thing at all. I mean, public speaking just frightens the life out of me, without getting up and acting in front of an audience. Frankly, it was hell. Never again!

G Best course I've ever done – by far. Just totally brilliant. I never realized the true power of the voice and the confidence it gives you when you can make it work for you. I'd definitely recommend this kind of training.

B So, there we have it. Time to shut down your laptop, brush up your Shakespeare and learn how to wow an audience with the professionals.

 **1.18**

If we are going to die, we are enough
To cause our country loss; and if to live,
The fewer men, the greater share of honour.
This day is called the Feast of Crispian.
He who survives this day, comes
safely home,
Will hold his head high when this day
is named
And stand up at the name of Crispian.
He that shall live today and see old age
Will celebrate it yearly with his neighbours
And say: 'Tomorrow is Saint Crispian'.
Then he'll roll up his sleeve and show
his scars
And say: 'These wounds I got on Crispian's
Day'.
Old men forget; yes, all will be forgotten;
But he'll remember all too well
What he achieved that day. Then will
our names:
Harry the king, Bedford and Exeter,
Warwick and Talbot, Salisbury and
Gloucester,
Be between cups of wine newly remembered.
This story will the good man teach his son;
And Crispian will never go by,
From this day to the ending of the world,
But we shall be remembered for it –
We few, we fortunate few, we band
of brothers;
For he today who sheds his blood with me
Will be my brother. However poor
and humble,
This day will make of him a gentleman.
And gentlemen in England, now in bed,
Will curse the fact they were not here,
And question whether they are really men,
While anyone speaks who fought with us
Upon Saint Crispian's Day!

05 PROBLEMS ON THE PHONE

 **1.19**

B Hello?
A Dan?
B Speaking.
A It's George. George Chatterton.
B Ah, George ... How are you?
A Couldn't be better, mate, couldn't be better! Someone happened to mention they'd bumped into you the other day. So I just thought I'd give you a call. See how you're doing.
B Oh, right. ... yes ... er, George ...
A So how's it going, mate? Just been promoted, so I hear.
B Er, yes, that's right.
A Glad to see they've finally started appreciating you.
B Er, yes, thanks. So, George, what can I do for you?
A Bit more money too, I imagine.
B Hm? Oh, a bit, yeah. Well, George, I expect you're calling about that project ...
A And how are your parents? Is the family doing well?
B They're all fine. Thanks for asking. Look, George, I am rather busy right now. I've just got back from holiday, actually, and you know what it's like. Was there something you wanted to talk to me about?
A Of course, how silly of me! You've just been on that safari you were planning last time we spoke, haven't you?
B Yes, and what with the new job and everything, there's a bit of catching up ...
A Kenya, wasn't it?
B What?
A The holiday – Kenya.
B Yes. Listen. George ...
A You know, I've always wanted to go to Kenya ...
B Well, now, George, I mustn't keep you.
A What's that?
B I'll let you get on. I'm sure you've got things to do, busy guy like you. It's been great talking to you, though.
A Yeah, likewise.
B We must get together soon.
A Yeah, yeah. As a matter of fact, I'm going to be in London for a few days next month.
B Oh, no!
A Sorry?
B I said 'Oh, nice.' Perhaps we can meet up for lunch or dinner.
A Yeah, that'd be great.
B But, erm, I'll have to let you go now, George. Someone just this minute stepped into the office.
A Oh, right, I see.
B And it looks like I've got an international call just come in on the other line as well. Yes.
A No worries. I'll call you back in half an hour, then. I haven't told you my good news yet. Wait till you hear it!
B What? Er, no. Erm, George? George?

 **1.20**

A Hello. Thank you for calling the iDeals customer service line. All our customer service advisers are busy right now. Please hold and your enquiry will be dealt with shortly ... This is the iDeals customer service line. Thank you for holding. All our customer service advisers are busy right now. Please hold and your enquiry will be dealt with shortly ...
B Oh, come on, come on!
C Good morning. Lisa speaking. How can I help you?
B Oh, hello. At last! I was just about to ring off.
C I am sorry about that. The waiting system is a bit frustrating, isn't it? It's the only way we can offer our 24-hour service, you see.
B Yeah, yeah. Look, it's about the computer I bought off you two weeks ago ...
C Yes? What seems to be the problem?
B Well, I was transferring my files to it from my flash drive and it's lost the lot. Everything!
C Okay, now don't worry. I'm sure we can sort something out. First, can you give me a few details? The computer has lost all your data, you say?
B Yes. But, you don't understand. It's wiped everything off the flash drive as well! My whole life, my whole life was in those files.
C Oh, my goodness! Are you sure? Sounds like the problem's with your flash drive.
B Of course I'm sure! And there's nothing wrong with my flash drive. I've had it years!
C Okay. I can understand how upset you must be. Now, I don't think we can deal with this on the phone, so I'm going to send a service engineer to see if they can retrieve your data. Can you give me your product reference number?
B Hm? Er, yes. It's ... here it is ... it's SF11–003.
C Thank you.
B I'll be expecting a total refund and compensation if this can't be fixed!
C Unfortunately, we're not authorized to give refunds, but what I can do is send you a brand-new computer. How would that be?
B This is supposed to be a brand-new computer. You think I want another one of these, after what the last one did to my files?
C Well, let's see what our engineer can do. Hopefully, it's not quite as bad as you think. Now, I've got your address here in your customer file. Oxford OX2 6BJ, right?
B Yeah, right.
C And it's Mr Harris, isn't it?
B Yes.
C Right, Mr Harris. We'll have an engineer with you this afternoon. And I'll ask him to bring a new hard disk with him. Is that all okay for you?
B Er, well, I suppose ...
C Good. Glad to be of assistance. Is there anything else I can help you with?
B Hm? Oh, no, no.
C Well, best of luck this afternoon. I hope we can solve the problem for you.
B Well, thanks. Erm, goodbye.
C Goodbye, Mr Harris.

 **1.21**

B Hello?
A
B Yeah, speaking. Is that you, Piotr? Aren't you supposed to be at the Trade Fair in Krakow?
A
B What?

A

B You haven't got a stand? Well, how did that happen?

A

B Maybe it's the laptop you're using.

A

B Well, what happened to our laptop?

A

B Those carriers! They're unbelievable! That's the last time we use them! I'll give them a piece of my mind when I speak to them.

A

B Where's Liesl?

A

B This just gets worse, doesn't it?

A

B What's gone wrong with the brochures?

A

B Portuguese! Oh, no ...

A

B That may be because I forgot to phone Tony. You remember we were going to attend the Lisbon Trade Fair originally.

A

B It completely slipped my mind. Oh, I'm really sorry, Piotr.

A

B Well, we're snowed under at the moment trying to get things ready for the Midas launch, but, look, don't worry. I'll sort something out. Can I call you back in an hour?

A

1.22

B Hello?

A Graham?

B Yeah, speaking. Is that you, Piotr? Aren't you supposed to be at the Trade Fair in Krakow?

A I am at the Trade Fair in Krakow, Graham. I'm just about the only thing that arrived here in one piece!

B What?

A Well, the stand got badly damaged in transit, so I've basically just got a table here, a few chairs and a couple of posters with nothing to attach them to! It's a complete disaster!

B You haven't got a stand? Well, how did that happen?

A Don't ask. Look, it's not just that. I've just tried out three of the promotional DVDs and two were defective – wouldn't play at all. I don't know how many more are like that.

B Maybe it's the laptop you're using.

A Wouldn't surprise me. I had to borrow it from another exhibitor.

B Well, what happened to our laptop?

A I'll give you three guesses.

B Those carriers! They're unbelievable! That's the last time we use them! I'll give them a piece of my mind when I speak to them.

A Yes, well, never mind that now. You've got to do something, Graham. I'm working flat out on my own here.

B Where's Liesl?

A She's come down with some sort of virus. I left her at the hotel.

B This just gets worse, doesn't it?

A Wait till you hear about the brochures ...

B What's gone wrong with the brochures?

A The English ones are okay. The others are all in Portuguese.

B Portuguese! Oh, no ...

A What?

B That may be because I forgot to phone Tony. You remember we were going to attend the Lisbon Trade Fair originally.

A And you didn't tell Tony about the change of plan?

B It completely slipped my mind. Oh, I'm really sorry, Piotr.

A Graham, you've got to get me out of this mess.

B Well, we're snowed under at the moment trying to get things ready for the Midas launch, but, look, don't worry. I'll sort something out. Can I call you back in an hour?

A Okay, I'll be waiting to hear from you.

1.23

A Hello?

B Hello, Piotr.

A Graham! You said an hour.

B Sorry. I got held up.

A What's happening, then?

B Right. I've been on to the carriers and they're sending a new stand out on the next plane. You should have that by tomorrow morning.

A Well, at least that's something.

B Can you get hold of the organizers and tell them we'll set up tomorrow at seven?

A Yeah, sure. I don't suppose you remembered to put another laptop in with the stand?

B I've sent two – just in case.

A Oh, right. Good. Thanks.

B And do you happen to have a phone number for the promotions people? Because if those DVDs are defective, I'll get them to send more by courier.

A I've got it somewhere. Graham, is there any chance of sending someone else out here? Kim, for instance.

B Piotr, you know how short-staffed we are here right now.

A What's this exhibition costing us, Graham? $18,000?

B You're right. I'll check with Liz and see if she can spare Kim for a few days.

A Thanks. It's murder here.

B Well, I'll see what I can do, but I can't promise anything.

A Hm. And would you mind getting some brochures to me in Polish, seeing as I'm in Poland?

B Yes, we're having a few problems with that – seem to have run out. Is there any point in sending the ones we've got in Russian?

A No, Graham, not a great idea. Send the German ones, if that's all we've got. But are you absolutely sure we didn't order a reprint of the Polish ones?

B I'll look into it the minute I get off the phone.

A Okay, but could I ask you to hurry that up a bit, please? It is pretty important.

B I know, I know. Would it help if we got a local Polish interpreter in? I know you speak Polish, but it might help you out a bit.

A Well, I wouldn't have much time to brief them on the product, but yeah, anything's better than nothing.

B Okay, I'll get on to that right away. Leave it to me.

A I did leave it to you and look what happened!

B Yeah, well. You're doing a great job Piotr. I owe you one!

06 LEADING MEETINGS

1.24

A Coming up on CBN Business: an interview with media king and head of News Corporation Rupert Murdoch, the stock market report and Katy Alexander with the week's business news round-up. But first, suffering from boardroom blues? Tired of taking minutes at meetings that take hours? Tess Liebowitz may have the solution ...

B According to diplomat and economist JK Galbraith, 'Meetings are indispensable when you don't want to do anything.' Therefore, logically, if you really do want to do something, it's the meetings you must dispense with. But can you dispense with meetings altogether? And what would take their place? At several well-known companies they think they've found the answer.

At leading hotel company, Ritz-Carlton, meetings have taken on a different twist. Hotel employees have short stand-up meetings styled much like the catering events they set up for their own guests. They stand, mingle and chat about the latest developments within the hotel. This stand and talk style provides high energy and motivation for the staff to keep maximizing hotel service.

Yahoo has gone one step further by holding regular Friday meetings in and around the work cubicles. Talk is casual and relaxed yet informative – centred around the snack and drink tables set up in the office area. This creates an inclusive communicative atmosphere that can't be replicated in any normal meeting room!

At media strategy company, Michaelides & Bednash they've come up with a different solution. All employees, irrespective of status, work around one enormous central table. Meetings become unnecessary when everyone in the company is sitting just across the table from you the whole time. The working day is a constant meeting!

 1.25

Extract 1

A Okay, thanks for coming, everybody. Erm, has anybody seen Lance, by the way? He was supposed to be here.

B Oh, yeah, he phoned to say his flight in from Chicago had a two-hour delay. He said to go ahead and start without him.

A Oh, I wanted his input on this one. Okay, never mind, let's get started, then, shall we? Erm, so, as I said in my email, the purpose of this meeting is to review last week's talks with the people from timeofyourlife.com and, secondly, to decide if we're interested in taking things further. Pieter is going to fill us in on the background. Pieter?

C Yeah, thanks, Ross. Well, now, timeofyourlife is a really exciting business proposition. Basically, the idea is that ordinary people can buy a kind of timeshare in various luxury goods that they could never afford to buy outright. What happens is you buy points online at the timeofyourlife website and you can use these points to buy, like, a Ferrari for a day, a Rolex Oyster for a weekend or a Jean-Paul Gaultier original for an evening! Neat, huh? I just love this proposal ...

D Er, sorry to interrupt, but is this going to take long, Pieter? Only I have an appointment at 11 and we have all read the summary on this company already.

A Jack, could Pieter just finish what he was saying? We're looking at $20 million in seed capital here. I don't want us rushing into anything. But perhaps we could speed things up a little, Pieter. We are short of time and by the end of this meeting I'd like some kind of decision on this.

 1.26

Extract 2

C So, as you can see, the advance publicity alone is attracting half a million visitors to the timeofyourlife website every day.

A Sorry, Pieter, but we seem to be getting side-tracked here. This is all very interesting, but can we go back to what we were discussing earlier?

C Oh, Okay. Sure.

A Perhaps we can come back to this later. Tell us about their logistics.

D Can I just say something here?

A Hold on a minute, Jack – you'll get your chance in a moment.

D It's just that I thought we'd agreed we weren't investing in any more dot.coms.

B No, Jack. That's what you wanted. But nobody actually agreed.

D Tania, we've been through this.

B Wait a minute. Who was it that said ...?

A Okay, okay! Let's all just calm down, shall we? We're here to talk about this proposal we have on the table. Tania, what's your position on this?

B Well, I agree with Pieter that it's a great business plan. Like you, I'm a little concerned about the logistics, though. The procurement and delivery system for a business like this would be extremely complex. And the insurance costs could be prohibitive.

C Now, hold on a second! This is all covered in the proposal, Tania. What are you saying? I thought you were with me on this one.

A Pieter, I think what Tania is trying to say is she likes the idea but the figures don't quite add up.

B Exactly.

A Okay, maybe we should take a short break at this point, grab a coffee and meet back here in 15 minutes.

 1.27

Extract 3

A Okay, so just to summarize what we've said so far. Basically, we like the timeofyourlife idea. At least most of us do. We're aware of the risks involved in a major investment in an e-business, but we think the concept has great potential. We need to make another appointment with these people because we have some doubts about their logistics. Pieter, can I leave that one with you?

C Sure. I'll get right on to it.

A We're also a little concerned about the amount of insurance a business like this would need. Tania, can you get back to me on that?

B No problem, Ross.

A Great. I think that's about as far as we can go at this stage. Thanks, everybody.

E Hi, guys. Sorry I'm late. Tania told you the story, right? Say, did I miss anything here?

07 COACHING

 2.01

Step 1, Goal

A ... Well, that's great, Jim. I'm pleased for you. It sounds like all that work we did on your presentation really paid off.

B It really did.

A I knew you could do it ... Okay, so what would you like us to work on today?

B Well, there was one thing. Actually, it's to do with the presentation.

A Uh huh.

B I mean, as I said, the talk itself went really well.

A Right.

B But then afterwards there was this networking event.

A Oh, yes?

B Yeah, and, obviously, a lot of people came up to talk to me about my presentation. And this was my chance to make some useful contacts, but, you know, I didn't feel I really made the most of it.

A Okay, and what makes you feel that?

B Well, I didn't seem to get all that many appointments with people. You know, I came away with the usual mountain of business cards, but not that many firm commitments to meet.

A Okay then, let's look at that, then, shall we? Now, what precisely would you like to get from this session?

B Well, I suppose I'd just like to be better at going beyond the small talk and doing more real business at these networking events.

A All right. And, on a scale from one to ten, how important would you say this issue is to you? Let's say one's not important at all and ten's extremely important.

B Um, well, at least an eight. Maybe a nine. I mean there's no point attending these events if I don't bring home the business.

A Right, so an eight or a nine. This is obviously a priority for you right now. Okay, so ...

Step 2, Reality

A ... Okay, then. So what's the most challenging thing about this right now for you?

B I think the most challenging thing is just making sure I don't end a conversation with a potential contact without trying to fix a definite appointment. But, you know, I don't want to look desperate or pushy. The problem is, once the event's over, it's much harder to follow up, you know?

A I understand that. So, ideally, how would you like things to be?

B Ideally, I'd like to be getting appointments with at least 60% of the people I'm meeting.

A Okay, and, in comparison with the ideal situation, where are you at the moment with this?

B Hmm, I'm getting maybe 30% – on a good day!

A So you're looking to double your effectiveness?

B Well, I know that sounds like a lot to ask, but yes, I suppose I am.

A All right. And can you give me a few examples of what you're finding most challenging?

B Well, I guess the trickiest thing is just making the switch, you know.

A The switch?

B Yeah, the switch from small talk to business.

A Oh, okay.

B It's like that awkward moment when you have to say: 'So, perhaps we could do some business together?' I mean, however you say it, it's difficult if they don't make the first move.

A All right, let's explore some options here ...

Step 3, Options

A Okay, now we've talked around the issue a bit, Jim; looked at some of the problems you're having. So what alternatives do you think you have here?

B Well, you know, as we've been talking, it's struck me that maybe I'm coming at this the wrong way.

A Uh huh. Go on.

B Well, maybe I'm focusing too much on what I'm getting out of these networking events, instead of focusing on the people I'm meeting.

A Sounds interesting. Would you like to say a bit more about that?

B Well, I could be spending more time thinking about what I can do for them rather than what they can do for me.

A Okay. And is there anything else you could be doing?

B I think maybe there is. I mean these events are hopeless for doing business, anyway. There's no privacy. Everyone's moving around, drink in one hand, food in the other. All I want is the chance to talk to them again after the event. So perhaps if I can do them a favour of some kind – send them some interesting data, introduce them to someone else – that's all the excuse I need to contact them again and start to build some kind of business relationship.

A Sounds like another good idea. So what's stopping you from pursuing these options?

B Well, nothing, I suppose – except that I'd need to know a lot more about the people I'll be meeting, before I meet them.

A Good point. Okay, let's think about how you might manage that ...

Step 4, Way forward

A All right, Jim, I think we're making some progress here. We've looked at some of the options you have for improving your networking – in particular, how to turn things around and focus on your contacts a bit more. So what are the steps you need to take now?

B Um, well, I obviously need to be doing a lot more research on the people I'm meeting at these events, so that I can have some ideas for ways in which I might be able to help them without actually having to talk business with them straightaway.

A All right.

B And I need to have a reason to contact them again at least once, maybe twice, before raising the subject of business. And, hopefully, I won't need to raise it at all, because they'll do it.

A Okay. So build the relationship first?

B Exactly. I think maybe I could also benefit from some kind of course on networking. Perhaps I could improve my communication skills there. You know, learn some tricks of the trade?

A That could help too. So, what do you think is the first thing you need to do?

B I'm not sure. I need to start getting my client research sorted out. That could take some time and I may need some assistance with it.

A Do you have someone to help you with that?

B Yes, I think so. And I should also find out about networking courses. Maybe that's my first step. I'd like to feel I'm taking some immediate action.

A Okay, and when are you planning to take that first step? Shall we commit to a date by which that will be done?

B Yes, I think that's something I can probably do by the next time we meet.

A In two weeks?

B In two weeks, yeah.

A All right, so shall we discuss that next time?

B Yes, let's do that. And in the meantime I'll also talk to my assistant about that client research.

A Good idea ...

08 PROMOTING YOUR IDEAS

 2.02

1 Erm, well, to tell you the truth, there's a part of me that's still scared I might just dry up completely. I mean, you know, your mind goes completely blank? Makes me sweat just thinking about it. I have this nightmare where the audience has gone deadly quiet, and everybody in the room's just staring at me and I haven't got a clue what to say next! It's only ever happened to me once, thank goodness, but I still lose sleep over it in case it ever happens again.

2 Technology. Well, if anything can go wrong, it will. About a year ago, I had not one, but two projectors break down on me. And then my mike went funny as well. I sounded like Darth Vader out of *Star Wars* for about half an hour until they fixed it. Completely ruined my whole presentation, obviously. I went mad with the technicians afterwards. But what can you do?

3 I always seem to run out of time and then have to rush the end of the talk or, even worse, run over schedule. Audiences hate that. I've had people tell me I overprepare, but it doesn't seem to matter what I do, I always have at least 20 minutes too much material. So, for me, every talk's a race against the clock!

4 Well, some people, older people especially, have told me that I move around too much when I speak in public – you know, that I pace up and down and wave my arms about. They say it's distracting. They can't concentrate on what I'm saying. But for me, as an Italian, you know, it's quite normal for us to jump around, be rather dramatic. So, now I worry about trying to stand still. And that just makes me feel tense and uncomfortable.

5 What was it Franklin D. Roosevelt said? The only thing to fear is fear itself? That's the thing I'm afraid of, still, after all these years in business – fear. Ridiculous, isn't it? But fear's an absolute killer in a presentation. Your mouth goes dry. Your heart speeds up. Your legs turn to jelly. In my experience, the first two minutes are usually the worst. Survive those and you're in with a chance.

 2.03

Extract 1

Er, well, I think the most important thing to remember is that people expect you to be an expert in your field of business. I mean a real expert. That means you should have all the technical information at your fingertips. Which is not to say they won't want to see it all in print after the presentation as well. And if you don't cover every detail in your pitch – costings, cashflow projections, everything – believe me, they won't be slow to interrupt you to ask for it. People here seem to like PowerPoint, the whole technology thing, you know. A word of warning, though: forget the jokes. If you try to be a comedian, they just won't take you seriously.

 2.04

Extract 2

Erm, I think the main thing here is to give your presentation the personal touch. That's what they value above everything else. You see, they're judging you as much as, if not more than, what you're actually talking about. But, erm, I think too many presenters worry about offending the local culture and then they end up sounding much too conservative. Don't. Be loud, be lively, be eloquent. They love all that. It's true that attention spans do tend to be a bit short sometimes and you'll get loads of interruptions, but just go with the flow. In any case, people will probably want to talk to you about everything all over again later.

 2.05

Extract 3

Well, it's almost a cliché, but the hard sell does actually work here. And, believe me, you really can't be too assertive. In fact, they want you to impress them and expect you to work hard to maintain their interest. So, be fast, be slick, make sure you have a few gimmicks up your sleeve. They like all that stuff. And you can say as many nasty things about your competitors as you like – especially if they're funny. Humour's nearly always appreciated, and, er, you don't need to be too subtle with that. They don't want dark sarcasm, though – so nothing too negative. Wisecracks, clever remarks – that's what they tend to go for.

 2.06

Extract 4

Erm, my main piece of advice here is: don't overwhelm them with your enthusiasm. Of course, they expect you to be highly competent and confident, but quietly confident. People will probably have read through all the paperwork beforehand, but they'll want you to go through all the main points again. For the sake of formality and politeness, they'll want to hear it directly from you. But don't get so carried away talking about your own ideas that you forget to point out why it's their company you especially want to do business with. That's very important – creating a sense of harmony and compatibility between you and them. Oh, and a long-term commitment for them, by the way, is 20 to 25 years, not three to five, as it is in the States.

 2.07

Extract 5

I suppose having a sense of humour's the main thing. In fact, you can't do without it really. Certainly, if you haven't made them laugh even once within the first five minutes, you probably won't be very popular. People may even switch off altogether. Speakers are kind of expected to be fairly entertaining as well as knowledgeable about their product or service. You don't actually have to crack jokes the whole time, but anecdotes and amusing stories seem to go down well. Making jokes at your own expense, especially, seems to help build rapport with an audience that can otherwise seem a bit cold and unfriendly. And don't try to wow them too much with technology. Be too techie and people'll just think you're showing off.

 2.08

Extract 6

Being stylish seems to be what matters here – both in terms of your personal appearance and how you actually come across as a person. It's true that you do have to keep up a certain formality and your talk should always be logical and well organized, but within those constraints you can be as imaginative and innovative as you like. In fact, unless you are offering something pretty special, something attractive – something unique that they haven't seen before, you'll find them very difficult to persuade. Obviously, knowing exactly who you're presenting to is always important, but here it really is essential that you do your homework. And, er, don't be surprised if the questions you get asked seem quite hostile. Tough questioning is all part of the business culture here.

 2.09

Extract 1

A Good morning, everybody. Thanks for coming. I'm Rachel White, area manager for the north-west division, and this is Brad Kennedy, head of our physiological research unit.

B Hi.

A As some of you already know, Brad and I have been working on a project of our own for some time now – a project, which we think you're going to be as excited about as we are. Brad?

B Thanks, Rachel. Well, now, as the USA's leading chain of health clubs with over a thousand centres in 35 states, we pride ourselves on providing the best in fitness training programmes. And for us, staying in shape is not just a business. It's a way of life. According to the National Center for Health Statistics, seven out of ten of us don't take regular exercise. In fact, figures recently published by the Surgeon General show that 70% of Americans are now seriously overweight. That's an alarming statistic. But, you have to admit, a tremendous marketing opportunity! The question is, how do we reach that market with something totally new?

 2.10

Extract 2

A A recent report claims that a mere 13% of Americans are satisfied with their physical appearance. And a staggering 92% are dissatisfied with their current level of fitness. So, why aren't they doing something about it? We did a nationwide survey of people who had previously shown an interest in joining a MaxOut club and then changed their minds. Full details are in the report in front of you, but this chart highlights our main findings. As you can see, 15% of respondents said joining a gym was simply too expensive. 53% said they'd love to join if they weren't so busy. And, interestingly, 32%, almost a third, admitted they were just too embarrassed to join a health club in their present physical condition. They wanted to get fit first! So, what does all this mean? We think the implications are clear. There's obviously a huge market for an inexpensive alternative to going to the gym for people who are conscious of their appearance but short of time. And this represents a golden opportunity to stretch the MaxOut brand and develop a new product that perfectly complements our existing business.

 2.11

Extract 3

B And here it is! The MaxOut Micro-GYM! 40% of our project budget went into constructing the prototype, and it's taken 18 months to get this far with the design, but isn't this just the coolest thing? I'll pass it around in a moment. Ladies and gentlemen, what you're looking at is the world's smallest full-body workout system – ever. It's the ultimate go anywhere exercise machine. And, we believe, it could be a significant part of this company's future. With its sleek, lightweight design, the Micro-GYM weighs just over a pound, or 450 grams. Disassembled, it fits easily into a coat pocket. The assembly itself is child's play. You can be ready to exercise in under 45 seconds. Now, I know what you're thinking. Can something so small possibly work? Yes, it can. The Micro-GYM offers 35 different exercises for upper body, lower body and mid-section. It can be adjusted from the five-kilo setting for gentle exercise right up to the 18-kilo setting for a real workout. In fact, it can do just about anything that much bulkier and more expensive equipment can. When you can't get to the gym, the Micro-GYM comes to you. You can get fit at home, on vacation, at the office, even in-flight!

 2.12

Extract 4

A You'll have to excuse Brad. He gets a little carried away sometimes. But we do think the Micro-GYM could be an enormously successful sideline to our main business. Okay, to wrap things up. The Micro-GYM has been fully costed – a complete breakdown is included in the report. Product testing is still being carried out, but we would obviously need the go-ahead from you before we proceed further with that. The Micro-GYM would probably be reasonably priced at around $35. It has been suggested that exercise demonstrations could be recorded on DVD and sold online. Both these suggestions would incur extra costs, but are currently being considered. The prospects for Micro-GYM are exciting. What we hope you'll give us today is the authorization to move on to the next stage. Thank you very much.

B Thank you, Rachel. Okay, we'd like to throw this session open now for questions and suggestions. Feel free to try out the Micro-GYM for yourself. But, sorry, you can't take it home. It's the only one we have at the moment!

09 RELATIONSHIP-BUILDING

 2.13

Extract 1

Yes, well, it's easy to say don't judge by appearances, but, I mean, we all do it, don't we? You take one look at somebody and you're already weighing them up, deciding how friendly they are, how confident, how interesting ... It's automatic. And then two minutes talking to them and you've got them labelled – successful, intelligent, pushy, funny, boring, potentially useful contact ... or not.

You know, I read somewhere that we actually evaluate people within 10 seconds of meeting them. And apparently that's it! It could then take 10 or 20 more meetings with that person to alter our first impression of them. I'm not so sure that's true, but I do think you can tell a lot about a person on first meeting them. It's the little things – a classy watch, a sharp suit, a nice smile, a nervous gesture, an ugly tie. Bitten fingernails are a no-no for me. Or a limp handshake. The wet fish! Absolute turn-off.

Actually, I think a good firm handshake is really important. I'm working in Germany at the moment. You know the Germans shake hands practically before every meeting? Even if they've already met you!

Extract 2

Actually, I think it's last impressions that we sometimes overlook. I mean, it's the impression you leave people with that counts. If you're meeting a lot of people all at the same event, it's easy just to drift around from group to group and never really make contact, like some kind of social butterfly.

I think you've got to be good at listening and drawing people out, investing some time in them and then making sure you close the conversation in a positive way. The old 'Oops, gotta go. Been great talking to you' thing is really bad. Or 'Here's my card. Give me a call.' Way too impersonal. You have to be careful how you end the conversation because that's what people are going to remember. And there's no point having the conversation in the first place if you're not going to try and make that person feel like it's been really worthwhile.

Extract 3

I think a good sense of humour is essential. At least, in Britain and America, it is. Humour's very much how we build relationships over here. On the other hand, have you ever done business in Finland? I have. Very different situation. You can forget the humour. They don't even really like small talk all that much. They'll lounge around with you in the sauna, no problem! But they don't give much away personally. Just not part of the business culture there.

Of course, it may be that they just don't understand our humour. I mean, humour's very cultural, isn't it? You watch a comedy on a foreign TV channel and it's hard to see what on earth they're laughing at. They probably think the same about our jokes.

But then I think jokes are usually a mistake, anyway, unless you know the other people very well. But you don't have to tell jokes to be humorous. Better just to make a few amusing observations. The worst thing is telling a long complicated joke and nobody laughs. Agony! Don't do it!

Extract 4

Of course, now that we live in the so-called 'network economy', everyone makes a big deal about networking. But it depends who you're networking with. Take the Russians. I mean, they'll have a serious conversation with you on any subject you care to name, but small talk is not really their thing. Same with the Germans, the Swiss, the Swedes – generally very good English, happy to talk about work, but not really keen on the social chit-chat.

But go out with a group of Russians after work and they really let their hair down! In that sense they're a bit like the Chinese. They like a big sit-down meal with plenty to eat. What they don't like is the mingling, the wandering around chatting to people.

Basically, it's the British, the French, the Latins and the Americans who are into the schmoozing thing. Americans, especially, have made an art of it. I mean, they're always easy to talk to. It doesn't get very deep usually, but they'll come right up to you and start a conversation and, actually, I quite like that. Working the room, as they call it, and that's what it is for them – work.

 **2.14**

Conversation 1

A Alessandro!

B Hello, Janine! How are you? I didn't expect to see you here!

A No, I don't normally come to these things. But a colleague couldn't make it, so I stepped in at the last minute.

B How long has it been?

A Oh, ages. A year, at least. You're looking very well.

B Just got back from holiday. St. Lucia.

A Lucky you! Look, Alessandro, I was just on my way to an appointment.

B Oh, okay. No problem. Don't let me keep you. Perhaps I'll catch you later.

A I hope so. As a matter of fact, I should be free in about an hour or so. Will you still be around then?

B Oh, yes. It's just me on the stand this year, I'm afraid.

A Oh, well, in that case, why don't I meet you back here when I'm done and perhaps we can go out for a drink – or grab a bite to eat if you're free. I've lots of news to tell you. And I want to find out all about your holiday!

B Great. No, I've no plans for this evening. See you later, then.

 **2.15**

Conversation 2

A Ms Mendoza?

B Yes.

A How do you do? I don't think we've been introduced. I'm Martin, Martin Shaw, the new assistant sales manager for our North American division. First week here, as a matter of fact.

B Oh, pleased to meet you. Welcome to Mexico!

A Thanks!

B So you're working with Richard, no?

A That's right.

B I head up the biotech team at Zantis here in Tampico. Perhaps Richard has mentioned me.

A Yes, of course. He told me all about your set-up here. Actually, Richard's just been detained for a moment. But I'm sure he'll be joining us shortly. Can I get you anything to drink, Ms Mendoza?

B No, I'm fine, thanks. And please, call me Victoria.

A Right, Victoria, well, you don't mind if I ...?

B No, no, of course not! What are you going to try?

A I'm not sure. Could you recommend something typically Mexican?

 **2.16**

Conversation 3

A Good morning. Ms Vatland?

B That's right.

A We haven't met. I'm Daniel Crane. Ana Lindstrom gave me your name. She might have mentioned me?

B Ah, Mr Crane! Yes, Ana said you'd be stopping by. Can I offer you anything? A coffee, perhaps?

A Thank you, that would be very nice.

B Okay. ... There you go. So how are you enjoying the Fair?

A Well, this is all new to me, but I'm hoping to make some useful contacts. It's certainly been an eye-opener so far. I'd no idea the industry was so developed here.

B Oh, yes. There's a lot of interest right now. I understand from Ana that you're looking for agents in Scandinavia, is that right?

A Yes, that's right. We're also looking for a good business lawyer with local knowledge to work with over here. I don't know if you happen to know of anybody?

B Well, I can think of several people who might be able to help you there. And, as far as agents are concerned, I can certainly put you in touch with some very professional operations.

A That would really be very helpful, Ms Vatland.

B Please. Lena.

A Lena. Ana said you were the person to talk to and I can see that she was right.

 **2.17**

Extract 1

A Stella! Max! You're just in time to join us for a little pre-match get together.

B Hi, Craig. Hi, Karen. Mmm ... is that coffee I can smell?

A Sure is. They use Arabica beans here – it's just fantastic! Would you like a cup? It really hits the spot.

C Oh go on then, I could do with warming up a bit.

A There you go. Stella?

B Yes, please. It is a little chilly this morning. Beautiful day, though.

A Isn't it? Well, now, we should probably be thinking of making a move quite soon. Unfortunately, we can't count on the weather staying fine at this time of year. Max, you're partnering Karen. And Stella, you're stuck with me, I'm afraid. Now, I've arranged for us to have lunch at the clubhouse – they've got an excellent restaurant there. So I thought we'd start at the tenth and just play the last nine holes, if that's okay with you. That way we should be able to get round the course in a couple of hours or so.

B Sounds perfect.

A And, Max, I think you'll find my game's improved a little since we last played.

C Splendid! I always like a challenge, Craig. You know that ...

 **2.18**

Extract 2

A Oh, come on! I don't know what's the matter with my game today. I just can't seem to get the ball straight. Sorry, Stella. You must be wishing you'd teamed up with Max.

B Well, you have been in two sand-traps and a lake, Craig! And this is only our third hole!

A I know, I know. Your shot, Max ...

B Craig, I've been meaning to have a word with you about this disposal operation of ours.

A Ah, I was wondering when you'd get round to mentioning that. Look, Stella, you know my position on that ...

B Now, Craig, listen to me. You know I want that oil platform disposed of at sea. It's by far the most cost-effective method. Oh, sorry, Max. I'm not trying to put you off your game. Oh, great shot! Wow, that's almost all the way to the flag! Craig, you didn't tell me Max was such a fantastic player.

A No, I, er, look, Stella, this oil platform – disposing of it at sea. Don't you think it's a bit risky? I know it's technically possible. But there must be 130 tonnes of highly toxic and radioactive substances on that platform!

B Craig, you're starting to sound like a Greenpeace activist, for goodness' sake! ... By the way, I understand you've applied for the top job here in Scotland.

A Yeah, so?

B So's Max.

A What?

B Yeah. And the way it's looking he may well get it. Seems the board like his competitive spirit.

A I see.

B Of course, I could probably put in a word for you. Let's talk later. For the time being, I'd like you to concentrate on your game! I'm not a good loser, Craig!

2.19

Extract 1

A Magda!

B Hello, Anne. Brrr! It's a bit nasty out there tonight.

A Horrible, isn't it? Come on in. Let me take your coat. You managed to find us okay, then?

B Well, I got a bit lost coming off the ring road, as usual. Sorry I'm a bit late.

A Oh, don't worry. Martin's still slaving away in the kitchen. Actually, he had a bit of a crisis with the starter just half an hour ago. You should have heard the language! Probably just as well you weren't here.

B Oh, right. So Martin's cooking, is he?

A Mm. He's quite an expert in the kitchen – fortunately for me. I can't boil an egg myself!

B Oh, I brought you this.

A Oh, thanks, you shouldn't have. I'll put it in the fridge. Come on through.

2.20

Extract 2

B Oh, what a fabulous apartment!

A Thanks. We like it.

B Have you been here long?

A Um ... about two years now. The whole place was an absolute wreck when we moved in. We had to do just about everything to it. Now, how about something to drink?

B Whatever you're having is fine.

A Okay. I'll be right back. Make yourself at home.

C Hi, Magda. I'm Martin. I don't think we've met.

B Hello, Martin. Pleased to meet you. You're the chef, I understand.

C Oh, yes. Doing a good job of setting fire to the kitchen at the moment. I had to rescue the starter.

B So I heard.

A Ah, so you two have met. Good. There we are, Magda. Let me know if you want a refill.

B Thanks.

A Are we nearly ready, then, darling?

C Er, yes, I'm just waiting for the sauce. In fact, I'd better go and check on it. I don't trust that new cooker.

A Oh, okay.

2.21

Extract 3

C Dinner's ready when you are.

C Right, Magda, sit wherever you like. Now, we're having duck in a berry sauce.

B Mm, smells delicious!

C Now, there's more duck if you want it. And help yourself to vegetables.

B Mm, this is absolutely delicious.

A It's one of Martin's specialities.

B Mm, it's really good. The duck's all crispy on the outside and juicy on the inside.

C I'm glad you like it.

B You must let me have the recipe.

C Oh, it's very simple, really. You just need the right ingredients.

A Magda, I've been meaning to talk to you about this business in Poland.

B Oh, yes, that.

A Do you know what's going on there? Because no one seems to be able to tell me anything.

C Right, well, excuse me a moment. If you two are going to talk business, I'll go and see to the dessert.

B Well, I ought to be making a move soon. Early start tomorrow.

C Oh, you don't have to rush off just yet, do you? How about some more coffee?

B Okay, just half a cup. And then I really must be going.

B Well, thank you both for a lovely evening. Martin, you're a brilliant cook.

C Oh, I don't know about that.

B Next time you must come to my place, although I can't promise you such a fabulous meal.

A Bye, Magda. Take care now. See you tomorrow.

10 MAKING DECISIONS

2.22

1 Don't even think about jumping from a moving vehicle. At 70 miles per hour the chances of surviving are remote. And crashing into the mountainside at this speed will almost certainly send you straight through the windshield. So, even though you may be scared of going over the cliff, your best chance of slowing the car down is to repeatedly run it against the crash barriers. After all, that's what they're there for.

2.23

2 Resist the temptation to run. You cannot outrun or outclimb a mountain lion. And put any ideas of playing dead out of your mind. While it may work with grizzly bears, to a mountain lion you'll just look like a free lunch. Your best bet is to shout and flap your coat at the animal to make yourself look bigger and fiercer than you really are. Mountain lions are not proud. If you look like more trouble than you're worth, there's a 50-50 chance they'll back away.

2.24

3 Water transfers heat away from the body 25 times faster than air. So trying to keep warm is more or less futile. And while you're staying calm and conserving energy, the chances are you're dying. You have to get out. Turn in the direction you fell and use your elbows to lift yourself onto the edge of the ice. Reach forward as far as possible and kick your feet as if you were swimming. Once you are back on the ice, crawl to shore. Do not in any circumstances try to stand up.

2.25

4 When landing a light aircraft, make sure that the nose of the plane is six inches below the horizon. As you approach the runway the plane should be flying at an altitude of about 100 feet. If you're higher, you'll overshoot the runway completely. The optimum speed on landing is about 60 miles per hour. Go faster and you may take off again. Go slower and you'll drop like a stone. Upon landing, it's a good idea to brake as soon as you've gained control of the steering. By reducing your groundspeed by 50% you triple your chances of survival.

2.26

5 The current world record for the long jump is just under nine metres, but most people can barely manage three or four. The chances are you can't either. To clear four and a half metres in conditions that are far from ideal you'd need a 20 to 30 metre run-up, perfect timing and a great deal of luck. Frankly, your chances are slim. The truck is a much better idea and it is quite possible to fall from the sixth floor and live. But don't jump out from the building unless there are balconies in the way. You'll be carried forward and miss the truck completely. Drop vertically and take care to land on your back to avoid breaking it.

2.27

6 The taxi could take anything from a few minutes to just a few seconds to sink. But there's not much point trying to force the door open because the water pressure will make this almost impossible. If the car does sink there'll be little or no air left anyway, so forget about trapping air inside. By far the most sensible thing to do is to open the window and actually let more water in. Even if you can't escape through the window, once the water pressure inside and outside the car are equalized, there's a fair chance you'll be able to open the door and save yourself – and maybe the driver too!

2.28

7 It's very unusual for both parachutes to fail, so by struggling with the emergency chute there's an outside chance you'll get it to work. But don't bet on it. You may just be wasting precious time. If you can share one of your friends' parachutes you're in with a chance, but just grabbing onto the nearest person is not a smart move. The G-force when the parachute opens will throw you apart. At 14,000 feet and falling at your terminal velocity of 120 miles per hour you've got about 75 seconds before your appointment with Mother Earth. So firmly attach yourself to the chest straps of another parachutist. You don't stand a chance unless you do.

2.29

8 You are 30 times more likely to be struck by lightning than to be attacked by a shark, but this is little comfort in your present position. Splashing around and making a noise will simply give the shark the idea you're in distress and easy meat. It's a common mistake to think the shark's nose is the best area to target. Punch it there and you are liable to lose a hand or arm – depending on the size of the shark. You'd do much better to strike at its eyes or gills since these are a shark's most vulnerable points.

2.30

Meeting 1

A Right, as you know, our last offer to the union was a 3% pay rise and a two-hour reduction in the working week to be gradually phased in over the next 18 months. The ball is now firmly in their court. Ragnar, do you have any idea which way they'll vote?

B Word is they'll turn it down. In fact, they might even be considering taking industrial action.

A A strike?

B I don't know, Dan. It's a possibility.

A With the current backlog of orders a strike's the last thing we need!

C Now, let's not jump to conclusions. They haven't announced the result of the vote yet.

B My sources are usually accurate, Per.

A Look, time is short. If the vote goes against us, I want us to be able to come straight back with an improved offer. So let's put our heads together and see what we can come up with.

2.31

Meeting 2

A Okay, we've weighed up the various pros and cons. Now it's time to reach a decision and stick to it. Our latest information is that the political situation in Somalia is worsening. In fact, it may only be a matter of days before the country is plunged into civil war. The proposal is that we should pull our people out of there immediately.

B Now, wait a minute, Richard. I don't want us rushing into anything. This whole issue requires long and careful consideration. This is our biggest production plant in North Africa and we're talking about closing it down here.

A I'm well aware of that, Hans. But I take it we're all in agreement that our first priority is to safeguard the well-being of our personnel.

B Of course.

A Well, then, I don't see we have any option but to give this proposal our full backing.

C Aren't we overlooking something here? I mean it's all very well talking about flying our management team home and closing the plant, but what about our factory workers? They'll all be out of a job.

A I'm afraid our responsibility to local workers is different, Andrea. When it comes to the crunch, we have to look after our European staff first …

2.32

Meeting 3

A Okay, you've all seen the results of the road tests. It looks like the two-litre model has some kind of a steering problem and we may have to authorize a total product recall while we conduct further tests.

B Isn't that a bit drastic, Simon? I mean, it's only a slight steering problem, isn't it? And it doesn't seem to be affecting the smaller-engined models.

A Well, that's what we're here to discuss, Matt. With a safety issue like this I don't think we should take any chances, but I'd like your input on this before committing us to any definite course of action. Laura?

C Hm, I'm in two minds about it. I mean, I agree with you that the safety of our customers must come first. But if we take the whole series off the market, I dread to think what the newspapers will do with the story. At this stage I think we should keep our options open. And these test results aren't conclusive, are they?

A Well, no, but I don't think we can just sit on the fence here. In the long run, failing to act quickly could do us a lot of harm.

B So what do you suggest?

A Well, in the absence of more reliable data, I think I'm going to have to go with my gut instinct on this one. I'm just not prepared to put our customers' lives at risk …

2.33

Step 1

The mighty Coca-Cola has been the world's number one brand for so long, it's hard to imagine anything threatening its position of global dominance. One of the company's own publicity brochures proudly declares: 'A billion hours ago human life appeared on Earth; a billion minutes ago the three great monotheistic religions emerged; a billion seconds ago the Beatles performed on the Ed Sullivan Show – a billion servings of Coca-Cola ago was yesterday morning.' Quite a claim. And one that makes a loss of consumer confidence unthinkable.

But take yourself back to May 1999. The unthinkable has just happened. Hundreds of people in Belgium and France have become ill after drinking what they claim is contaminated Coke. And when the cause of the problem cannot quickly be established, the famous soft drink is officially banned in both countries as well as Luxembourg and the Netherlands. The price you pay for being the brand leader is that customers expect quality, as Coca-Cola's CEO is the first to admit. 'For 113 years,' he says, 'our success has been based on the trust that consumers have in that quality.' Now that trust is shaken.

In fact, the four countries banning Coke only represent 2% of the company's $18.8 billion in annual sales. But within a week consignments exported from Belgium to other countries as far apart as Germany and the Ivory Coast have also been seized by officials. Though no definite proof of contamination has yet been found, the panic is starting to spread …

2.34

Step 2

1999 is not a good year for soft drinks companies. Though the Dow is up 25%, both Coke and Pepsi, normally well ahead of the market, are down by around 13%. Coca-Cola is not going to rush into a highly expensive product recall.

In any case, early examinations of the Belgian bottling plants find nothing unusual and an official toxicologist's report concludes that the 200 cases of sickness are probably psychosomatic.

But while Coca-Cola is deliberating over what action to take, rivals Pepsi and Virgin Cola are quick to fill the gaps left on the supermarket shelves. And Coke's refusal to react until it has conducted a thorough investigation is starting to look like a denial of responsibility …

2.35

Step 5

This is how Coca-Cola actually handled the problem.

Initially, full-page advertisements were taken out in European newspapers to reassure the public that the quality of Coke was 'irreproachable'. This was not totally successful as the public at that time could still remember a similar contamination scare at Perrier some years before and all the talk was of pesticides on fruit and mad cow disease.

But, fortunately, the source of the Coke contamination was eventually traced to a strange fungicide on cans shipped from Dunkirk and poor carbon dioxide at Coca-Cola's bottling plant in Antwerp, which makes the Coke taste a little different but does no real harm. It wasn't the Coke itself but the cans that were contaminated.

Coke took the necessary measures and, at enormous cost to the company, all 17 million cases of Coke were withdrawn. Finally, in a spectacular public relations coup, and as an apology to the Belgians who had been ill, Coca-Cola offered a free one-and-a-half litre bottle of Coke to each and every one of Belgium's ten million citizens! Coke was immediately back in the stores.

11 STRESS

2.36

Now, this next slide shows how performance varies with the level of stress. At very low levels, as shown by the yellow area, performance, health and motivation are low. This state is referred to as Under-stressed; it may be experienced by people who are unemployed, or who have very boring jobs with too little to do.

As the level of stress increases, in the green area, performance improves and people feel more motivated. This state is known as Eustress, that's E-U-S-T-R-E-S-S, or 'good stress'. Many people need a moderate amount of stimulation and pressure in order to perform at their best.

However, if the level of stress increases beyond a certain point it becomes destructive and reduces levels of performance, motivation and health. This red zone is called Distress. The first step in managing both your own and other people's stress is learning to recognize the symptoms of Distress.

2.37

1

A I'm sorry, Mark, you must think I'm so unprofessional!

B Not at all. You're frustrated because the customer keeps changing his mind. It's perfectly normal, and it's better to get it off your chest.

A Thanks.

2

C I just never seem to finish my 'to do' list. There just aren't enough hours in the day.

D You obviously need to prioritize. HR run a really good time-management course. If I were you, I'd register straight away. In fact I'm surprised you haven't already done it!

C Oh, yeah. Erm, thanks, Jacky.

3

E Look, Corey, even if I write the whole thing again, I'm sure it still won't be good enough for you!

F I understand how you feel. Would it help if Martha took over some of your regular work for a couple of weeks? That would give you more time, and then maybe you could work from home some days?

E Oh, yes, that would be great. Erm, thanks.

4

G Brett, I just can't go on like this!

H What's the matter?

G I don't ... I don't want to talk about it.

H Was it Pete Jennings? Has he upset you again?

G Mm.

H Was it something he said? D'you want me to talk to him?

G No!! ... erm, no ... thanks.

5

I Listen, Jo, how can you ask me to transfer to London when you know my partner's just found a good job here?

J Well it's hardly my fault! I don't decide company policy; I'm just trying to do my job.

I Oh, right! Well thanks!

6

K That's the third time this week I've left after 8 pm. I'm burning out here, Perry!

L It's just the time of year. It's always like this in November. You'll get used to it. Anyway, it's not as bad as January.

K Oh great – thanks!

7

M What's the matter?

N I've just had my head bitten off by Production. I ordered the wrong components again. I can't seem to go a week without putting my foot in it. I must be stupid or something!

M Oh, come on! It could happen to anyone. You're just going through a difficult period. It was an honest mistake, there's no need to feel guilty about it.

N Yeah, I suppose so. Thanks, Chris.

8

O I'm never going to meet the new sales objective. It's just not fair!

P Not fair?

O Yeah, just because Marcus is always over target, you've raised everybody's objectives! I mean come on, Georgie, we're not all sales superstars like he is!

P Hmm. What would happen if you didn't meet your target?

O Well I wouldn't get my bonus for a start!

P Uh huh. How big a problem would that be?

O Well ... not really that disastrous actually, since the basic's gone up. It's just the principle, isn't it? But yeah, if you look at it like that, I suppose it's not the end of the world. Thanks.

12 EMAILING

2.38

Welcome to the *In Company* Business Podcast Career Spot.

Forget about spelling, switch off your grammar check, and you just might email your way to the top of the corporate ladder. According to research by Professor David Owens of Vanderbilt University into what your email says about your career prospects, sloppy, hastily written emails are a clear sign of leadership potential. 'High-status people in a company' he says, 'send short messages and they have the worst grammar and spelling in the firm. This isn't because they are the least educated. They just don't have time to waste on the small stuff.'

Owens's study shows that high-fliers invest more time in 'face-mail', face-to-face meetings with those they need to liaise with or persuade. This leaves them just a few brief moments during the day to dash off emails confirming what was decided, making last-minute changes and tying up any loose ends. Frequently the emails of natural-born leaders are no more than a phrase: 'Fine by me', 'Let's do it!', 'Okay, see you at the meeting'.

The neatly paragraphed 300-word email with a 5Mb attachment, on the other hand, is strictly for corporate losers. The message it sends is: my job is so undemanding and lacking in challenge or responsibility, I have hours to craft this email into a work of art. 'Reply to all' usually indicates a time-waster, whilst anyone who uses the 'blank carbon copy' to secretly involve the boss in emails to colleagues, is a poor player of office politics and definitely not to be trusted.

Owens's research also reveals that anyone who has a habit of forwarding jokes or sending animated electronic greetings cards is destined never to reach the level of senior management. An overuse of smileys and other more elaborate emoticons further undermines professionalism and guarantees you won't be taken seriously. According to Owens, office jokers play an important social role – they boost morale and are unlikely to be fired, but they don't very often get promoted.

But is it really true that bad email is good? A study attributed to Cambridge University and widely circulated on the Internet, claims that bad spelling, at least, is not much of a barrier to communication. And surveys suggest that when native English speakers receive emails from non-natives, the last thing they care about is the grammar. So, if you want to stay on the executive fast-track, don't waste your time on email – you're supposed to be much too busy!

2.39

A This week on CyberReport Terry Lancaster takes a look at some of the biggest email blunders ever made.

B In April 2000 millions of computer users received an unexpected email. The subject line was intriguing. It said 'I love you.' Those whose curiosity got the better of them opened the message and unleashed what later became known as the Love Bug – a virus so lethal it has so far infected 45 million PCs and caused $8.7 billion worth of damage to computer networks worldwide.

Computer viruses like the Love Bug sound like every company's worst nightmare. But the real danger these days is not so much what can get into your email system as what can get out. You just never know where that email you now regret sending may end up.

The first high-profile blunder occurred in 1997 when employees at the Norwich Union insurance company started spreading a rumour about a competitor on their internal email system. Western Provident, they said, was about to go bankrupt. Western Provident was not about to go bankrupt, and when the emails suggesting it was came into their possession, it sued. The case was eventually settled out of court for a cool £450,000.

In yet another email blunder instance, Devon schoolgirl Claire McDonald found herself receiving emails containing top secret information from the Pentagon after being accidentally added to a cc list by a naval commander. One of the emails was offering advice to the UK on how to prevent secrets from being leaked. She received so many secret files, it caused her computer to crash!

And the corporate email blunder stories just go on. When Dow Chemical discovered hundreds of controversial emails being exchanged between members of staff, the company took no chances. It fired 74 employees and suspended a further 435.

But disciplining your staff electronically isn't always a good idea, as the CEO of Cerner, Neal Patterson, found out to his cost. When Patterson reprimanded 400 managers by email, his criticisms somehow found their way onto the Yahoo! website – for all the world to see. Cerner stock fell by 28% within the week.

And at Merrill Lynch in 2002, the company ended up paying out $100 million when Henry Blodget, an Internet stock analyst, strongly recommended buying stock in a company he had previously described, in what he thought was a private email, as totally useless.

But perhaps the most famous business emails in history came to light during the Microsoft® antitrust trials. When Netscape was still operational, CEO Jim Barksdale claimed his company never wanted to collaborate with Microsoft in the Internet browser market – until, that is, Microsoft lawyers unearthed an email from Netscape president Jim Clark to a senior executive at Microsoft stating clearly: 'We do not want to compete with you.' And Microsoft, for its part, denied any attempt to push Netscape out of the market – until an email from Bill Gates to AOL executives was submitted as evidence. The email clearly expressed Gates' desire to sabotage Netscape. Oh, dear!

So the message is clear. With email, honesty is not always the best policy. And if you must tell the truth, think twice before clicking that send button.

A That was Terry Lancaster talking about the biggest email blunders ever made. And now a sneak preview of the latest in wireless technology ...

13 MAKING AN IMPACT

3.01

1 Did you know that of the world's 100 biggest economies only 56 are actually countries? That's right, 56. The other 44 are companies! In fact, if companies were allowed to join the G8 group of the world's richest countries, Microsoft would take the place of the poorest country! I think it's getting a little scary, don't you, when a corporation can outperform a nation? And maybe it's time to stop and ask ourselves: should business really be that powerful?

2 You know, the joke books of the world are probably full of more lawyer jokes than just about anything else. One of my favourite lawyer jokes is: this guy's having a quiet café latte at a coffee bar when an angry man starts shouting 'All lawyers are criminals!' The man jumps to his feet and cries 'I resent that remark!' 'Why?' says the angry man. 'Are you a lawyer?' 'No' says the man, 'I'm a criminal!' But I'm here to tell you that not all lawyers are corrupt. It's just 99% of them who give the others a bad name.

3 Good morning. Erm, I'd like to start off by thanking Dr Jensen, Dr Tan and Dr Martinez for inviting me to speak today. Our company has a long history of collaboration with this university and it's always a great pleasure to address the robotics experts of the future. Erm, yes, before I begin, perhaps I could just take a moment or two to introduce you to the rest of my team, who are here with me this morning ...

4 I think it was Thomas Edison who said: 'I have not failed. I've just found 10,000 ways that don't work.' Of course, Edison was an inventor, but he could just as easily have been talking about sales. In sales, our success rate is nowhere near as bad as one in 10,000. At least, it better not be! But we have to go through an awful lot of 'no sales' to make one sale. And the ability to deal with failure is the single most important characteristic of the successful sales professional. Could you just raise your hand if you failed to make a sale yesterday? ... Just about everybody, right? Well, congratulations! You're obviously on the right track!

5 I was looking through the appointments pages the other day and came across this unusual job advertisement. Here it is: 'Good hours, excellent pay, fun place to work, paid training, mean boss! Oh, well, four out of five isn't bad.' Wouldn't you like to be interviewed by that boss who admits he's mean? How powerful that little touch of honesty is. And that's exactly what I want to talk to you about this morning: honesty in advertising. And how you get people's attention when you simply tell the truth ...

6 Whenever I'm asked about Total Quality, I think of the story of the American steel magnate, Andrew Carnegie. It seems Carnegie was doing a factory tour one day, when he stopped to speak to one of the machine operators – a grey-haired old guy obviously coming up to retirement. 'Wilson,' he said, reading the man's name badge, 'how many years exactly have you been working for me now?' '39, sir,' Wilson replied with a proud smile. 'And may I add that in all those years I made only one very small mistake.' 'Good work,' mumbled Carnegie, 'but from now on, please try to be more careful.'

3.02

Extract 1

In the long history of the world, only a few generations have been granted the role of defending freedom in its hour of maximum danger. I do not shrink from this responsibility – I welcome it. I do not believe that any of us would exchange places with any other people or any other generation. The energy, the faith, the devotion, which we bring to this endeavour will light our country and all who serve it – and the glow from that fire can truly light the world. And so, my fellow Americans, ask not what your country can do for you – ask what you can do for your country. My fellow citizens of the world, ask not what America will do for you – but what together we can do for the freedom of man.

3.03

Extract 2

I say to you today, my friends ... so even though we face the difficulties of today and tomorrow, I still have a dream. It is a dream deeply rooted in the American dream. I have a dream that one day this nation will rise up and live out the true meaning of its creed: 'We hold these truths to be self-evident; that all men are created equal.' I have a dream that one day on the red hills of Georgia the sons of former slaves and the sons of former slave owners will be able to sit down together at the table of brotherhood. I have a dream that one day even the state of Mississippi, a state sweltering with the heat of injustice, sweltering with the heat of oppression, will be transformed into an oasis of freedom and justice. I have a dream that my four little children will one day live in a nation where they will not be judged by the colour of their skin but by the content of their character. I have a dream today.

 3.04

Extract 3

These are the two great challenges of our time – the moral and political challenge, and the economic challenge. They have to be faced together and we have to master them both. What are our chances of success? It depends on what kind of people we are. What kind of people are we? We are the people that in the past made Great Britain the workshop of the world, the people who persuaded others to buy British, not by begging them to do so, but because it was best. We are a people who have received more Nobel prizes than any other nation except America, and head for head we have done better than America, twice as well in fact. We are the people who, among other things, invented the computer, the refrigerator, the electric motor, the stethoscope, rayon, the steam turbine, stainless steel, the tank, television, penicillin, radar, the jet engine, hovercraft, float glass, carbon fibres, et cetera – and the best half of Concorde.

 3.05

Extract 4

We are both humbled and elevated by the honour and privilege that you, the people of South Africa, have bestowed on us, as the first president of a united, democratic, non-racial and non-sexist South Africa, to lead our country out of the valley of darkness. We understand it still that there is no easy road to freedom. We know it well that none of us acting alone can achieve success. We must therefore act together as a united people, for national reconciliation, for nation building, for the birth of a new world. Let there be justice for all. Let there be peace for all. Let there be work, bread, water and salt for all. Let each know that for each the body, the mind and the soul have been freed to fulfil themselves. Never, never and never again shall it be that this beautiful land will again experience the oppression of one by another ...

 3.06

a What's the main problem we're facing? The main problem is cash flow.

b It's so risky, so problematic, and yet so critical to our success.

c It's faster, cheaper and easier to use. But, above all, it's more reliable.

d Even if we can never again be the biggest, we can still be the best.

e The point is, more and more graduates are fighting over fewer and fewer jobs.

f Not only are we number one in Brazil. We're now number one in Latin America.

g In this market, no company has outperformed us, not one – ever!

h Not once, in over 30 years of business, have we ever had a complaint – not a single one!

 3.07

1 Ladies and gentlemen, we are truly on the brink of a revolution in biotechnology. I'm reminded of the words of futurist and science fiction writer Arthur C. Clarke: 'People go through four stages' he said, 'before any revolutionary development. Stage one: it's nonsense, don't waste my time. Stage two: it's interesting, but not important. Stage three: I always said it was a good idea. And stage four: I thought of it first.' In gene therapy we're about to enter stage four. And I'd like this company to honestly be able to say 'We thought of it first.' Thank you.

2 Uh-oh. Sorry. Looks like we've run out of time. Erm, so I'm going to have to cut it short. Er, yeah, I was hoping to show you some of the figures in our comparative study. But, erm, never mind. I think you'll find all the main points are covered in the handout. So I'll, er, I'll just leave the copies here and you can pick one up on your way out. Okay. So, sorry about that. That's it. Thanks.

3 Well, that just about brings me to the end of my presentation, except to say that the future of this company is now in your hands. For if there's one central message I'd like to get across to you this morning it's this: that this consultancy is no more and no less than the consultants who represent it. And whilst our reputation as a firm may have been damaged by the recent unfortunate events, our expertise as a team is in no way diminished. I want to see each and every one of you raising this company to new heights. I know you can. We built our reputation on crisis management, and it would be ironic indeed if we were unable to successfully manage this crisis of our own – and come out on top. So thank you very much.

4 So, how do you sum up the new Spearing Silhouette ocean cruiser? I could tell you that it has won just about every boat show in the USA and Europe this year, that the orders for it are coming in so fast we already have a five-year waiting list; that the first three names on that waiting list, though strictly confidential, include a famous Hollywood actor, a member of the Saudi Royal Family and one of the world's greatest sporting legends. I could also mention that, so impressed are they with our award-winning design, the directors of the Museum of Modern Art are actually proposing to place a full-size model on permanent exhibition. But all that would fail to do it justice. For the fact is that the Silhouette is in a class of its own. It is a masterpiece of marine engineering. It is, quite simply, the most stunningly beautiful boat ever built. Ladies and gentlemen, I give you ... the Spearing Silhouette!

14 OUT AND ABOUT

 3.08

Traveller I'm sorry I'm so fat. Name's Lucas Loomis.

Leary Macon Leary.

Traveller You a Baltimore man?

Leary Yes.

Traveller Me too. Greatest city on the earth. One of these seats is not really enough for me. And the stupid thing is, I travel for a living. I demonstrate software to computer stores. What do you do, Mr Leary?

Leary I write travel guidebooks.

Traveller Is that so? What kind?

Leary Well, guides for businessmen – people just like you, I guess.

Traveller 'Accidental Tourist'!

Leary Why, yes.

Traveller Really? Am I right? Well, what do you know? Look at this. Gray suit – just what you recommend, appropriate for all occasions. See my luggage? Carry-on. Change of underwear. Clean shirt. Packet of detergent powder.

Leary Oh, good.

Traveller You're my hero. You've improved my trips a hundred per cent. I tell my wife, going with *The Accidental Tourist* is like going in a cocoon.

Leary Well, this is very nice to hear.

Traveller Times I've flown clear to Oregon and hardly knew I'd left Baltimore.

Leary Excellent.

Traveller I see you have your book for protection there. Didn't work with me, though, did it?

 3.09

1 Emma

A So Emma, what's your worst flying experience?

B Well, I think the worst one's probably flying back from Bangladesh to Heathrow. It's quite a few years ago now, but I can still remember it. We were at the gate, ready to taxi to the runway, and suddenly there was this terrible hammering noise from outside the plane.

A A hammering noise?

B Yes, and the strange thing was that the cabin crew just seemed to be ignoring it. But all you could hear was this bang, bang, bang on the fuselage. After a while, some of the passengers were starting to get nervous, me included.

A I'm not surprised.

B Anyway, eventually, after we'd been sitting there for about ten minutes with no announcement and the plane still not moving, I said something to one of the stewards and they went and opened the door to see what was going on.

A And what happened?

B The pilot got in!

A You're joking!

B No, they'd locked him out. Seems quite funny now, but it didn't at the time.

2 Enrique

A Enrique, what's the worst flight you've ever been on?

C Definitely the time I was flying from Malaga to Stansted in the UK. This was around the time of security alerts on international flights and people were very nervous about flying.

A Oh, yes, of course.

C I was travelling on business, but most of the passengers were British tourists.

A Uh huh.

C Anyway, we were cruising at 30,000 feet and I looked out of the window and saw this French air force fighter plane flying alongside us.

A What? Oh, yes, I read about this. Didn't they think the plane had been hijacked or something?

C Well, apparently, air traffic control had lost radio contact with our plane, so they weren't sure what was going on and they weren't taking any chances. I mean, this French jet was armed with missiles and everything.

A Sounds terrifying!

C It was.

A So, what happened?

C Well, the jet was there for about ten minutes checking us out. Fortunately, the captain of our plane managed to keep everybody calm. And anyway, to cut a long story short, everything turned out okay. We even landed on schedule!

A But I bet you were glad to be back on the ground, weren't you?

C You can say that again!

3 Joe

A Joe, have you had any bad experiences on planes?

D Oh, yes, several. One flight I was on, I couldn't understand why they were making us go through the lifejacket drill for landing on water.

A But don't they always do that?

D What, on a domestic flight from Manchester to London?

A Oh, right. I see what you mean.

D I'm not sure which flight path they were planning to take but it goes nowhere near the sea. But that's nothing compared to one of my recent trips to Frankfurt.

A What happened there, then?

D Well, we didn't land in Frankfurt.

A You were diverted?

D No, no, the pilot just landed in completely the wrong country!

A What, you mean he didn't know?

D Hadn't got a clue. Just about everybody on the plane was looking out the windows and saying 'Er, look, I'm sorry to be a nuisance, but this isn't Frankfurt.'

A So where did you land?

D Luxembourg.

A Oh, my goodness! I don't believe it!

4 Selina

A Selina, you've flown all over the world. You must have some stories to tell.

E Hm, quite a few. I'll never forget the time I was flying in Asia and the cabin crew asked me to sit on the toilet during take-off.

A What?

E Yeah, they wanted my seat next to the emergency exit.

A Doesn't inspire much confidence in the airline, does it?

E Not a lot, no. And then, to top it all, I ended up sitting next to a guy with a rattlesnake in a basket!

A Incredible!

E Yes, that's what I said. Apparently, he just brought it on as hand luggage.

 **3.10**

a

A Ugh, isn't it dreadful? And we'd got plans for the weekend as well. Thought we might have some friends round for a barbecue.

B Well, it's always the same, isn't it? You plan anything, it always lets you down. And it was so fabulous yesterday.

C Yes, wasn't it? Never would have thought it could turn so nasty in just 24 hours. But that's Britain for you, I suppose. Heatwave in the morning, a downpour in the afternoon and a howling gale by dinner time. Unbelievable weather!

b

A What on earth is that?

B Don't think you'd like it? Look, it's seasoned with a bit of cinnamon and dried mint.

A Smells off to me.

B Nonsense! It's really delicious. How about trying it?

A Cinnamon sounds a bit odd. And dried mint? As seasoning?

B Well, that's normal for Middle Eastern dishes! Ian is giving it a go, so why don't you? It's really good!

A Hm. All right, if you insist! But if you ask me, cinnamon belongs in sweets!

B Oh, give it a chance, Roger! We'll order you something else if you really can't handle it.

c

B No, it's not my thing at all, I'm afraid.

A Oh, but I thought it was marvellous! And it was so well done. Because it must have been a very difficult adaptation, don't you think?

B Hm, yeah. It went on a bit, though, didn't it? I mean, what was it, two and a half hours?

A Well, I found the whole thing absolutely fantastic. Brilliantly directed. And the special effects were incredible!

B Yes, well, they were good, I'll admit, but they've all got those nowadays, haven't they? I mean it's all just CGI digital animation. Like all those sci-fi, superhero things ...

d

B I'd really appreciate it, because I'm just snowed under at the moment, what with all this backlog to deal with.

A Yes, I'm sorry to have dumped all that on you. Couldn't think of anyone else I could trust. And with the deadline coming up so fast ...

B It's no problem, but if you could let me borrow Kim for a couple of hours, I'm sure that together we could polish the whole thing off that much faster.

C You overworking this poor boy, Susan? That's how she lost her last assistant manager, you know, Ian.

A Oh, ignore Roger. I'll speak to Kim about giving you a hand as soon as we get back to the office.

B Thanks.

15 DELEGATION

 **3.11**

1

A Daniel, can I have a quick word?

B Yeah, sure.

A We've just had confirmation for the Ericsen order. You worked on it last year with Maggie, didn't you?

B Yes, that's right.

A So this year, I'd like you to handle it on your own. Are you comfortable with that?

B Yes, no problem.

A Great. So basically, the deliverables are exactly the same as last year. You'll find all the specifications in the file. The only difference is we got a bit squeezed on price this time, so if we can manage to keep costs down as much as possible, that would be great.

B Okay, I'll do my best. What's the timeframe?

A We've scheduled delivery for July 31st. Do you think that's feasible?

B Yes, should be fine. I'll get started straight away.

A Excellent. Let's schedule a meeting every couple of weeks, then, so we can look at any problems together and think about ways of keeping costs down, okay?

B Sure.

2

C Hi Gina, how's it going?

D Not too bad, thanks. But there's a lot to remember!

C Yes, well, everybody says the first week is the hardest; it gets better, believe me!

D Okay, that's good to know!

C Listen, could you call these people as soon as you can? They're old customers, so you don't need to tell them a lot about the product, just try to get appointments for me. Tell them we've got a special offer on upgrades, so I'd like to meet them. You've got my schedule, haven't you?

D Yes. Shall I email them first?

C No, just keep calling until you can speak to them personally. You'll probably have to call some of them back outside office hours; if you need to work overtime, that's fine, just keep a note of the extra time you put in, okay?

D All right.

C I'd like us to contact everyone on the list by this time next week. Book the appointments into my schedule as you go, and we'll see how you're getting on when I get back from Spain on Friday, okay?

D Okay.

C If you have any questions while I'm away, feel free to ask Mandy. Is that all right?

D Erm, yes. That seems fine.

C Brilliant. Thanks, Gina, I know you'll do a great job!

3

E Technical support?

F Pete? Frank here.

E Uh-oh!

F Yeah. Look, I know it's late, but the server's down again at Captain Discount.

E Oh for goodness sake! All right, I'll get over there asap.

F Thanks, mate. Give me a ring when you've finished, would you? Just to let me know how things stand?

E All right. Will do.

F Cheers.

3.12

This next slide shows how you can adapt your management style to different members of staff. The horizontal axis indicates an increasingly directive style from left to right, and the vertical axis measures a supportive style, less at the bottom and more at the top.

So, as you can see, there are four quadrants representing four main management styles. At the bottom right we have Directing. Here the focus is on giving very explicit instructions: you tell people exactly what you want them to do, why, how and when they should do it, and you follow them very closely to make sure they do it right. It's the kind of approach you need for young, inexperienced or new members of your team.

As people get to know the job, you can gradually move up into the top right quadrant, which is Coaching. Here you can spend less time telling them what to do, and more time working with them to develop their skills. Gradually you can then move to the top left quadrant, which is Supporting: here your main role is to make sure that they have the resources they need to do the job, and of course to continue setting objectives and checking achievement. If there are problems, you may sometimes need to move back towards a more directive style.

Finally, the most experienced and expert members of your team will be happiest with a Delegating style, here in the bottom left-hand quadrant. They are almost completely autonomous, setting their own objectives and evaluating their own results. Of course, they will always welcome a few words of support and thanks from time to time.

16 TELECONFERENCING

3.13

A Since you're new here, I want you to meet your teams in London, Bangalore and Tokyo. You need to do it right away.

B Oh, I'm really looking forward to meeting them, but it's going to take a week or more to get to all those places.

A Actually, they're right down the hall.

B Oh! ... A video conference.

A I wouldn't call it that.

B No?

A I think you'll be pleasantly surprised.

B Wow.

A Hello, everyone. This is Patricia.

C Hello from London. Tania and Owen here.

D I'm Mohan. This is Seema. Greetings from Bangalore.

E And I am Hiro with my colleague Kumi from Tokyo. Hajimemashite!

B I really feel like I'm in the same room with all of you.

Voiceover This isn't the future. It's right now. With Cisco TelePresence you feel like you're sitting across the table from other meeting participants. Seeing them in full life-size images. Making direct eye contact. Hearing them talk left and right ... and centre. Making everyone sound like they're in the same room. TelePresence creates an in-person meeting experience over the network, where the quality's so good, it's as if you took a conference table and just split it in half.

3.14

A Ugh! Who on earth can that be? Where's the ... the light switch! Ow! Er ... hello?

B Pete, is that you?

A Er, yes. Who is this?

B It's Max.

A Max! ... Max, it's ... it's two o'clock in the morning!

B I'm sorry, Pete, but this is an emergency.

A Well, it had better be, I've got to be up in a few hours.

B I think you'd better get up right now, Pete. All hell's broken loose here. We're going to have to shut down the Hamburg plant immediately.

A What!

B It's the heat exchanger. We've got a leakage between the hydrogenation section and the oil heater. There's nothing we can do but stop all production straightaway. Otherwise, the whole thing could go up!

A But Max, do you have any idea what you're saying? If you authorize a plant shutdown, everything grinds to a halt. We'll have container lorries backed up from Hamburg to Lübeck!

B Pete, do you think I don't know that?

A Tell me this isn't happening. It cost us millions last time ... Okay, look, I have no idea how long it will take me and Monica to get a flight, but we're on our way.

B I think that's best, Pete.

A I'll phone you to fix up a teleconference once we're airborne. Contact Françoise and Otto right away, will you? There's not a moment to lose ...

A Monica? It's Pete. Look, I'm sorry to get you up at this unearthly hour, but there's been a disaster at the Hamburg plant. Yeah. Better get dressed. I'll tell you about it on the way to the airport.

3.15

Extract 1

A Okay, so we're just waiting for Otto. Françoise, you told him when to call in, right?

C Yes, I did. Perhaps he's still at the plant or he may just be having problems getting through.

B Pete, where are you and Monica?

A Just left Vancouver about half an hour ago, Max. Should be back in 13 hours or so.

C Pete, I think we should just start.

B Yes, I think so too.

A Okay, we really need to talk to Otto, but let's go ahead and get the meeting started and hopefully he'll join us later on ... Right, well, as you all know, we've had a serious mechanical failure at the Hamburg plant and, basically, we've had to shut it down. There'll be time for a proper analysis of what went wrong later but right now we need a rescue plan. Max, could you first of all just fill us in on what's going on? When can we expect to get the plant up and running again?

B Well, Pete, it's difficult to say at the moment. My technicians tell me they can't get a replacement heat exchanger for at least 48 hours. And then it'll have to be fitted, of course. We're probably looking at three days.

D Three days!

A It's worse than I thought. And is that your best estimate? Three days?

B I'm afraid so, Pete.

A Well, that's that, then. But I want us back in production no later than Thursday, Max. Okay?

B Okay, Pete, I'll see what I can do.

3.16

Extract 2

E Excuse me, Mr Manser has joined.

A Otto! Thank goodness you got through. Have you been to the plant yet? What's the situation there?

F It's pretty bad Pete. We've had to clear the whole site for the fire service to run safety checks.

A I see. Otto, is there any chance we can rewrite our production plan? I mean, can we make sure our key customers get priority on orders?

F I'm already working on that. The problem is it doesn't look as though we'll be able to meet any of the orders completely.

A What's the stock situation?

F Not good.

A Oh, great. Just what I needed to hear. Don't we keep any stock in reserve for this kind of thing?

F What, for a complete plant shutdown? No, Pete, we don't.

A Okay, okay. Well, what about transferring stock from one of our other European plants?

F It'd take too long. And, besides, they're already overstretched as it is.

A Right ... Monica, is there any point in us buying in traded goods from another supplier to cover the shortfall? Just for the time being.

D You mean buy products from our competitors to keep the customers happy?

A Just for the time being.

D Pete, you know how I feel about buying from the competition. How are we supposed to build a reputation with our customers if we end up selling them other people's products instead of our own?

A It's not as if we haven't done it before, Monica. And what alternative do we have?

3.17

Extract 3

A Okay, now, we've got to make up this backlog of orders somehow. How about Handelsmann?

C Er, can I come in on that?

A Go ahead, Françoise.

C Well, I've already been on to Handelsmann. They owe us a favour, actually. We helped them out a few years ago when they were in a similar situation, if you remember. Anyway, it looks like they may be able to do something, but probably not until tomorrow morning.

A Well, at least that's something, I suppose. Okay, get back to them and see if we can hurry things up a bit. And get somebody in after-sales to ring around all our biggest customers and smooth things over with them.

C Okay, I'll see to it now.

A Now, Max. Are you sure this thing can't just be fixed? I mean, if I gave your technical people, say, 24 hours ... Max, you still there?

B Still here. I've just been told the leakage area has now been made secure.

A Well, thank goodness for that. Anyway, okay, that's it for now. We're going to try and get some sleep. I suggest we schedule another conference call for midnight European Time. But, Otto, keep me posted if there's any change in the situation, won't you?

F Will do, Pete.

A Okay, thanks everyone ...

17 NEGOTIATING DEALS

3.18

The activity you just did is designed to demonstrate the critical importance in the negotiating process of relationship building.

In your first negotiation you probably didn't think much about your opponent's interests. And why should you? After all, it was just a stranger who you'd never meet again. But by concentrating on only one objective, you reduced the whole encounter to a single issue negotiation with little room for manoeuvre. This made it a simple zero-sum game – if I get what I want, you don't, and vice-versa.

In order to win at all costs, perhaps you became hostile and tried to pre-empt negotiation altogether by just grabbing the box off the other person. Or maybe you gave in completely, deciding it simply wasn't worth the hassle. Many professional negotiators act the same way if they think they are negotiating a one-off deal. As the negotiation ended in deadlock, perhaps you became desperate and resorted to emotional blackmail, inventing all sorts of reasons why your kid was more deserving than the other kid.

In the second negotiation, on the other hand, there was a long-term relationship you wanted to maintain. The circumstances were exactly the same, but the prospect of one of you 'losing' was no longer an option. By accepting the need to reach some kind of compromise, you were able to turn a head-on conflict into a problem-solving meeting. Now your main objective was to generate options in the hope that you could create a win-win situation, where you both got something you wanted.

3.19

Extract 1

A Okay, so, do I take it we're in agreement on volume?

B Er, well, just a minute, wouldn't it be a good idea to talk prices before we go any further?

A Yes, of course. But in principle you're happy about taking 40 cases, right?

B Er, well, in principle, yes, if the product's as good as you say it is ...

A Splendid, that's settled then.

B ... But, look, getting back to price for a moment. This would be just a trial order, you understand? Sale or return. Until we see how it sells. So, can you give us some idea of what kind of figure you were thinking of?

A €50.

B €50 per case.

A Er, no. Per pack.

B Per pack? There seems to have been a slight misunderstanding. A pack is just 12 bottles, right?

A Yes, that's right.

B Is this meant to be some kind of joke or something? €50 per pack? That's over €4 a bottle. By the time we've added a decent margin, you realize we're looking at a retail price of €7 minimum. How am I supposed to sell a one litre bottle of water for €7, Mr Koivisto?

A Ms Barrett, O-Zone is an innovative, premium product. A pure oxygen-enriched drink. We're not talking about a bottle of Perrier here.

B Well, that's as may be, but €7!

A O-Zone is an exciting opportunity to get in at the start of a new trend in luxury health drinks.

B Well, there's no way on earth I'm paying you €4 for a bottle of oxygenated water, Mr Koivisto. With respect, your prices are simply not competitive.

A Ms Barrett, there are no competitors in this market. O-Zone is a unique product and at €4 – well, I'm afraid that really is our absolute bottom line.

B So you're saying it's take it or leave it?

A I'm afraid so.

B Well, then, I think I'll have to leave it ...

A What ...? Now, just a minute. You said on the phone you might want 100 cases.

B That was before I knew your water was more expensive than Chanel No 5, Mr Koivisto. Okay, look, let's set the price issue to one side for the moment, shall we? Tell me a bit more about the product ...

3.20

Extract 2

A Okay, I'll tell you what I'll do. If you order 250 units today, I can offer you not our usual five but a 6% discount, free delivery and I'll throw in 12 months' free parts and service as well. Now, I can't say fairer than that, can I? Of course, that's only if you can give me the order today. Can't hold the offer, I'm afraid.

B Well, erm, Robert, isn't it?

A Rob. Call me Rob.

B Well, now, Rob, we appreciate the free service and delivery, but to be honest with you, what we'd really like to see is a bit more movement on price. I'm afraid a 6% discount is not quite what we had in mind. We were hoping for something a bit closer to 10%.

A 10%? I don't think I could stretch as far as that. Not unless this was a substantially bigger order.

C Oh, come on! You'll have to do a lot better than that, Mr Hayes. You're not the only precision tool manufacturer, you know.

B Hold on, Gavin. Let's hear Rob out.

C Well, frankly, I think we're wasting each other's time here. We've already been offered a much better deal by Magnusson's.

B Now, wait a minute, wait a minute. Surely we can sort something out here. Rob, would you be willing to meet us halfway?

A How do you mean?

B Well, if you were to offer us an 8% discount, we might be in a position to increase our order, say, by 50 units. But we'd need to see a bit more flexibility on terms of payment. Maybe on installation costs too.

A Erm, well, I suppose there may be some room for manoeuvre there. I'd need to check. Can you give me a moment to have another look at the figures?

B Sure. In fact, let's take a short time out, shall we? And meet back here in, say, half an hour?

A Okay, fine.

C I still say we'd be better off going with Magnusson's.

3.21

Speaker 1

Well, frankly, I get a bit tired of hearing people go on about win-win negotiating. I mean, let's face it, a lot of negotiations are basically win-lose, and your opponent's interests are the last thing you should be worrying about. Buying a house, a car, double-glazing – all win-lose situations. And you'd be surprised how many business negotiations are basically one-off deals as well. In my opinion, in a win-lose situation the tougher you are – without actually being aggressive – the further you'll get. That's because your opponent takes your attitude as an indication of what's possible and what's not. And the friendlier you seem, the higher their expectations will be. It's like the old saying: give them an inch and they'll take a mile.

3.22

Speaker 2

'You always know who is going to win a negotiation – it's he who pauses the longest.' I forget who it was who said that but it's pretty good advice – basically, shut up! And remember that silence is very often your best weapon. It's a very difficult argument to counter. Faced with prolonged and uncomfortable silences, your opponent is liable to make another concession or give away their strategy or weaken their own position by becoming defensive. So play your cards close to your chest. Talk less, learn more. There's an old Swedish proverb: 'Talking is silver. But listening is gold.'

3.23

Speaker 3

I think the biggest trap less experienced negotiators fall into is to turn the whole negotiation into a debate, which it isn't. This is sometimes called 'positional negotiating'. Both sides end up arguing the whys and the wherefores, rationalizing their position, trying to justify themselves. They can talk till the cows come home but it's a complete waste of time. Besides, you're not there to convince your opponent that you're right. He doesn't care if you're right or not. And neither should you. You're there to explore both sides' interests, generate options and trade concessions – preferably giving away things that mean little to you but a lot to him and receiving the opposite in return. This is 'interest-based negotiation' – discovering the needs, desires and fears behind your opponent's position and working on those. The two phrases you need most of all are: 'If ..., then ...?': If I give you that, then what do I get? And 'What if ...?': What if we looked at this another way? What if we did this instead?

3.24

A Tess?

B Mr Logan. It's Kate and Miles to see you.

A Ah, good. Send them right in.

C Hi, Ronnie.

A Kate, good to see you. You're looking great as usual. Miles, come on in. Erm, sit anywhere you like. Can I get you something to drink?

C Do you have an Evian?

A No problem. There you go. Miles?

D I'll just have a black coffee.

A Good idea, Miles! You really look tired; coffee ought to perk you up! So, I hear you two had quite a late evening at the Marquee.

D You could say that.

C Ronnie, you have to sign this band. You could hardly move for A&R people last night. If we don't snap them up, someone else will. I saw Jimmy Armstrong from Sony sniffing around.

A Uh huh. Well, he usually is.

C Yeah, and EMI were there as well. This band's hot. You listened to the demo I sent you, right?

A I did.

C And?

A Well, ...

C Oh, come on, Ronnie. These guys are the best thing to come out of Ireland since U2 and you know it.

A I wouldn't go as far as that, Kate. They sound a little inconsistent on the demo. They need to work on a clear musical identity, if you ask me.

C Well, maybe they need a little help in that direction. We can work on that. But you have to admit the lead singer's voice is just amazing. In fact, they're musically really strong all round.

A Okay, I'll give you that. Apart from the drummer, that is, who's pretty second-rate. So he'd have to go.

C She.

A She? They have a female drummer? Interesting. Well, anyway, she's no good.

C Could be tricky to fire. She's the lead singer's girlfriend.

A Hm. I'm going off them already.

C Ronnie, believe me, The Penitents are a class act. And I'm not easily impressed, you know that.

A True, you're not. Miles, meet the woman who turned down Oasis.

D Fine by me. I never liked them.

C I thought we weren't going to talk about that any more.

A Okay, okay. Well, what do The Penitents look like? No, let me guess. Like they haven't eaten a hot meal for a week and they cut their own hair, right?

D Not at all. The lead guitarist looks like Keanu Reeves. The drummer's fabulous even if her drumming's a little off. In fact, they're all pretty glamorous. Ronnie, I have a good feeling about this one.

A Okay, call their manager and set something up. But not next week. I'm at the MTV awards.

C Okay, I'll do that. Oh, and by the way, you might want to tune in to VH1 at eight this evening. They're being interviewed live.

A They are? Well, why didn't you say so before? Look, give me their manager's number, I might just call him myself this afternoon ...

18 MEDIATION

3.25

A Okay, take a seat. Now, look, you both know why we're here. Henri, you've been struggling to get the Panama project completed for weeks.

B What? ...

A No, hear me out, Henri. I've got another meeting in an hour and we really must sort this situation out today. In fact, I probably should have intervened earlier. Now, for one reason or another, you've been having difficulty bringing this project to completion. I brought Elena in to help you out, thinking it would make your life easier. And since then you two have done nothing but fight, and the project seems to be further behind schedule than ever! Now can somebody please tell me what on earth's going on? Elena?

C Well, it's Henri. He's totally disorganized. I mean, I'm not surprised he's so far behind schedule. He can't work to a deadline. We've got no proper milestones in place for this project. I've tried working with him, but it's just hopeless ...

B I am not totally disorganized, Elena. Just because you're obsessed with ticking boxes at every stage of the project, and I'm not, does not make me disorganized. In fact, I never asked for your help in the first place. I was getting along just fine without you, thanks very much.

C How could you be 'getting along just fine'? Why do you think I was brought in?

B I've no idea. I certainly didn't request your assistance.

A People, people ...

C And I didn't ask for the job either, Henri. I've got better things to do than sort out your problems!

A Right, everybody just hold it right there!

B Okay, that's it! I've had enough of this! I'm sorry, James. If you want to discuss this matter with me in private, we'll need to arrange another meeting.

A Henri ...

B I'll be in my office if you want me.

A Well, that went well!

 3.26

A Okay, let's get started, shall we? Well, I'm Kaye and, as you know, James has asked me to mediate this session. He thought that maybe someone from a different department might be in a better position to help you resolve your issues. Is that okay with both of you? Okay, good. Now, it's Elena and Henri, isn't it? All right, well, first of all, let me say, that everything you say in this meeting is totally confidential. Nothing goes outside this room. And, of course, I'm completely impartial in all this. I have no personal interest in how you resolve your differences. I'm just here to try and make sure we explore every option, okay? Now, one or two rules to make this meeting more productive. We'll speak one at a time if possible. So please try not to interrupt each other. If you've anything to say, make a note of it, so you can make your point when it's your turn to speak. And if you need to talk to me privately at any stage, just let me know. All right? Now, Henri, let's start with you, shall we? How do you see the situation? ...

B ... So, frankly, I don't see what kind of help Elena can possibly offer when she hasn't been involved in this project, knows nothing about it, in fact ...

C Now, hang on, Henri! I know as much about this project as you do. I ought to by now, for heaven's sake – I've been working on it 24/7 for the last three weeks! You see what he's like? Just no respect for anybody else's point of view.

A Okay, I understand your position, Elena. But just let Henri finish what he has to say and I'll come back to you in a moment, okay? Now, Henri, as I understand it, you're not happy about sharing responsibility for this project with Elena, is that right?

B Well, of course, I'm not. It's my project. James had no right bringing Elena in at all. I had everything under control. I just needed a little more time. Maybe some more IT support would have been a nice idea too. What I didn't need is someone else coming in and taking over!

C I have not taken over!

B Only because I haven't let you!

A Okay, clearly, we have a misunderstanding about roles here. Elena, what was your brief from James when he brought you in?

C To make sure this project is completed on time and on budget. At the moment, it's five weeks behind schedule.

A But James did not ask you to take charge of the project?

C Well, of course he didn't. I can't take responsibility for all this. I've got three other projects I'm involved in at the moment.

A So you agree with Henri that this is his project and that you're just trying to do what you can to prevent any further delays?

C That's right.

A Henri, are you reassured by what Elena just said?

B Well, ... yes, all right. I mean, if she'd just made that clear at the start instead of storming in.

A All right. And, Elena, can you see how Henri might have thought you were taking control?

C Well, I suppose so.

A Good, we seem to be making some progress.

C Look, Henri, I'm just trying to bring a bit of organization to this project. I mean, you're great on the creative side, but you have to admit you're not strong on the details. We're still sorting out things from phase one and we're supposed to be on phase three!

B I've got all that covered, Elena.

C So you say, but how do I know that? You never send me progress reports or anything ...

A All right. It looks to me as though what we have here is a conflict of working styles. Shall we talk about that a bit more?

 3.27

A ... Okay, so, can I just summarize what you've agreed? Henri, you're going to remain in charge of this project, but you're going to send weekly reports to Elena, so she can keep track of progress – especially on the details – and help out just where she's needed. Otherwise, though, meeting deadlines is going to be your responsibility – and yours alone. Is that acceptable to both of you? Okay, now it's just a suggestion, but you might like to consider having scheduled daily chats over a coffee just to keep everyone up to speed.

C Good idea.

B Yes, sure.

A Now, Elena, you've agreed to get that extra IT support Henri requested, which will free him up to concentrate on the creative side of things, and free you up to get on with some of your other projects. Now, does this new arrangement sound like something you can both live with?

C Yes, I think so.

B Okay, let's give it a try.

A Great, now I'll ...

Macmillan Education
Crinan Street, London N1 9XW
A division of Macmillan Publishers Limited
Companies and representatives throughout the world

ISBN 978-0-230-45532-0

This edition published 2014
First published 2004

Designed by emc design limited
Illustrated by Rosie Scott (NB Illustration) p98
Cover design by emc design limited
Cover photo Getty Images/E+
Photo research by Alison Prior

The publishers would like to thank the following people, schools and institutions for their help in developing this third edition: Pat Pledger, Pledger Business English Training, Hamburg; Louise Bulloch, Intercom Language Services, Hamburg; Elbie Picker and David Virta, Hamburg; William Fern, KERN AG IKL Business Language Training & Co. KG, Frankfurt; Belén del Valle, ELOQUIA, Frankfurt; Katrin Wolf, Carl Duisberg Centren, Cologne; Andrina Rout, Fokus Sprachen und Seminare, Stuttgart; Gerdi Serrer, ILIC, Paris; Sylvia Renaudon, Transfer, Paris; John Fayssoux, Accom Formation, Paris; Kathryn Booth-Aïdah, Araxi Formations Langues, Paris; Fiona Delaney and Allison Dupuis, Formalangues, Paris; Francesca Pallot and Susan Stevenson, Anglesey Language Services, Chatou, France; Paul Bellchambers, Business and Technical Languages (BTL), Paris; Louise Raven, marcus evans Linguarama, Stratford-upon-Avon.

Many thanks also to all the teachers around the world who took the time to complete our *In Company* online questionnaire and who have contributed to the development of the *In Company* series.

The authors and publishers would like to thank the following for permission to reproduce their photographs:

Alamy/Alaska Stock p64(tl), Alamy/All Canadian Photos p39, Alamy/Thomas Russ Amestad p64(tr), Alamy/Arterra Picture Library pp110, 111, Alamy/Blend Images p31, Alamy/Steve Bloom Images p114(b), Alamy/Remy Boprey p124(hotel), Alamy/Cultura Creative p86, Alamy/dpa Picture Alliance p84(tl), Alamy/Imagebroker p67, Alamy/Image Source pp34, 52, Alamy/Johner Images p50, Alamy/Juniors Bildarchiv GmbH pp63(br), 124(shark), Alamy/MBI p135(b), Alamy/David Noton Photography p57, Alamy/OJO Images p115, Alamy/Onoky-Photononstop p44(b), Alamy/PhotoAlto p8, Alamy/Prisma Bildagentur AG pp76, 77, Alamy/Peter Probst p45, Alamy/Daniel J Rao p63(bl), Alamy/David Soulsby p124(car), Alamy/Stock Connection Blue p104, Alamy/Homer Sykes Archive p84(bl), Alamy/Kristoffer Tripplaar p25(t), Alamy/VStock p49, Alamy/Wavebreak Media Ltd UC1 p24, Alamy/Woodystock pp2(Guggenheim), 7(c); **Carol Simpson**/www.solidarity@cartoonwork.com p70(t); **www.Cartoonstock.com** pp20(t), 44(t), www.Cartoonstock.com/©WileyInk.Inc/Distributed by Universal Click via Cartoonstock p114(t); **Corbis**/Blue Images p37(r), Corbis/Blue Jean Images p71, Corbis/Richard Cummins p58, Corbis/Dream Pictures/Blend Images p70(cl), Corbis/John Hicks p15, Corbis/Les & Dave Jacobs/Cultura p13, Corbis/Ocean pp63(t), 102, Corbis/Pascal Perich pp2(JackWelch), 6(r), Corbis/Tony Rodriguez p93, Corbis/Sullivan p17, Corbis/Per Windbladh p26; **Getty Images** pp2(relay race), 2(a), 2(b), 20(t), 84(br), 96(b), 97(l), 97(c), Getty Images/AFP pp2(c), 97(r), Getty Images/Blend Images/Hill Street Studios p70(bl), Getty Images/Bloomberg pp2(Stanford), 6(l), Getty Images/Peter Dazeley p60(c), Getty Images/Nick Dolding p89, Getty Images/Odilon Dimier p60(b), Getty Images/Jon Feingersh p92, Getty Images/Oliver Furrer p124(parachute), Getty Images/Gamma-Rapho p20(b and inset), Getty Image/Troels Graugaard p85, Getty Images/Hill Street Studios p27,Getty Images/Jetta Productions p55, Getty Images/Jetta Productions/Dana Neely p32, Getty Images/Thomas Kokta p107, Getty Images/David Lees pp16, 109, Getty Images/Dan Moore p83, Getty Images/NBAE p100(b), Getty Images/Poba p91, Getty Images/Mike Powles p48, Getty Images/Kim Sayer p60(t), Getty Images/Time & Life Pictures p84(tr), Getty Images/TommL p74, Getty Images/Jonas Velin p82, Getty Images/Yellow Dog Productions p70(tl); **Goodshoot** p65; **Image Source** p121; **Kobal**/Renaissance Films/BBC/Curzon Films p28; **Plain Picture**/Johner p78, Plain Picture/Zak Kendal/Cultura p37(l); **Press Association Images**/Jae C Hong p25(b); **© Rambod Rambod**/Geometrical Inc p131(b); **Randy Glasbergen**/www.glasbergen.com pp2(cartoon), 96(t); **Reuters**/Mike Blake p66; **Rex Features**/David Sandison/The Independent p100(t); **© Tagonthat.com** p135(t); **Thinkstock**/iStockphoto pp2(London Eye), p7(b); **winnsbaker@suddenlinkmail.com** p131(t).

Commissioned photography by Paul Bricknell pp22, 23, 46, 47, 72, 73, 98, 99, 116, 117

The authors and publisher would like to thank the following for permission to reproduce the following material.

Excerpt from 'The Ultimate Business Presentation Book' by Andrew Leigh. © Andrew Leigh 1999. Published by Random House. Used with permission; Excerpt from 'The Accidental Tourist' by Anne Tyler. Published by Random House; Excerpt from 'Contemporary Public Speaking' by Courtland L. Bovee. Published by Rowman & Littlefield 2003. Reprinted with permission; Excerpt from 'You have to Start Meeting Like This!' by Gina Imperato. Published in Fast Company Issue 23, 1999. Reprinted with permission; Extracts from 'Innovation Intraprenuring-The Five people of innovation' Published on www.pinchot.com; Extracts from The Worst Case Scenarios series website, reprinted with permission of Quirk Books, Philadelphia, USA. www.Quirkbooks.com/Worst-Case-Scenarios; Extract from 'Effective Decision Making' by John Adair Pan Macmillan, 2009. 'Coke Products Banned in Belgium' published by The Associated Press. 15.06.1999. Reprinted with permission; Extract from 'What are the Biggest Email Mistakes?' by Tim Sanders. Published by Krup NYC. Extract from 'SEND, The Essential Guide to Email for Office and Home' by David Shipley and Will Schwalbe. Published by Knopf Double Day / Random House 2007. Extract from 'I Have a Dream' speech by Dr Martin Luther King Jr. Reprinted by arrangement with The Heirs to the Estate of Martin Luther King Jr., c/o Writers House as agent for the proprietor New York, NY; Extract from Conservative Party Conference Speech, by Margaret Thatcher 10.10.1975. Reprinted with permission from the Margaret Thatcher Foundation; Extract from Nelson Mandela Inauguration speech 10.10.1994. Reprinted with permission from the Nelson Mandela Foundation; Material from 'Jet Lag Hater's Guide to Business Travel' by John Cassey / George Mackintosh Originally published in the Guardian 14.9.1999. © Guardian News & Media Ltd 1999. Reprinted with permission; Extract from 'Should Genetic Tests Decide Job Prospects?'. Originally published in The Sunday Times, 24.01.1999. Reprinted with permission; Extract from: "In a high-tech world, it's a cinch for employers to spy on workers" by Liz Stevens, Knight Ridder Newspapers, originally published December 6, 2002. © McClatchy-Tribune Information Services. All Rights Reserved. Reprinted with permission; Extract from 'Creative Way to Better Management' by Francis Beckett. © Francis Beckett. Originally published in The Financial Times, 08.11.1999. Reprinted with permission.

Printed and bound in Thailand

2018 2017 2016 2015 2014
10 9 8 7 6 5 4 3 2 1